LIZZIE COLLING

Lizzie Collingham writes in a garden shed near Cambridge. She taught History at Warwick University and was a Junior Research Fellow at Jesus College, Cambridge before becoming an independent historian. Her books include *Curry: A Tale of Cooks and Conquerors*, *The Taste of War: World War II and the Battle for Food* and *The Hungry Empire: How Britain's Quest for Food Shaped the Modern World*. She is currently an Associate Fellow of Warwick University and an Advisory Fellow for the Royal Literary Fund.

ALSO BY LIZZIE COLLINGHAM

Imperial Bodies: The Physical Experience of the Raj, c.1800–1947

Curry: A Tale of Cooks and Conquerors

The Taste of War: World War II and the Battle for Food

The Hungry Empire: How Britain's Quest for Food Shaped the Modern World

LIZZIE COLLINGHAM

The Biscuit

The History of a Very British Indulgence

VINTAGE

1 3 5 7 9 10 8 6 4 2

Vintage is part of the Penguin Random House group of companies
whose addresses can be found at global.penguinrandomhouse.com

Penguin
Random House
UK

Copyright © Lizzie Collingham 2020

Lizzie Collingham has asserted her right to be identified as the
author of this Work in accordance with the Copyright,
Designs and Patents Act 1988

First published in Vintage in 2021
First published in hardback by The Bodley Head in 2020

penguin.co.uk/vintage

A CIP catalogue record for this book is available
from the British Library

ISBN 9781529112245

Printed and bound in Great Britain by Clays Ltd, Elcograf S.p.A.

The authorised representative in the EEA is Penguin Random House
Ireland, Morrison Chambers, 32 Nassau Street, Dublin D02 YH68.

Penguin Random House is committed to a sustainable future
for our business, our readers and our planet. This book is
made from Forest Stewardship Council® certified paper.

MIX
Paper from
responsible sources
FSC
www.fsc.org
FSC® C018179

For
Sophie Calypso

To make Bisket Bread Stif

Put to a pound of flower half a pound of sugar, nyne whites
and six yelks of eggs, finelie beaten, mould it together, &
make it up in a roule to bake it, when it is baked slice it & drie
it, in the oven on a gredyron, you must put in some anniseeds,
& coriander in the moulding.

Lady Elinor Fettiplace's manuscript cookbook

CONTENTS

LIST OF ILLUSTRATIONS

Ancient Roman bread, Pompeii. Alamy Stock Photo.

Andrea Mantegna, *The Circumcision* (1462). Alamy Stock Photo.

Wafers made by Ivan Day with a set of early-seventeenth-century English wafering irons. Reproduced by kind permission of Ivan Day.

Frontispiece for Hannah Woolley, *The Queen-like Closet, or Rich Cabinet: stored with all manner of rare receipts for preserving, candying and cookery. Very pleasant and beneficial to all ingenious persons of the female sex* (1675). LUNA Folger Digital Image Collection, The Folger Shakespeare Library.

Jan van Halbeeck, *Vrouw bij een schaal lekkernijen* (1610–1680). Rijksmuseum. Amsterdam.

William Hogarth, *The idle 'prentice executed at Tyburn* (1747). The Lewis Walpole Library, Yale University Library.

Emigrant and pretzel vendor, New York. The Library of Congress, Washington DC.

Migrant mother making biscuits in her tent home, Mercedes, Texas. Library of Congress, Washington DC.

Jean Charles Devell, 'Les Biscuits: scene in a pastry shop', design in progress for a painted porcelain plate, rondel, for the Service des objets de dessert (1783), Sèvres porcelain manufactory, France. Cooper Hewitt, Smithsonian Design Museum.

Mould for making House of York toasting biscuits to celebrate the wedding of the Duke and Duchess of York, England, *c*.1790, unidentified wood, Fitzwilliam Museum, Cambridge.

Sketches in a biscuit manufactory (1874). Private collection.

Huntley & Palmers trade card. Private Collection.

Advertisement for Henderson's Digestive Pufnels (*c.*1900–1930). Private collection.

International Health Exhibition, Peek Frean (1884). Private collection.

Huntley & Palmers Breakfast Biscuits (1907). Private collection.

Interior of W. S. Dustin's confectionery shop in Wanganui, 1909, photograph by Frank J. Denton. Alexander Turnbull Library, Wellington, New Zealand.

British Army soldiers suffering from frostbite lying on hay in a shelter made from Huntley & Palmers biscuit boxes at Suvla, Gallipoli Peninsula, Turkey, 1915. Australian War Memorial, Canberra, Australia.

Emboitage des 'Petit-Beurre Extra: Biscuits Olibet', postcard. Private collection.

Soldiers with military supplies in a French farmyard, Bus-lès-Artois, 21 April 1918, photograph by Henry Armytage Sanders. Alexander Turnbull Library, Wellington, New Zealand.

El Agheila, Cyrenaica, Libya, 7 December 1942. Australian War Memorial, Canberra, Australia.

S. W. Fores, *Genuine Tea Company* (1825). Lewis Walpole Library, Yale University Library.

Profile of a young woman reading a book and eating. Everett Collection/Bridgeman Images.

Colour plates

Bread distribution, Roman fresco from the Praedia of Julia Felix in Pompeii. Museo Archeologico Nazionale (Naples), The Picture Art Collection/Alamy Stock Photos.

Theriaca, an illustration from Ibn Butlan's eleventh-century Taqwim al-sihhah or Maintenance of Health, published in Italy as the Tacuinum Sanitatis in the fourteenth century. CPA Media Pte Ltd/Alamy Stock Photo.

Andrea Mantegna, *The Circumcision* (1462). Alamy Stock Photo.

Alexander Hugo Bakker Korff (*c.*1850–1882), *The Waffle Maker*. Rijksmuseum, Amsterdam.

Recreation of an English Renaissance sugar banquet for a wedding, *c.*1610, conceived and made by Ivan Day, consisting of replicas of wafers, rolled and flat, pressed from seventeenth-century wafering iron; alphabet jumbles; knotted jumbles. Fitzwilliam Museum, Cambridge.

Gingerbread mould with pressings of gingerbread figures, by Ivan Day, 2019. Fitzwilliam Museum, Cambridge.

William Hogarth, 'Evening – La Sorée', 23 June 1740. Lewis Walpole Library, Yale University Library.

Jan Havickszoon. Steen, *The baker Arent Oostward and his wife, Catharina Keizerswaard* (1658). Rijksmuseum, Amsterdam.

Mate to 'Le grand dessert', print (1879). Library of Congress, Washington DC.

A selection of Huntley & Palmers trade cards. Private collection.

Huntley & Palmers Biscuit Factory, Reading, advertising postcard. Private Collection.

McVitie & Price biscuit tin. Private Collection.

McVitie's Digestive biscuits 'at any time of the daily round' (1936). Chronicle/Alamy Stock Photos.

PREFACE

On 28 April 1789 William Bligh and 18 of his crew were set adrift in the *Bounty's* longboat in the Tongan archipelago. The mutineers supplied them with a sextant, a compass, nautical tables, a tool box and 150 lb of biscuit, 20 lb of salt pork, 3 bottles of wine, 5 quarts of rum and 28 gallons of water. Bligh and his men's attempt to find more provisions on a nearby island ended in disaster when the islanders killed the quartermaster, John Norton. They decided their best option was to make their way to the nearest European outpost, the Dutch settlement of Kupang on the island of Timor, 4,000 miles to the west. To make this journey they would each have to ration themselves to a quarter of a pint of water and an ounce of biscuit a day.[1]

More than 200 years later I found myself in a similar predicament on a small island overlooking the same stretch of sea. We had booked a home stay on the tiny island of Uiha, only to be told when we arrived that our hosts had been possessed by an evil spirit and taken to see an exorcist on another island. An islander came to show us the makeshift kitchen and our sleeping hut, told us to make ourselves at home and then left us to our own devices. A search through the kitchen cupboards turned up a tin of tuna, plenty of tea and some bananas. We had brought with us a loaf of bread and half a dozen packets of Marie biscuits. Unfortunately, the bread was devoured by ants as we did not think to put it in the insect-proofed cupboard. We realised that we would have to ration ourselves to 28 biscuits a day.

Because biscuits are a convenient and durable way of preserving the nutritional value of wheat, for centuries they have been the food of seafarers and soldiers, travellers and explorers. Indeed, biscuits have always been the most fundamental of foodstuffs, baked to tide people over periods of scarcity and hardship. Bligh's ability as a navigator and the frugal biscuit ration saw the men through their gruelling six-week voyage. Biscuits also saw us through our week on Uiha. However, while we were a little hungry, eating sweet biscuits while lying in a hammock gazing out over the Pacific Ocean felt more of an indulgence than a hardship.

Biscuits are the most versatile of foodstuffs, associated with hardship and endurance as well as luxury and indulgence. In the 1930s, a food writer observed that because they could 'be eaten at all moments in the day ... [were] the easiest most durable and digestible auxiliary food to transport, and ... the most aristocratic sweet transformation of wheat', biscuits were 'destined to become among all people one of the most widespread and democratic foods'.[2] In Britain this is certainly the case. No other nation buys and eats more biscuits. Indeed, while sales of chocolate and sweets have fallen in recent years, biscuit sales have risen. The average British household buys more than a hundred packets a year, and for many a cup of tea is incomplete without a biscuit.[3]

Biscuits are as embedded in British food culture as fish and chips or the Sunday roast. And yet it was only in the last half of the twentieth century that they became integral to the British diet. In the preceding centuries only soldiers and sailors ate savoury biscuits, and they heartily disliked the hard, weevil-ridden things. The gentry occasionally ate sweet biscuits, and with their mass production during the Industrial Revolution they became a bourgeois food. But biscuits barely featured in the diets of the majority of the population. It was only after the Second World War that a biscuit and a cup of tea became a normal part of the British daily routine.

In which the slaves in the Modestus bakery over-bake their bread

On the morning of 24 August 79 CE, the slaves in the Modestus bakery in Pompeii were still busy making bread. It seems likely that by now many of the town's inhabitants would have taken heed of the earth tremors that had been felt in the area for several days and fled. But the owner of the Modestus bakery must have thought there were still enough potential customers to make it worth baking a batch of loaves. In any case, his slaves would have had no choice in the matter. 'All work' graffitied on the bakery wall suggests that their owner was a hard taskmaster. Hopefully the slaves were not in as pitiable a state as the fictional ones described by the narrator of *The Golden Ass*: miserable creatures covered in 'dirty flour ash', clothed in tattered tunics, their bodies 'a welter of inflamed bruises; their backs scarred by the rod'. But the Modestus bakery slaves would no doubt have worked in a similarly 'steamy dank' and 'dusty darkness'.[1] Little light can have entered the enclosed atrium where they laboured. At its centre was a large domed oven and several stone mills for grinding the wheat. Beyond were the stables which housed the donkeys that turned them. The bakers mixed and kneaded the bread dough in large stone bowls. Once it had proved, they shaped it into circular loaves and tied a piece of twine around the edge to form a handle, which made it easier to carry the bread when baked. Once the slaves had made four cuts across the top of each loaf, dividing it into eight sections, the bread was ready to be baked.

It was still in the oven when Vesuvius erupted at midday. Within an hour Pompeii was plunged into darkness as a mushroom-shaped cloud blew southwards and pumice and ash began to rain down on the town. No bodies have been found in the bakery. Like the painters decorating the garden room of a residential house on the other side of town, who fled virtually mid-brushstroke leaving behind their mixing bowls, jars of plaster and pots of paint, the bakery slaves must have bolted.[2] The 81 loaves they had baked that morning were taken out of the oven by Victorian excavators – nearly 2,000 years over-baked.

The first biscuits were simply dried bread, made in order to store this most fundamental of foods. At some point in the sixth millennium BCE the people living on the fertile plains of the Tigris–Euphrates river system domesticated wild

One of the eighty-one loaves of bread found in the oven at the Modestus bakery by Victorian excavators.

cereals and began cultivating barley and wheat. Over time the varied meat-rich diet of hunting and gathering was displaced by a farming diet dominated by cereals. A grain-based diet was less nutritious, but it had the advantage that it supplied as many as a hundred times more people with a comparatively secure source of food, which with care could be stored for years.[3]

By the third millennium BCE, the Mesopotamians had discovered that twice-baking grain not only made it sweeter but also meant that it could be kept for longer. They would soak barley grains in water until they began to germinate, thus releasing the sugars stored in the kernels. Then they would arrest the process by drying them in the sun or a warm kiln. A second, slightly hotter bake turned the partially germinated grains into sweet malted barley. Pounded and sieved to remove the chaff, malt barley flour could be stored for several months in sacks or jars. But if the flour was baked into a loaf of bread, which was then sliced and these slices were dried in the residual heat of the wood oven, the barley was transformed into hard, dry rusks that could be stored for years. The baking and drying process removed water and air but retained most of the grain's nutritive value. The rusks were in effect durable condensed bread. However, it seems the Mesopotamians did not use these first barley biscuits as a foodstuff but as a way to preserve the base for making beer. Soaked in water and heated in a mash vessel, the rusks formed a wort that could be sweetened with honey or date juice and left to ferment.[4]

The ancient Greeks used the same method to preserve bread. Both Hippocrates and Aristotle refer to *dipyros artos*, which again means 'twice-baked bread'. But a more common name for bread rusks in ancient Greece was *paximadia*, presumably in honour of Paxamus, a Greek writer who lived in Rome in the first or second century. Unfortunately, none of his writings have survived but because other classical authors refer to his works we know that he wrote on a wide variety of subjects ranging from farming to sexual positions. Perhaps his agricultural handbook included particularly good instructions on how to make barley bread biscuits.[5]

In the seventeenth century these twice-baked bread rusks were still being made on the Greek island of Santorini, where the French traveller Jean de Thevénot encountered them. 'The Inhabitants of this Island live very meanly,' he wrote. 'Their Bread...is Bisket...as black as Pitch, and so harsh that one can hardly swallow it.' Thevénot thought the islanders' food matched their home. As a consequence of a volcanic eruption in the harbour three years earlier, it was 'a frightful place...like Hell; for the Sea in the Harbour and about the Coast is black, and all seems Burn'd and Scorched'. The islanders of Santorini lived on biscuit rather than fresh bread due to their lack of firewood. Thevénot explained that they had to buy all their wood 'by the pound' from the neighbouring island of Nio, which made baking an expensive business, and so the islanders 'never heat the Oven but twice a Year'.[6] Hence it made sense to store their bread as biscuit.

In the drier parts of the Greek world the climate was better suited to the cultivation of barley but as Rome rose to political and cultural ascendancy, barley became the grain of the poor, slaves and the peasantry. The Italians preferred wheat as it made better bread due to its higher gluten content but if they ate bread at all, the poor in the countryside had to make do with black barley bread thick with chaff. More often they boiled whole barley grains into a porridge. If they grew wheat, they sold it in the towns and cities. Wheat bread was the staple food of the Roman town dweller.[7] There were at least 30 bakeries in Pompeii and these would have been supplemented by numerous street sellers touting rolls and loaves from baskets. While what seem to be shopping lists scratched on the walls of the houses show that Pompeiians were keen consumers of olive oil, wine, pork, whitebait, cheese, lard, onions, cabbage, beetroot, leeks, mustard, mint and salt, most of their food budget would have gone on bread.[8] It would have provided at least three quarters of the calories in the urban Roman diet (see page 1 of the picture section).[9]

The Romans made a wide range of breads. In his third century CE work *The Banquet of the Learned*, the Graeco-Egyptian author Athenaeus describes the different sorts of bread enjoyed in the ancient world: 'raised bread, unleavened bread, bread made with fine flour, with groats, with unbolted meal … of rye, of spelt and of millet'. He goes on to mention 'oven bread … so named, from being baked', 'thin wafer bread made over the ashes', bread enriched with honey and oil or lard, griddle cakes and cheese bread, hot rolls sprinkled with poppy seeds, brazier bread, which was a delectable speciality of Rhodes, where they dipped it in sweet wine, and the glorious twisted barley rolls of Thessaly. *Obelias* was made by winding a sausage-shaped length of dough around a spit and then roasting it over an open fire.[10] This spit bread was said to be popular with soldiers on campaign.[11]

Like the Greeks, the Romans twice-baked their bread to make biscuit. Athenaeus mentions biscuit made from 'voluptuous loaves'.[12] This appears to be a reference to biscuit made from fine white bread, which would have had the consistency of desiccated toast. The Romans also made hard rusks with coarser breads. They called bread rusks *panis bicoctus* – twice-baked bread – and it is from the Latin (via the French) that the English word is derived. Thus, the original method for making biscuit is embedded in its name. As a durable and easily transportable form of bread, it was used by the Roman navy and army.[13] The biscuit distributed to soldiers was sometimes shaped into bagel-like rings. These may have been made by first dropping rings of dough into hot water and then drying them before they were baked to a crisp. The soldiers would string them on a cord and hang them from the cross-shaped pole they used to carry their equipment.

Charred though the carbonised loaves found at Pompeii are, across the millennia we can still imagine the pleasure that a hungry Roman might have taken in tearing off one of the still-warm wedges. The loaves divided into sections were made to be broken and shared.[14] Indeed, to 'break bread' became synonymous with the idea of eating together. The poet Antiphanes praised the generous host who furnished his guests with good bread, asking, 'How could a man of gentle breeding ever leave this roof, when he sees these white-bodied loaves crowding the furnace in close ranks?'[15] A simple Roman meal consisted of bread, fish and wine. This was what Jesus and his disciples ate at the Last Supper, and through this symbolic meal, bread, fish and wine were transferred into the Christian world as foodstuffs that symbolised membership of the Christian community.[16]

The Christian anchorites who withdrew from the world to lead solitary lives of contemplation in the Egyptian desert restricted themselves to a frugal diet of bread, water and salt. Out in the desert they would have had limited access to firewood and like the inhabitants of Santorini, they made their bread into long-lasting biscuit. Coptic accounts of the life of St Anthony, an Egyptian farmer who renounced the world to live alone in an abandoned Roman fort, tell how twice a year he would bake barley bread and then dry it into biscuit in the sun. In the third and fourth centuries anchorites began to abandon their solitary rock-cut tombs and caves in favour of living together in religious communities.[17] A veteran of the Roman army called Pachomius founded the first monastery on the Isle of Tabennisi. In the set of rules he drew up to guide his fellow devotees, he instructed them to fast on Wednesdays and Fridays and to eat only bread, salt and water on the other days of the week. From Pachomius's rules we can see that bread-making was a solemn business. He ordained that from the moment the flour was sprinkled with water no one should be allowed in or out of the bakery and that the bakers were to keep silence: not only draughts but also noise was thought to prevent bread from rising.[18] Like St Anthony, the monks on the island of Tabennisi would only have gone to the expense of firing up their ovens to bake once or twice a year and they would have converted most of their bread into biscuit.

Pachomius's first monastery gave rise to others throughout the Nile delta and eventually monasteries were founded all over Europe.[19] We can see from the frequent reference to twice-baked bread in their regulations that biscuit was a staple of the monastic diet. The twelfth-century charter of the Greek Kosmosoteira monastery has instructions on how to make a brew of onions, herbs and olive oil to pour over a bowl of crushed rusks.[20] This was still how the islanders of Santorini prepared their biscuit five centuries later. The French priest François Richard noticed that just as the islanders reconstituted dried beans and fish in water, they first soaked their rusks before covering them with a stew of vegetables.[21] In many parts of Europe villagers took the same precautions as the monks when baking bread, protecting the proving dough from noise and draughts. And linguistic evidence suggests that like the monks, they converted some of their bread into biscuit and that this was a commonplace food throughout the European countryside.[22] In Slovene the word *prepecenec* implies over-baking; *dvopek* in Serbo-Croat and *Zwieback* in German both mean twice-baked. The Venetians rendered the Greek *paximadia* as *pasimata*, and the Serbo-Croats pronounced it *peksimet*; it became *pesmet* in Romanian.[23]

Geoffrey the Grammarian's fifteenth-century Latin–English dictionary tells us that the English used the term *krakenelle* for 'brede twyys bakyn'.[24] Just as there were different types of bread, ranging from white wheaten manchet loaves to coarse maslin bread made with a mixture of wheat, rye and barley flour, so there was a range of biscuits.[25] Maslin biscuits would have been as hard and black as the pumice-like biscuit of Santorini, but white biscuit was considered suitably fine for ambassadors to offer as a gift to distant rulers. When Friar William of Rubruck set out on an expedition to the Tartars on behalf of King Louis of France in 1253, he took with him wine, apples and fine biscuit. The nomadic tribespeople he met while travelling through Central Asia were unimpressed and advised him to add valuable cloth to the offering.[26]

The Dutch, German, Danish, Swedish and Norwegian words for what we would think of as crackers – respectively *knäckebröd, knäckebrot, knaekbrød, knackebröd* and *knekkebrød* – may all derive from the same root word as *krakenelle*. These northern European twice-baked breads were, however, of a different character. Oats and rye grew better than barley and wheat in cooler climates and stonier ground. In these regions people made thin 'cakes' with their rye- or oat-based doughs. In Lancashire these were known as 'clap bread' because they were made by placing a ball of oatmeal dough on a wooden board and then beating or 'clapping' it with the hand until it was spread as thin as paper.[27] These oat cakes could be toasted when propped against a tripod in front of the fire or baked to a crisp on an iron griddle over a flame to form 'thin wafers as big as Pancakes', so dry and 'short' that they 'easily broke into shivers'.[28] Labourers would make a large batch and then store them piled in a basket hung from the roof beams. In Scotland and Scandinavia they fashioned holes in the centre of these 'cakes' so that they could be strung on a pole, which was then balanced across the ceiling beams. Although oat and rye crackers were different from bread rusks, they derived from the same principle. They were all a dried version of the staple bread. Throughout Europe and North Africa, the Middle East and Asia Minor, freshly baked bread was the ideal food but it was preserved and stored as biscuit to ensure that a reserve supply was available year round.

DAKOS SALAD

On his 1933 walking tour from the Hook of Holland to Constantinople, Patrick Leigh Fermor encountered *paximadia* in the wild Kravara region of western Greece. This region's 'inhabitants had been famous for living exclusively by mendacity', and he was surprised to discover they were happy to talk openly about their disreputable past. He was sent to meet a 90-year-old man who described how when he was young, the youth of the area would take a *'tagari*, a roomy woven bag, slung on a cord [and fill it with] *paximadia*, bread twice-baked and hard as a stone, once the diet of hermits … and now the sustenance of shepherds', and thus equipped would set off to make their living as itinerant quack doctors, relic pedlars, beggars and pickpockets.[29]

The Greeks took *paximadia* to the olive groves at harvest time and softened it in their wine at lunchtime. In the 1970s it was still available in bakeries but generally 'relegated to untidy heaps in the back'.[30] But since the 1990s it has become popular again, and now the shelves of Greek supermarkets abound with *paximadia* in all shapes and flavours, from hard black barley rusks to bagel-shaped rings studded with sunflower seeds, and light toast-like biscuits made with olive-oil-enriched bread. The island of Crete is known for producing the best *paximadia*. Here they eat it in a salad known as *dakos*:

> Crush a handful of barley biscuits (*paximadia*) and cover with chopped tomatoes, and *myzithra* cheese. This is the local Cretan cheese, you can use feta as a substitute. Pour over some olive oil and sprinkle with oregano. The biscuit softens in the tomato juice and oil but is still pleasingly crunchy.[31]

In which Ibrahim bin al-Mahdi writes a poem about sweet biscuits

In ninth-century Baghdad, the Abbasid prince Ibrahim bin al-Mahdi wrote a poem to thank his nephew for a gift of biscuits. In his cookbook, Ibn Sayyar al-Warraq reproduced the poem. According to Ibrahim, the biscuits, shaped into discs, resembled the moon and tasted as luscious as honey or a sweetly perfumed breeze. They were decorated with consecutive lines of sesame seeds, almonds and pine nuts, dripped with almond oil and were coloured yellow by saffron, making them shimmer like nuggets of gold. Ibrahim tells his nephew that the kind and generous present proves his affection, and ends by asking God to protect him so that he might 'live a thousand years, forever happy', untouched by harm.[1] This effusive thank you for the simple gift of a few biscuits conveys the unashamed pleasure Arabs took in the consumption of sweetmeats.

Islamic confectioners were the first to add sugar to the dough for twice-baked bread – *baqsamat* in Arabic – to produce *baqsamat bi sukkar*: sweet biscotti-like rusks. Sugar transformed the Christian monks' storeroom staple into a luxurious food of indulgence. Although the ancient Greeks and Romans were aware of a honey-like substance that was 'brittle to the teeth' and was harvested from 'reeds' in India and Arabia, sugar played no part in the culinary and medical concoctions of the ancient Europeans.[2] Their sweetener was honey. But while honey had good keeping qualities and was therefore an excellent substance in which to preserve quinces, for example, honey is hygroscopic, which means that a dough sweetened with it attracts water. Thus biscuits sweetened with honey quickly became soft, defeating the object of making them in the first place.[3] Biscuits made with sugar, on the other hand, remained hard and good for just as long as any unsweetened variety.

Originating from New Guinea, sugar cane had spread throughout South East Asia and India, where people enjoyed chewing pieces of cane and sucking out the sweet juice. At some point in the fourth century BCE, northern Indians appear to have discovered how to manufacture hard lumps of crystalline sugar by boiling and filtering cane juice. 'Stone honey' then spread from India to Iran, and when in the eighth century the Abbasid Arabs established the city of Baghdad, they took sugar cane with them to Iraq. Soon the fertile flood plains of the Tigris and Euphrates were dotted with sugar-pressing factories.[4]

The method for transforming cane juice into sugar improved in Arab hands. In the factories the cane was cleaned and cut into small pieces, which were put through a stone mill to extract the juice. This was then strained into a cauldron, where it was brought to a rolling boil and then strained again. Once it had been boiled and strained three times, the juice was poured into cone-shaped moulds and left in a drip house. As the sugar slowly crystallised, a residue of liquid molasses drained out of the cone. When the sugar had dried into hard cones of what the Arabs called red and we would call brown sugar, these were taken back to the boiling house, dissolved in water with milk and boiled again. This produced white sugar and a more refined molasses. And if the process was repeated once more, pure rock sugar was the final product.[5] Unlike the juice, which went sour within a few hours, this crystallised sugar could be kept for years. This process in itself appeared to be one of miraculous alchemy. But if the crystallised sugar was dissolved in water and boiled again, it underwent further transformation, turning first into a hard, glass-like substance and after additional boiling into a thick fudge or fondant. While quince juice cooked in honey produced an opaque red paste, when cooked in a sugar solution it became a translucent jelly, which seemed 'to capture the very essence of quince'.[6] Sugar appeared to have magical qualities.

In the minds of ancient and medieval medical practitioners, no line separated food from medicine. Every substance was thought to possess humoral qualities and, if they were ingested, these qualities were then absorbed by the body. Wet, cold foods such as fish could cause an excess of black bile and induce melancholy. This could be countered by eating them alongside warm, dry foods such as nuts to boost the choleric humours. Diet not only affected a person's mood but reached into the realm of their soul.[7] The ideal was to maintain a humoral balance that preserved the body in a state of both internal equilibrium and harmony with the environment. Arab medics now integrated sugar into this humoral understanding of health.

By the eighth century the Islamic world had supplanted the Roman Empire as the centre of scholarship and culinary innovation. In Baghdad an unprecedented transfer of knowledge from one culture to another took place. The Abbasids conceived the city as a crossroads at the centre of the world and welcomed people of all faiths and ethnicities. In their libraries the elite amassed works of medicine, philosophy and natural science from across the known world and patronised Christian, Zoroastrian, Buddhist, even pagan, as well as Arab scholars to translate and interpret them. In Arab hands the ancient Greek medical–dietary repertoire of remedies was transformed as honey was replaced with sugar. Arab medics classified sugar as hot and moist like the blood and therefore a neutral substance in that it did not disturb the body's equilibrium; they advised that it was suitable for everyone of any age or humoral disposition and could even restore harmony to those in an unhealthy state of imbalance.[8]

Islamic cookery embraced this perfect food. Sugar can be found everywhere in Sayyar al-Warraq's tenth-century cookbook, which provides us with a record of elite Islamic cuisine at its height. We can see that Muslim cooks used sugar as a spice, adding it to stuffing for fish or to a sauce that could be poured over meat; but at the same time a new branch of cookery used sugar as a main ingredient.[9] Sugar was the basis for about a third of the recipes in the cookbook: an array of pastes, conserves, jellies, puddings, pancakes, pastries, sherbets and, of course, biscuits. Some of these confections were used medicinally to treat stomach, bladder and kidney ailments, eye diseases and the pains caused by agues and fevers. The Syrian physician Ibn al-Quff recommended a lemon and quince sherbet drink to warm a cold stomach and clear the throat of phlegm.[10] But sugar was not just consumed as a remedy. It was seen as a health food, and was eaten as a prophylactic to ensure that the body stayed in tune with the environment. When the weather was hot, Ibn Butlan, a Nestorian physician and theologian born in Baghdad in the eleventh century, advised the consumption of sugar confections made with camphor and rose water; when it was cold he recommended fig and nut sugar confections.[11] Eating sweet biscuits could thus be seen as a form of preventive medicine, as a means of keeping the body in a state of harmony with the cosmos.

The first sweet biscuits were made by simply adding sugar to the dough for twice-baked bread. Islamic bakers made twice-baked bread rings that resembled the biscuits distributed to Roman soldiers. The dough was often flavoured with flower waters.[12] The translation of ancient Greek texts had enabled Islamic alchemists to perfect the art of distilling the essence of flower petals. The invention of new apparatus now enabled the commercialisation of the process and the distilling factories dotted throughout the Islamic world made rose and orange-blossom waters so widely available that they became ubiquitous flavourings in Islamic confectionery.[13]

A second line of sweet biscuits known as *ka'k* evolved as Muslim confectioners invented a more economical way of twice-baking enriched biscuit breads by baking them in small clay tandoors rather than large, fuel-hungry bread ovens. The discs of biscuit dough received their first baking stuck to the side of the tandoor. They could then be dried in the sun or receive a second, gentler baking placed in a net at the top of the oven. More elaborate adaptations involved pressing discs of dough into concave moulds and filling them with mixtures of nuts or dates and then sealing the filling with a second disc. They could be baked either pressed on the side of the tandoor or in an oiled pan lowered into the bottom. These little filled biscuits (ancestors of modern-day fig rolls) were finished by dipping them in rose-water-flavoured sugar syrup and sprinkling them with grains of white sugar.[14] Thus in the Arab world two lines of sweet biscuit evolved: sweetened rusks and sweet dough confections.

A RECIPE FOR *KA'K* MADE FOR ABU ATA SAHL BIN SALIM AL-KATIB

Flour, sesame seeds, almond oil, salt mixed to a dough. Sugar and saffron. Kneaded with yeast and water. When dough is fermented rub it with a little fat and rose water beaten together. Roll out on a board into a square and cut into small squares. Bake them in the tannur by sticking them onto the inner wall. When done leave them at the top of the tannur for a short while to dry out.[15]

Ibn Sayyar al-Warraq

In the eleventh and twelfth centuries, the economic and cultural centre of the Islamic world shifted from Iraq to the North African Fatimid empire, with its capital in Cairo. Sugar cane and the pressing industry had by this time spread along the Jordan valley into coastal Syria and Egypt. On his travels through the Arab world at the beginning of the fourteenth century, the North African explorer Ibn Battuta remarked that even the small town of Mallawi on the Upper Nile had eleven sugar-pressing facilities. Here he was surprised to observe beggars and Sufi mendicants wandering into the refineries to soak their bread in the pots of boiling juice. These factories shipped raw brown sugar down the Nile to large refineries near Cairo, where it was processed into white sugar.[16]

The art of confectionery spread with the sugar industry. In Cairo confectioners perfected the art of sugar sculpture. By mixing sugar with oils or vegetable gums it could be formed into a clay-like paste, which was fashioned into all manner of shapes and then baked hard. An eleventh-century visitor to Cairo during Ramadan marvelled at a lemon tree with a thousand branches, leaves and fruit, all fashioned out of sugar paste.[17] Sugar was expensive – a kilo cost about twenty-two times the price of a kilo of wheat – but not so expensive that minor merchants, artisans, scholars, scribes and notaries could not afford to wander through Cairo's sweetmeat bazaar and choose a delectable treat from the confections displayed on huge brass trays in the shopfronts, such as a sugar candy moulded into the shape of a lion or a pomegranate, to give to their children at Ramadan.[18] Cairo even had its own biscuit bazaar – the *suq al-ka'kiyyin*.[19]

Muslim and Jewish merchants grew rich exporting Egyptian sugar down the Red Sea to Aden and Calicut and across the Mediterranean to Venice and Genoa – and the art of confectionery and sweet biscuit baking travelled with it.

3

In which Bartolomeo Scappi serves Pope Pius IV *mostaccioli* biscuits

In Mantegna's painting of *The Circumcision* (*c*.1460), a small child in red leans against his mother's legs, a ring-shaped biscuit in his hand. Perhaps the model had been given something to chew to alleviate the tedium of posing. In placing the biscuit in the child's hand, Mantegna's scene – painted to illustrate a moment in the life of Christ – affords the modern viewer a glimpse into the everyday life of Renaissance Italy. It seems that centuries after the collapse of the Roman Empire, Italians were still making ring-shaped biscuits of the kind that Roman soldiers had carried with them on campaign. But appearances may be deceptive: the little boy's bread ring may well have been a different kind of biscuit altogether. We know from contemporary records that a range of biscuit sellers were touting their wares on the streets of Italy's cities. Vendors sold biscuits that looked like Roman military bread rings but were in fact Italian versions of the Islamic *ka'k*, with almonds added to the dough and dipped in sugar syrup.[1] It is likely that the snack in the little boy's hand was one of these new sweet biscuits that had arrived in Italy through contact with the Muslim world.

Andrea Mantegna, *The Circumcision* (1462). One of a triptych of paintings
Ludovico III Gonzaga of Mantua commissioned to adorn his private chapel.

Between the seventh and ninth centuries the Arabs conquered Cyprus, Spain,
Crete and Sicily, bringing with them sugar cane and the knowledge of how to process it.[2] In fact, in the ninth century Sicily became North Africa's main supplier of
sugar. At the same time, in the kingdom of al-Andalusia, established after the Ber-
bers had crossed the Straits of Gibraltar in 711, the Moors renovated the Roman
irrigation systems and rejuvenated Spanish agriculture. As well as sugar cane,
they introduced a host of new foodstuffs, including citrus fruits, figs, pomegranates, saffron and rice. Consequently, in Catalonia, Arab and European styles of
cookery fused to create a sophisticated cuisine characterised by complex sauces
layered with flavour, a preference for the sour–sweet combination of meat cooked
with dried fruits, and the use of bitter citrus juices or fragrant flower waters to

heighten flavour.[3] And of course, along with sugar, the full repertoire of Islamic confectionery was also introduced to Spain.

The first written evidence of the arrival of the Arabic art of confectionery in Europe is to be found in the *Libre de totes maneres de confits*, a Catalonian cookbook compiled in the 1400s.[4] This was the first in a long line of European cookbooks to contain a strange medley of instructions on how to make sugary confections such as fruit preserves and marzipan alongside remedies for a host of medical complaints. In the fifteenth century the Catalan fusion cuisine was spread to Italy by the resurgence of the kingdom of Aragon, which pushed the Moors back to southern Spain and incorporated Catalonia into its realm. It then went on to conquer Majorca, Corsica, Malta, Sicily and, in 1443, the kingdom of Naples on the Italian mainland.

Long before then, Italian cities like Venice and Genoa had traded in grain, olive oil, salt, wine, sugar and Eastern luxuries with Alexandria, Constantinople and ports around the Levant.[5] In the enclaves that European merchants established in the Muslim cities, Latin scholars met Arab and Greek philosophers. A syncretic culture emerged from this contact and flourished at the court of the Norman Emperor Frederick II in Sicily and in university towns such as Toledo and Salerno. Here classical Greek texts were reintroduced to the West and Islamic medico-moral learning made inroads into medieval Europe.[6]

The revival of classical learning in Europe eventually blossomed into the Italian Renaissance. The first cookbook to document the cuisine of Renaissance Italy was *On Right Pleasure and Good Health* (1470) by Bartolomeo Sacchi, more commonly known as Platina. Platina was no cook himself: he took all but 10 of the 250 recipes from a manuscript cookbook by his friend Maestro Martino, whom he hailed as 'the chief cook of our age'.[7] What he brought to the table was his scholarship. He had studied under two of the pioneering humanists in fifteenth-century Italy and he now embedded Martino's cookery in an Arabic *regimen sanitatus* while also applying Greek humoral classifications to foodstuffs.[8] Most importantly for the history of the biscuit, he added sugar to the *materia medica* and reiterated the Arabic appraisal of the substance as 'warm and damp so that it is of good nourishment...and soothes whatever discomforts there are'.[9] Martino's recipes reveal how heavily fifteenth-century Italian cooking had been influenced by Catalan cuisine. A good number of the recipes are explicitly introduced as 'Catalan', and Islamic influences can be traced in the use of dried fruits, rice, dates, bitter oranges and pomegranates. Like Islamic cooks, Martino made liberal use of sugar as a spice for seasoning, flavouring many of his sauces with it or sprinkling it over his finished dishes. More significantly for the development of the biscuit, he was among the first European cooks to follow Muslim practice and use sugar as a main ingredient in a range of sweet confections.[10] Crucially, Platina observed that 'the [good] quality of sugar...crosses over into the qualities of those things to which it clings in the preparation'.[11] By defining sugar as nutritious, he gave Renaissance diners carte blanche to indulge in sweetmeats and the Italian elite enthusiastically integrated Arabic confectionery into their dietary regimen.

Platina stipulated that sugary confections were most appropriately consumed at the beginning of a meal to 'induce appetite' and at the end to 'seal the stomach'. Antonio Cammelli's contemporary poem, 'When I dined with Marco Nigrisolo', describes the kind of meal Platina would have enjoyed with his friends, men like himself, scholars, poets and philosophers, who acted as secretaries, chamberlains, scribes, pages and cooks to ecclesiastical dignitaries. The meal begins with 'a mug of sweet Malvasia [wine] and candied fried dough' and continues with a succession of fine dishes including stuffed and roasted fowl, lamb, mutton, fatty pork and beans, a veal pie, cheese and wine. But according to Platina, not only the quality of the food but also the atmosphere in which it was eaten was of supreme importance. Cammelli's diners illustrate Platina's ideal: seated at a beautifully laid table covered in a cloth 'as white as snow' they enjoy good conversation with erudite friends. The poem tells us that when the meal was over and their conversation at an end, not only were their bodies 'satiated' but their souls were 'consoled'.[12]

The last victuals to be served to Cammelli's diners were melon seeds coated in marzipan. Like the sugar-coated coriander and anise seeds, known as comfits, that Platina recommended eating at the end of a meal, these were supposed to suppress rising vapours and sweeten the breath. While digesting a meal the stomach was thought to work like an internal cooking pot, giving off vapours just as a pot of bubbling stew gave off steam.[13] These vapours were regarded as potentially harmful; therefore, as sugar was thought to 'seal the stomach', it made a perfect end to a meal.[14]

A niche for confectionery was thus created at the beginning and end of a meal, but Martino and Platina did not yet include biscuits in their confectionery recipes. A century later, however, Italian versions of both the sweet rusks and the sweet dough biscuits of the Arab world appeared among the various confections served at Renaissance feasts. Bartolomeo Scappi, chef to popes Pius IV and V in the 1560s, was one of the first of the grand Renaissance chefs to include biscuits in his cookbook. In *Opera* (1570), he wrote that he often served *mostaccioli* biscuits as part of the first course of a banquet, alongside marzipan confections, pots of clotted cream, olives and a salad of borage flowers.[15]

Mostaccioli were hard brown biscuits made with ground almonds, heavily spiced and flavoured with musk – *muschio* in Italian – hence their name. In *L'Arte di ben cucinare* (1662), Bartolomeo Stefani gave a recipe that used four ounces of cinnamon and two grains of musk to three pounds of almonds and two of flour. The last of the great Italian chefs Antonio Latini dropped the musk and instead flavoured his biscuits with a heady mixture of powdered lemon, cloves, pepper, nutmeg, cinnamon and candied lemon rind, and glazed them with a thin sugar icing. These spicy biscuits are still popular in Naples at Christmas today.[16] *Mostaccioli* were a staple of the Renaissance kitchen. Chefs pounded them into crumbs and used them as a thickening agent. Crushed *mostaccioli* appear throughout Latini's *The Modern Steward, or the Art of Preparing Banquets Well* (1692–96) in custards, creams and meat stuffing mixtures, including a mixture of candied citron, pepper, ox marrow, rich cheese, egg yolks, sugar and lemon juice which he used to fill small pastries that sound a little like the forerunners of English mince pies.[17]

FINE MOSTACCIOLI

Take three pounds of peeled almonds, dry them and pound until very
smooth, sprinkling them with cedar flower water, you will add
four ounces of powdered cinnamon, and two pounds of flour,
be sure to add it little by little; take a pound and half of
clarified sugar, and cooked, you will put it in
the mortar over a charcoal brazier,
mix with a spoon making sure the
mixture does not stick, ground
two grains of must
with a little sugar,
put it in
the
jar, pulverizing it to a paste on the heat,
then when it is chilled, you will
form Mostaccioli in the
usual stamps.[18]

Bartolomeo Stefani,
L'Arte di ben cucinare (1662)

An Italian version of the Islamic *baqsamat bi sukkar,* mostaccioli were bound together with sugar water. At some point in the Renaissance, chefs began using egg to bind their biscuit mixtures. If the egg was thoroughly beaten it acted not only as a binding but also as a leavening agent. The base for these biscuits took on the character of what we would think of as a sponge rather than a bread. Scappi refers to the mixture as *pan di Spagna* – Spanish bread – suggesting that the innovation originally came from Spain. We may take this as evidence of the culinary influence of the Spanish kingdom of Aragon in southern Italy. Just as with bread rusks, once baked, the sponge biscuit bread was sliced and the slices were then dried to a crisp in a slow oven. Reflecting the proportions of flour, sugar and eggs, the various mixtures differed in density. Those made with more flour and where the eggs were only lightly beaten, resembled the hard sweet rusks of Arabia; we would now think of these as *biscotti.* The batters made with a mixture of sugar and eggs, first beaten into a thick frothy mass with only a little added flour, were often poured straight into narrow pans to produce light, friable sponge fingers.

By the sixteenth century, sponge finger biscuits were a stock part of the Italian chef's repertoire of sweetmeats. There were numerous variations on the basic recipe. The sponge base made a good vehicle for digestive seeds such as aniseed or coriander. More refined versions were enriched with milk and flavoured with musk or rose water.

Biscuits were eaten both at the beginning and the end of a meal. When they were served with the final course, diners would soften them by dipping them in sweet wines or hippocras. At the beginning of a meal, they were often dipped into creams or custards. To titillate the appetite, Antonio Latini recommended serving a 'tasty and noble' custard of egg yolks, candied peel, cinnamon and sugar in a silver bowl with a decoration of mint leaves and sponge fingers.[19]

Marzipan was another ubiquitous feature of the first and last course of a Renaissance meal. The name derives from *mauthaban,* which in Arabic denotes a type of money box. Muslim cooks initially fashioned a stiff paste of ground almonds and sugar into a sort of box to contain sweet fillings which is how Martino used marzipan.[20] Later, marzipan began to appear on Renaissance banquet tables as a sweetmeat in its own right, baked into a flat cake. Martino also created a sort of marzipan 'porridge' out of a mixture of water, ground almonds, breadcrumbs, sugar and rose water cooked over a gentle fire.[21] This was sometimes used as a filling for pastries but if beaten egg white was added to the mix rather than water, it formed a sticky 'dough' that could be baked into little cakes or biscuits. This was the origin of a range of Italian macaroon-like almond biscuits such as *ricciarelli*, *pasticcini* and *amaretti*.

In the Renaissance Italy of competing city states, power and status were projected through competitive conspicuous consumption. Who could commission the most impressive buildings or the most beautiful paintings, patronise the most inventive poets and the cleverest scholars or employ the best chef to give the most flamboyant banquets? In May 1475, the families of Constanzo Sforza and Camilla Marzano d'Aragona flaunted their wealth at the couple's wedding feast in Pesaro with a frivolous display of expensive sugary creations. The table was decorated with sugar sculptures of castles, birds and animals; four of the courses were made up entirely of sweet confections, including what appeared to be lilies and garlic cloves fashioned out of pine nut marzipan and sugar paste; comfits, quince paste, spiced wine, and twisted wafers. Ballet dancers brought round sugar caskets filled with sugar jewellery, and the bride and groom were given what appeared to be majolica bowls and glass goblets, all made from sugar.[22]

At the time of the wedding feast sugar was still an expensive luxury, but elite families could afford to put on such lavish displays because between 1350 and 1550 the price of sugar dropped by 75 per cent.[23] This was because during the course of the fifteenth century sugar production shifted into Portuguese hands. In the 1450s, Portuguese settlers on the island of Madeira realised that the climate was ideal for growing sugar cane. With Genoese finance and the skills of Sicilian technicians, they set up cane-processing mills. By 1480 seventy ships a year were plying the route between Madeira and Antwerp, making the former Eastern luxury good widely available in northern Europe.

Biscuits played only a minor role in lavish Renaissance banquets. Sponge fingers and macaroons were just one of the many ways in which sugar could be consumed, and they did not lend themselves to the fanciful sugar sculpture displays that allowed chefs to help their aristocratic masters outshine each other.[24] But if biscuits have left only a faint trace in the Renaissance cookbooks written by the chefs who worked for ecclesiastical and political dignitaries, they would have been popular among the middling commercial classes. As increasing amounts of New World sugar reached Europe and the price fell, a taste for confectionery spread downwards through society. The biscuit clutched by the small boy in Mantegna's painting might well have been bought from a street seller. In Italian cities vendors touted a variety of biscuits to those who could afford the indulgence of an S-shaped *susamielli* covered in dried fruit and almonds, a fennel- and aniseed-studded *taralli* ring, or a sugar-syrup-coated *panesigli*. The latter were precursors of the pretzel, as they were boiled before they were baked. Latini has left us a recipe that required that eleven pounds of flour, four ounces of rose water, four pounds of milk, two pounds of fine sugar, twenty-five eggs and six ounces of butter should be mixed together with hot water. Once the dough had risen, the *panesigli* were formed, presumably into rings or knots, and then dropped into boiling water before being baked.[25]

Antonio Latini's *The Modern Steward* was the last of the great Italian cookbooks. In the seventeenth century French *nouvelle cuisine*, with its emphasis on simple, natural flavours, rose to occupy the position of dominance in Europe.[26] As Italy's spicy, multi-layered syncretic cuisine fell out of fashion, the Islamic art of confectionery was preserved in an unlikely home: the convents of the Catholic Church.

In the fifteenth and sixteenth centuries the young girls who entered holy orders rarely did so out of religious conviction. Religious dowries were often less expensive than if the girl were to marry into a well-connected family, and yet valuable social links would still be forged that could be used to the advantage of her family. Nuns were required to spend their time productively. Well schooled in the accomplishments expected of the daughters of patrician households, they passed the hours sewing and embroidering as well as preparing medical remedies and confections.[27] The well-endowed religious houses had access to all the expensive ingredients needed to excel in the art of confectionery: they could afford plentiful supplies of New World sugar, the convent orchards produced an abundance of fruit and nuts, and the use of egg whites to make starch left plenty of egg yolks that would otherwise have gone to waste. Convent kitchens were well equipped with charcoal and wood ovens and all the necessary paraphernalia of graters, skimmers, sieves, pots and moulds. The nuns gave the confections they produced to aristocratic donors and benefactors, or sold them to raise funds. The Franciscan order of St Clare in particular gained a reputation for making the loveliest confections, and as the order expanded and opened new religious houses throughout Europe, the nuns took the art of confectionery to France, the Netherlands and Madeira.[28]

In the 1950s, in the Sicilian town of Erice, the inhabitants would still make their way down one of the town's narrow winding streets to the Instituto San Carlo to pick up a box of confectionery from the nuns living there. When they rang the bell a shadowy figure would appear behind the iron grating to take their order, and they would place their coins on one side of a revolving hatch; as the nun turned it, a box of sweetmeats would emerge from the other side.[29] The convent's staple product were *mostaccioli*, the same hard brown biscuits that Bartolomeo Scappi made for the Pope's guests to dip in their sweet wine at the end of a meal, and which Latini crushed into crumbs to thicken a sauce. People would buy half a kilo from the nuns to give to friends or relatives, or to the farmer when they went to buy olive oil.[30]

Eleven-year-old Maria Grammatico and her six-year-old sister Angela entered the Instituto San Carlo in 1952 when their father died, leaving their pregnant mother unable to feed six children. They joined fifteen other orphans and about the same number of cloistered nuns. Torn away from a happy childhood on their farm, it was daunting for the girls to learn that some of the nuns had entered San Carlo at the same age as Angela and never left the convent buildings. Even the Mother Superior had begun her life at the convent as an orphan.[31]

Maria was set to work helping the nuns make the biscuits and other confectionery that generated the convent's small income. On the fortnightly baking days she had to get up at one in the morning to light the fire in the cavernous brick oven, as it needed at least six hours to reach the necessary temperature. She would check the heat by rubbing a fennel stick on the floor of the oven: if sparks flew, it was ready for the first batch of *mostaccioli*. The nuns would bake about five or six batches of these, followed by a few batches of milk biscuits and finally some soft almond *bocconcini*. By now the oven would be cool enough for the *pasta di conserva*, little jam-filled marzipan shells iced with a special sugar glaze that turned white as it dried so that the pastries shone as if they had been polished. At the very end, often as late as eleven at night, when the oven was barely warm and Maria's eyes were red and sore from the smoke, they would put in the *amaretti* biscuits.[32]

The nuns produced 40–50 kilos of *mostaccioli* every other week and stored them in a large wooden chest.[33] During Lent they would make the more austere *quaresimali* biscuits, which contained neither egg yolks nor fat; just flour, almonds, sugar and egg whites. Other biscuits could be specially ordered. For weddings they baked batches of *miliddi ri badia* (my lady of the abbey), an aniseed-flavoured version of the ancient Greek *paximadia*: 'We made a bread dough, flour with a little leavening and a little anise and that's all and then shaped it into biscuits and let it rise. And they were crisp, we baked them twice until they were very crisp.'[34] At the end of October people would put in orders for the marzipan fruits they gave to children as presents from the dead on All Saints' Day. As Easter approached, Maria would painstakingly fashion curls of wool out of marzipan to decorate Paschal lambs. And before Christmas, she would grind figs together with oranges, nuts, spices and honey to make a stuffing for the *biscotti al fico*, which were versions of the filled biscuits made in Baghdad in the tenth century.[35]

The important place of confectionery in Catholic religious orders meant that in Italy and Spain biscuits and pastries became an integral part of the liturgical calendar. Bone-shaped biscuits are still made in some Italian towns for the day of the dead, and many of the confections are associated with saints. The little cream-filled pastry domes called *genovesi* are also known as 'virgin's breasts'; they are made to commemorate the martyrdom of St Agatha, whose breasts were cut off. Some legends suggest that these associations may go even further back, as saints often took the place of ancient gods in the affections of locals. In Calabria, for example, folklore suggests that the *mostaccioli* made to celebrate the feast of St Rocco have phallic symbolism derived from older pagan fecundity festivals. Women from the town of Cosimo are said to have purchased *prucitani* biscuits formed in the shape of female genitalia to give to their husbands at Christmas.[36]

In fact, virtually every city and town in Italy to this day produces its own distinctive biscuit; and just as the biscuits Maria made in the convent of San Carlo had barely changed since they first entered the Italian culinary repertoire during the Renaissance, many of these local recipes have been preserved over the centuries. It was to be in England in the seventeenth century that sweet biscuits underwent the next stage in their evolution.

SPICE BISCUITS

This recipe is from Frederick Nutt's *The Complete Confectioner* (1789). Nutt learned the art of biscuit making from Domenico Negri, a confectioner from Turin who in the 1750s founded the *Pot and Pineapple* in Berkeley Square, London. Nutt was his apprentice. The initial dough, made with sugar syrup, is a less spicy version of the Renaissance *mostaccioli* but the method of first baking the mixture in a 'loaf' and then slicing it follows the method for making sweet rusks.[37] These biscotti were meant to be dipped in sweet dessert wine but they also taste good dunked in tea or coffee. Indeed, Italian coffee shops usually keep large glass jars of biscotti on hand for this purpose. I like them best dipped in a single malt whisky.

Two words of warning: weigh your sugar carefully and err on the side of less rather than more and be careful with your oven temperature. Too much sugar or too hot a bake can result in a melted nut brittle rather than a 'loaf' that can be sliced.

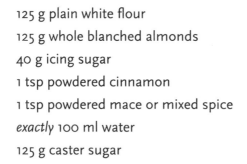

125 g plain white flour

125 g whole blanched almonds

40 g icing sugar

1 tsp powdered cinnamon

1 tsp powdered mace or mixed spice

exactly 100 ml water

125 g caster sugar

Sieve the dry ingredients into a large mixing bowl. Add the blanched almonds. Mix well with a wooden spoon.

Make the sugar syrup: put 100 ml of water in a pan and bring to a rolling boil. Then add the caster sugar. Do not stir. Swirl the water around until every sugar crystal has melted. Then boil for 1 minute until you have a thick viscous syrup.

Gradually pour the syrup into the dry ingredients while mixing with a wooden spoon. Once the syrup has cooled you can use your hands to bring the mixture together until it forms a pliable dough.

Form into a thick sausage about 30 cm long. Flatten it slightly with the palm of your hand and then press the sides down firmly with the side of your hand so that the centre is elevated.

Place the length of dough on greaseproof paper on a baking tray.

Bake at 160°C for 40 minutes.

Take out and turn off the oven. Turn the loaf onto a board. Nutt suggests wetting the back of the paper with a brush dipped in water. If you wait a few moments the paper will then peel off easily. Discard the paper.

Cut the loaf on the diagonal into thin slices about 3 mm thick.

Place the slices back onto the baking tray and return to the oven.

Dry in the oven for 40 minutes.

WAFERS AND WAFFLES

Although we think of wafers as a form of biscuit, they are not descended from twice-baked bread rusks. Wafers and waffles emerged out of the Jewish ritual of eating unleavened bread during Passover. The Book of Exodus tells us that the Israelites fled from Egypt in such a hurry that they did not have time to let their dough rise and so had to bake flat unleavened bread. As a reminder of this bread of affliction, for the eight days of the Passover festival Jews eat only unleavened matzo bread. In the first and second centuries CE they began making thin wafers by pouring an unleavened batter onto the bottom face of a pair of hot iron tongs. The tongs were then closed and held over a fire. It took a few minutes to make a brittle wafer that melted in the mouth.[1] If the face of the tongs was embossed with a pattern, this was transferred to the surface of the wafer. Passover wafers could therefore be elaborately decorated with animals and flowers.[2]

Until the ninth century Christians used leavened bread for the Communion, probably in order to distinguish the host from the Jewish matzo. But in 819 the Roman Catholic Church ordained that the bread used for Holy Communion should be unleavened, and Christians now adopted the Jewish technique for making matzo wafers, replacing the nature designs with Christian symbols.[3] This meant that no matter how primitive their surroundings, all that itinerant Christian preachers needed to make the Communion host was a bowl to mix up the batter, and a pair of tongs, which they could heat over a campfire. In response, Jews appear to have abandoned Passover wafers and returned to making matzo in the form of flat breads.[4]

It was traditional for the Christian Church to distribute communion wafers to the poor and the infirm on the Thursday before Easter. When in the thirteenth century the clergymen of Paris commissioned local bakers to make the *oblatum* (the Latin designation of the host) for the Easter distribution, wafers began to move out of the ecclesiastical and into the secular realm. A guild of *oblayeurs* (host makers) was founded in Paris in 1270, and they soon began selling wafers for non-ecclesiastical purposes. They added sugar and spices to the batter, and because the wafers were liable to crumble, they would roll them into tubes while they were still warm and malleable.[5]

In Italy wafers were often served with the Pope's medicinal goblet of hippocras at the end of a meal, transforming this Arabic practice into a ritual that echoed the Eucharist.[6] As Arabic influence on European cuisine spread the use of sugar across Christendom, it became standard practice for European monarchs to be given hippocras and wafers to finish a meal. In 1287 Edward I's Great Wardrobe accounts record the purchase of 667 lb of ordinary sugar,

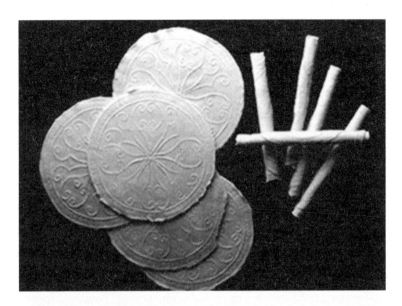

Wafers made by Ivan Day with a set of early seventeenth-century English wafering irons.

300 lb of violet sugar and 1,900 lb of rose sugar, some of which would have been used to sweeten his wine and wafers.[7] This practice spread into the wider population. The first detailed account of an English feast is found in a mid-thirteenth-century Anglo-Norman poem written to help a gentlewoman teach her children French. After describing the dishes eaten by a fashionable yeoman at a banquet, including 'rabbits in gravy, all covered with sugar', the poem describes how at the end of the meal, the company was served with 'sweet spice powder with large dragées, maces, cubebs and enough spicerie, and plenty of wafers'.[8]

Le Ménagier de Paris, a fourteenth-century household guide, confirms that the practice was also established in France. The treatise recommended that a generous wedding feast should allow eight wafers between two guests to accompany the hippocras at the end of the meal. Delicate wafers were made with batters enriched with wine, eggs, flour, a little sugar, and spices such as ginger. But most of the recipes in *Le Ménagier* suggest that by the fourteenth century wafers had developed from simple melt-in-the-mouth morsels into complex waffle-like creations. Recipes now included eggs and cheese in the batter; and one English medieval recipe even suggested adding the ground stomach of a pike.[9] By the fifteenth century, the English royal households of Henry VI and Edward IV had their own wafery, employing a yeoman in charge of an assistant and a page.[10]

When in 1582 Pope Gregory XIII changed the official beginning of the ecclesiastical year to January rather than March, the Dutch transferred the tradition of giving wafers to the old and the poor from Easter to New Year's Day. In 1770, when the city of Coevorden tried to put an end to the distribution, claiming that it placed too much of a financial burden on the better-off families, a furious crowd gathered in front of the city hall. As the council members fled, a few had their clothes torn when they were grasped in the wafer irons held by the irate protesters.[11] By the eighteenth century the Dutch were adding yeast to wafer dough and enriching it with sugar and butter to make what we would now think of as waffles, eaten with a spiced wine and butter sauce. The elaborate decorations on the face of the irons had by now given way to the honeycomb weave that makes the distinctive pattern we associate with waffles today. Wafer and waffle irons were often given as wedding gifts in the Netherlands and these were handed down through the generations as heirlooms (see page 2 of the picture section).[12]

IRMGARD'S BUTTERMILK WAFFLES

This is my German mother-in-law's recipe for waffles, from a 1978 cookbook endearingly entitled *Backvergnügen wie noch nie* (*Backing Enjoyment Like Never Before*). The buttermilk gives them a distinctive flavour (although if you don't have any handy you can substitute plain yoghurt). They are very good with maple syrup, black cherry jam or strawberries and cream. In my family we eat them for breakfast on Christmas morning (you can make the batter the night before and leave it in the fridge overnight).

125 g butter
50 g sugar
2 tbsp vanilla sugar
pinch of salt
4 eggs
250 g self-raising flour
250 ml buttermilk
oil for the waffle iron

Beat together the butter, sugar, vanilla sugar, salt and eggs until they are foamy.

Sieve the flour. Mix alternate spoonfuls of flour and buttermilk into the butter/sugar mixture. This should result in a fairly thick batter.

Grease the waffle iron with oil and heat. Put a small spoonful of batter in the hot iron and bake for 2–3 minutes until the waffle is golden brown.

4

In which Lady Elinor Fettiplace
bakes 'stif bisket bread'

If Lady Elinor Fettiplace was not to be found in the brewhouse, overseeing the mashing of the wort; or the dairy, supervising the production of cream and butter; or the bakehouse, checking whether the bread dough was proving; or the kitchen, tasting a sauce, she was probably in her still room. This was one of a collection of outbuildings clustered around the long, low Cotswold-stone house of Appleton Manor, a few miles south-west of Oxford, where Lady Elinor lived with her husband Sir Richard after their marriage in early 1589.

Throughout the summer and autumn she spent a great deal of time in her still room, drying herbs and flowers, pickling vegetables, preserving fruits and making fancy confectionery. The room was the realm of an alchemist, physician and confectioner. The central piece of equipment was the alembic still. Lady Elinor grew hundreds of damask roses for their petals, which she distilled into rose water, a flavouring that in the seventeenth century found its way into virtually everything, from savoury sauces to macaroons. Her still room was also equipped with special ovens for drying out herbs and flowers, a sugar boiler and preserving pans, pearling pots for sugar-coating seeds, wafering irons, charcoal stoves and braziers, and special chafing dishes with indented lids on which embers could be placed to gently heat the dish's contents from above and below. There were mortars and pestles for grinding spices into a fine powder; silk sieves for sifting sugar and cane ones for pulping fruit; bundles of birch twigs for beating eggs; marble slabs for pastry work; a syringe for squeezing biscuit dough into fanciful shapes; cutters and modelling tools for fashioning pastry and sugar paste; and moulds for shaping fruit pastes and biscuit dough into figures.[1]

Here Lady Elinor performed the alchemy of clarifying and refining sugar. In the sixteenth century there were only two sugar refineries in England, so most sugar had to be clarified at home. First the sugar cone had to be ground into a powder and dissolved in water with a clarifying agent such as bullock's blood or egg white. If it was brought to a rolling boil, the scum that rose to the surface could be skimmed off. The mixture then had to be strained into a drip cone and left to crystallise.[2] This process had to be repeated several times before fine white sugar could be obtained. This was then ground into coarse sugar crystals, 'double refined' (caster) or powdered (icing) sugar. With that, Lady Elinor had her base ingredient for her medicines, preserves, pickles and confections.

With the appearance of the first flowers in spring, she began candying them to create delicate decorations for her creams and custards, and mixing up syrup of violets to make soothing medicines to treat fevers. Yellow dye could be extracted from cowslips, red from roses and green from spinach to colour sugar fondant. In May the first tender vegetables were ready for pickling and the still room's shelves filled with jars of herbs steeped in olive oil to form the base for various remedies. In August the season for preserving fruit began with gooseberries and apricots and ended with the autumn harvest of apples and quinces. Fruit was boiled down with sugar to form thick, unctuous pastes, preserves and marmalades.[3]

Amid all this activity Lady Elinor also made biscuits. Indeed, besides fruit pastes, preserves, pastilles and sugar fondant, biscuits were her preferred form of confection. At the turn of the sixteenth century biscuits still belonged in that

In the frontispiece for Hannah Woolley's *The Queen-like Closet, or Rich Cabinet* (1675) the gentlewoman can be seen at work baking, preparing remedies and making confections.

strange halfway zone between medicine and food: as confections made of sugar they were perceived as both a sweetmeat and a remedy. Biscuit recipes were found not in ordinary cookbooks, but in the handbooks that began to appear in the second half of the sixteenth century promising to admit the uninitiated into the secret world of the confectioner. The first of these to be published in England was *The Secrets of the Reverende Maister Alexis of Piemont* written by Girolamo Ruscelli, an Italian alchemist, and translated from the French in 1558.[4] To modern eyes it is a peculiar book, which muddles together household tips on how 'to take all manner of spots out of silk' with remedies 'against the wormes in little children' and 'a very good Parfume against the plague' as well as 'the stinch of toes'; fanciful instructions on how 'to find Golde with Salamanders' with recipes for preserving fruit and vegetables in sugar. There is also one for making 'little morsels as they use in Naples' – the hard, spicy *mostaccioli* biscuits that we saw were a stock confection in the Italian chef's repertoire of sweetmeats.[5]

Lady Elinor's biscuit breads were versions of Italian sponge biscuit doughs, leavened by eggs, which needed to be beaten by themselves for at least two hours before the sugar was added and then for a further couple of hours until the sugar melted into the eggs. The idea was to produce a stiff batter thick enough to hold the tracks of the whisk when it was withdrawn (as we do now for a Swiss roll sponge). Then the flour could be added and the entire mixture would be beaten again before being poured into little dishes or pans. Lady Elinor's 'light bisket bread' and 'bisket bread' would both have turned out as crisp sponge fingers. Her 'stif bisket bread', the plainest of all her confections, made denser biscuits more akin to biscotti. This mixture contained more flour and did not require quite as much beating. Like bread, the dough was formed into a roll that was baked before being sliced and dried 'in the oven on a gredyron'. The resulting hard, dry rusks could be rubbed with sugar and, if boxed up, would keep for years. A store of them was kept on hand to offer to guests as they sat before the fire with a jug of posset.[6] We can see a direct line of descent from Lady Elinor's English biscuits back to the egg-leavened biscuit doughs of the Spaniards and Italians which were themselves descended from the sweetened rusks of the Arabs and the twice-baked bread of the ancient world.

'Maister Alexis' claimed that his Naples biscuits were 'very savorous, do comforte the stomacke, and make a swete breath'.[7] It was for the same purpose that Lady Elinor flavoured her biscuit breads with seeds: coriander to aid digestion and aniseed to sweeten the breath and suppress the vapours rising from the stomach. Her light bisket bread she flavoured with caraway, a distinctively English addition to biscuit flavourings. In his herbal, Nicholas Culpeper recommended caraway seeds to dispel 'the windy colic'; and in Shakespeare's time apples, which were thought to induce wind, were customarily served with a dish of caraway comfits.[8] Thus biscuits entered the English culinary repertoire as a form of prophylactic against digestive disorders.

We know about these activities in the still room at Appleton Manor from Lady Elinor's manuscript cookbook which is one of very few to have survived from the period. At the front, the manuscript is inscribed 'Lady Elinor Fettiplace, 1604'. Like the *Secrets of Alexis* it contains a hotchpotch of recipes, with instructions for how 'to bake a rabbit' interspersed with an egg nog 'for a great cold' and various versions of bisket bread. Three quarters of the text appears to have been copied out in one session by a scribe with a fine Italianate copperplate. This seems to have been a copy of Elinor's mother's household manual made for her to help her in setting up her own family home at Appleton Manor. The annotations noting extra ingredients, quantities and timings indicate that she used it as a working cookbook.[9]

Some of the recipes are attributed to friends of the family; others may have been copied out from the many manuals and advice books that followed the publication of the *Secrets of Alexis*. These enabled aspiring gentlewomen to buy expert knowledge rather than acquiring it by study or connections.[10] The manuals allowed the social climber entry into the sophisticated world of *The Accomplisht Cook* and instructed her on how to create *Delights for the Ladies*. This wealth of titles was aimed at the ambitious class of families who rose to prominence under the Tudors. Both Elinor's paternal and maternal grandfathers had fought for Henry VIII and were knighted on the battlefield. Lady Elinor's father, Giles Poole, continued the socially upward trend, prospering under Henry's heirs and eventually serving as Elizabeth I's provost martial for Ireland.[11]

The manuals were one of the means by which the Italian cuisine, and with it the Arab-Greek medico-culinary philosophy, was transmitted to England. Indeed, Lady Elinor's cooking reflects new trends in English cuisine. By the end of the sixteenth century increased foreign travel had exposed the wealthy to different food cultures and made them open to innovation; with the Dissolution of the Monasteries in the 1530s, the gentry's manor houses took on the role once held by the religious houses as centres of horticultural and culinary experimentation. Gentlemen employed foreign gardeners to assist with growing new fruit and vegetables. Italian cuisine was regarded as the height of culinary sophistication and household stewards were sent on regular shopping trips to London to stock up on the figs, currants, raisins, citrus fruits, pomegranates, olive oil, onions, garlic, spices, preserved ginger and sugar that were essential to replicating it.[12] The wealthy could afford to employ an Italian chef, but others had to content themselves with consulting Platina's *On Right Pleasure and Good Health*, which was translated into English as early as 1475.[13] The influence of Arab-Catalan-Italian cuisine is noticeable in Lady Elinor's liberal use of rose water, citrus juices and dried fruits. In her kitchen, sugar was used as a spice and considered a healthy addition to any dish. Her 'sauce dorfine' was a mixture of red wine, breadcrumbs, Seville orange juice and vinegar, to which she added a pinch each of cinnamon, ginger, galingale and sugar. At the end of the cooking process she added beef marrow to give depth of flavour. The sauce was poured over roast chicken, and to finish, she sprinkled the dish with red and white sugar-coated anise and caraway seeds.[14]

Although it was by now commonplace to serve spiced, sweetened wine and wafers while the table was cleared ('voided') at the end of a meal, until the 1540s only royalty and the superbly wealthy could afford to lay on a profusion of sugary confections such as were commonplace at the Renaissance courts. This changed with the flooding of the north European market with Portuguese-produced New World sugar. In the 1540s, the Portuguese settler Duarte Coelho successfully introduced sugar cane to Pernambuco on the Brazilian coast. Within a few years Brazil had become the world's major producer of sugar and the price of sugar halved.[15] This substantially increased the availability of the sweet comfits that Platina recommended should be consumed at the end of a meal. In Lisbon, London merchants bought confections from the Catholic convents and the confectioners' shops that proliferated in the city. Sephardic Jews, who had been heavily involved in the Mediterranean sugar trade and confectionery business until they were driven out of the Iberian peninsula in 1492, now set up confectionery shops in London and Amsterdam.[16] Boxes of Portuguese quince paste, 'biskets' and macaroons were added to the list of items the steward was to secure on his shopping trips to London. Now when the guests filed out of the great hall for the 'void', they entered little anterooms where an array of sweetmeats had been set out on a bench or 'banquet'.[17] Among the nobility it became fashionable to build banqueting houses in rooftop turrets or the gardens of their country houses (see page 3 of the picture section).[18]

Skill in making confectionery items was added to the list of desirable accomplishments for the gentlewoman. In *Country Contentments, or the English Housewife* (1613), Gervase Markham listed among the skills that a 'compleat woman' should possess 'physick, chirogery, cookery, extraction of oils, *banqueting stuff*, ordering of great feasts, preserving of all sorts of wines, conceited secret distillations of perfumes', as well as more prosaic skills such as 'ordering of wool, hemp or flax, making cloth and dying; the knowledge of dairies, the office of malting oats, their excellent uses in families, of brewing, baking and all other things belonging to a household'.[19] The spread of the art of confectionery throughout the manor houses of England was confirmed by a member of James I's entourage when the recently crowned king stopped at Sir Anthony Mildmay's manor at Apethorpe

THE USUALL BISKET SOLD AT
COMFIT-MAKERS

Take a peck of flower and foure ounces of
Coriander-seed, one ounce of Anniseed: take
three eggs, three spoonfuls of ale-yeast, and
as much warm water as will make it as thick
as paste for manchets [white wheat loaves]:
make it in a long rowle, and bake it in an
Oven one houre; and when it is a day old,
pare it, and slice it, sugar it with searced
sugar, and put it again into the Oven: and
when it is dry, take it out, and new sugar it
againe, and so box it, and keep it.

A Closet for Ladies and
Gentlewomen (1651)

in Northamptonshire on his progress from Scotland in 1603. 'The tables were newly covered with costly banquets wherein everything that was most delicious for taste proved more delicate by the Arte that made it seeme beauteous to the eye: the Ladye of the house being one of the most excellent confectioners in England, though I confesse many honourable women very expert.' Lady Mildmay was so proud of her accomplishments that when she had her portrait painted in 1613, she had the artist include two of her stills as well as her household receipt book in the painting – just as a gentleman might have had himself painted with signifiers of learning such as books or a globe.[20]

Lady Elinor too would have aimed to create a colourful display on her banqueting table. The translucent fruit jellies she produced were supposed to shimmer gem-like in the candlelight. Alongside bowls of white creams and bright yellow custards she served crisp fingers of bisket bread and delicate white wafers curled into cigar-shaped rolls. Wine-soaked sippets of biscuit were used as a base for a cream 'foole' in an early version of what would become trifle.[21] Her almond macaroons were finished with a layer of icing that shone like polished glass. Biscuits fashioned into letters of the alphabet, twists and knots added structure to the display, which would have been strewn with crystallised flowers and tiny candied fruits.[22]

In 1641 England established its own sugar-producing colony on the island of Barbados. James Drax imported sugar cane and the processing technology from Portuguese Pernambuco, and by the 1680s, the island was producing as much sugar as Portuguese Brazil. Sugar imports into London more than doubled, and in contrast to the price of other foodstuffs, which either remained stable or rose, the price of sugar fell again, from a shilling a pound in 1660 to 6d or 7d a pound in 1685. Although sugar would still have been an expensive luxury for a skilled craftsman earning 36d a day, it was now within his reach.[23]

In 1681, just as sugar prices were falling, 21-year-old Rebecca Price began compiling her own manuscript cookbook of receipts. The daughter of a successful London draper, Rebecca belonged to the growing middle classes whose wealth was based on trade and commerce rather than land. Many of Rebecca's recipes were gleaned from family or friends. Aunt Rye was a frequent source, but she seems to have been a muddled cook. The transcriptions of her recipes read as though her words tumbled out too quickly, and she goes backwards and forwards in her instructions, remembering an earlier stage when she has already moved on to a later one. Often she warns not to let something boil too long or spoil in the oven, as if this was something that frequently happened to her. To her recipe for 'Almond Bisquittes' Rebecca appended the note, 'I having made them did not approve them' and the recipe was crossed out.[24] But her Cousin Clerk's recipe for biscuit was one of Rebecca's staples. The detailed set of instructions gives an insight into the hard work that went into making confectionery. First the ingredients themselves had to be prepared: the flour dried and sieved, the sugar cone ground and sifted, the eggs separated. Before the laborious process of beating air into the mixture began, it was necessary to heat the oven. Whether the correct temperature had been reached could be ascertained by how quickly a paper placed on the oven floor browned. Although she instructs that the biscuits should lay on a cloth until quite dry, Rebecca includes no instruction for a second baking of her cousin's biscuits: the 'bis' (twice) in biscuits had become redundant.

In this seventeenth-century illustration for a sonnet a Dutch gentlewoman is eating a sponge finger biscuit in her closet or private chamber. Rebecca Price kept a sweetmeat cupboard in her closet and no doubt sponge fingers were among the confections she kept in it. French women referred to their closet as a boudoir, a term English women adopted, hence sponge fingers were sometimes referred to as boudoir biscuits.

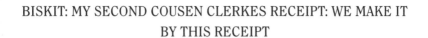

BISKIT: MY SECOND COUSEN CLERKES RECEIPT: WE MAKE IT BY THIS RECEIPT

Take a pound of fine flower dry it, and searce it through a tiffany sieve, take also a pound of fine sugar beaten and sifted; then take six eggs and three of the whites, but be sure to take none of the tridles; beat with your eggs four spoonfuls of rosewater till they are enough, then put your sugar in by little; and little, at a time till all be in; keeping it beating all the while; and always one way, for an hour by the clock, as fast as you can, but when you first go beating put fire into the oven, for you must not stay for that, make it as hot as for white bread; be sure to have it hot enough, when you have cleansed it very well you must take a mop wetted and wipe the top, and sides, of the oven, then shut up your oven a little while, when your oven is ready put your flower into your sugar, and eggs, keeping it stirring till you put it in your pans, which you must have ready buttered, and put them in the oven as fast as you can, first trying with a paper if it not colour too much, keep down the lid all the while they are in, take them out when they are enough which will be before they are co-loured, you must be sure not to stay for too long in your oven, for that will spoil them quite; when they are done, take them out of the pans, and lay them on a cloth with their bottoms up, for a day or two till they be dry; if you have not pans to put them in, you may drop them upon plates buttered, and that will do as well: instead of rose- use orange-flower water which is much better, 4 spoonfuls is enough.[25]

Rebecca Price's cookery manuscript (1681–1740)

Many of the recipes in Rebecca's cookbook are annotated 'my mother's receipt'. But her mother died when she was ten and she was sent to school in Hackney.[26] In the 1650s, Hannah Woolley, one of the most popular cookery writers of the second half of the seventeenth century, had run a school there. By the time Rebecca attended one of these establishments in the 1670s, Hackney was so overcrowded with schools for young ladies that it was known as 'the ladies' university'. Samuel Pepys made a special point of attending Sunday service in Hackney church on 21 April 1661, 'chiefly to see the young ladies of the schools whereof there is a great store, very pretty!'[27] The girls were taught the accomplishments appropriate for a gentlewoman: French and Italian, bookkeeping and verse-making, cookery, pastry work and the art of confectionery. From the recipes Rebecca learned at school we can see the influence of French cuisine on English culinary practices.

In 1660, the year Rebecca was born, the restoration of the monarchy hastened the influence of French cuisine on English cookery. Charles II had spent his years of exile living in France, and when he returned, he brought with him a French cook. French food soon became fashionable. Rebecca's school employed a Frenchman to teach confectionery; next to many of her recipes she noted 'given me at Schoole' or 'given me by Monsieur le Marqui Achiolier'. Monsieur Achiolier taught her how to confect a *trompe l'oeil* dish of bacon and eggs entirely from sugar paste, as well as a range of Italian biscuits including 'Naples Bisquets' (sponge fingers) and 'Ratafie Cakes' made with ground apricot kernels.[28]

From these recipes it is possible to see how Italian biscuits were gradually evolving in French and English hands. Her cookbook contains recipes for 'Almond puffs' and 'Jumbles', which are Italian almond biscuits, but it also contains 'Mrs Whitehead's recipe for very fine cakes' made from a paste of flour, marzipan, nutmeg, grated lemon rind and eggs, an English interpretation of Italian macaroons. Coated in a sugar and rose-water icing, they would have been intensely sweet.[29] Rebecca's cookbook also includes a version of what Lady Elinor called 'white bisket bread'. Lady Elinor's was composed mainly of whisked egg whites and sugar, but contained a handful of flour to give the 'dough' substance.[30] In the 'sugar or Italian biskets' Monsieur Achiolier taught Rebecca, the flour had been dropped from the recipe and her biscuits were musk- and aniseed-flavoured meringues.[31] Monsieur Achiolier also taught her how to make 'Melinde' using the Italian method of making meringue by heating the mixture of sugar and egg whites.[32] Long before 'meringue' appeared in any printed cookbook, Rebecca's manuscript indicates that it was firmly established in the English repertoire of confectionery. She gives many recipes for fruit puffs, biscuits and drops that are all versions of meringue with the addition of fruit juice or pulp.[33] Although we no longer think of meringue as a biscuit, for a seventeenth-century confectioner they were a version of egg-leavened biscuit bread.

TO MAKE MELINDES: A FRENCH RECEIPT: GIVEN ME BY MONSIEUR LE MARQUI ACHIOLIER

Take halfe a pound of lofe suger beat very fine, and three whites of eggs, put them with the suger into a copper or silver skillitt, then with a wooden spoone stir it till it be as white as snow, then set it over a few hot embers till it becomes like pap, keeping it stirring and not letting it boyle; take it off and put to it a good halfe spoonfull of orange-flower water, then set it over the fire againe, that the humidity of the water may be dryed, be sure not to let it boyle, then lay it upon white paper (strewed with suger) in what fashon and bigness you please to have them, then bake them in a temperate oven that is not too hot, I thinke the best fashion to make them in is rather longesh, that is to say about an inch and halfe longe, and almost an inch broade.[34]

Rebecca Price's cookery manuscript (1681–1740)

Even before they acquired their own sugar-producing colonies, the English exhibited an excessive fondness for sugar. Already in 1603 the Spanish ambassador to England commented that English gentlewomen ate prodigious amounts of bonbons, comfits and sweetmeats.[35] In the 1660s, about half the semi-refined muscovado sugar that arrived at the London docks from the English West Indies was re-exported to Europe. By 1700, raw sugar imports had doubled but the amount the English were retaining for their own use had increased to two thirds of all imports.[36] The sugar trade fostered the growth of a new class of planters, merchants, financiers, industrialists, craftsmen and shopkeepers, all of whom also made up a large part of the increasing number of people who consumed sweetmeats. As sugar became established in English kitchens as a staple rather than an exotic luxury, the English expanded the range of confectioneries they made, including the varieties of biscuits. But if sweet biscuits were a product of England's access to abundant sugar from its growing empire, the empire that afforded them this indulgence itself depended on biscuits. Not the sweet biscuits of the banqueting course, but the ancient, unsweetened twice-baked bread that was the staple food of the early Christian monks.

SPONGE FINGERS

This modern version of seventeenth-century sponge fingers is quick and easy to make with an electric beater, and is an ideal base for a trifle.

    3 eggs, separated
    100 g ground almonds
    1–2 tsp rose water or orange-flower water or the grated
    rind of 2 lemons
    160 g caster sugar
    100 g white or wholemeal flour

Pre-heat the oven to 160°C.

Whisk the egg whites until they just hold their shape, then beat in the ground almonds.

Whisk the egg yolks with the flower water (if using) and the sugar until pale and the mixture leaves a ribbon-like trail when the beaters are lifted out of the mixture.

Combine the two mixtures. Sieve in the flour and add the lemon rind (if using). Mix well and spoon into well-greased baking tins – a large teaspoonful should be enough for each biscuit. Sprinkle them with caster sugar and bake in a moderate oven for 40 minutes.

Remove from the tin and cool on a rack.[37]

In this eighteenth-century recipe for trifle from Margaretta Acworth's manuscript cookery book the layer of fruit jelly has not yet been added to trifle. I add a layer of fruit purée on top of the sponge fingers.

To make a Trifle. Take Savoy biscakes [another name for sponge fingers] and lay them in a China Dish. Cover the Bottom [and] wet them through with white wine. Boyl a thick Custard and pour it over them, then whip up a sullibub and put it on the Custard. It must be made overnight. You may make it what size you will.

To make Whip Sullybubs. Take a pint of Cream, put to that half a pint of sack…[sherry], half a nutmeg grated, some Lemon peel grated, [juice of] two or three lemons, sugar as you like. Beat these together to a sullibub then put them in your glasses. You may if you will Boyl your cream first.[38]

GINGERBREAD

Buy any gingerbread, gilt gingerbread! Will your worship buy any gingerbread, very good bread, comfortable bread?[1]

The cry of Joan Trash, the gingerbread seller in Ben Jonson's comedy *Bartholomew Fair*, would have been familiar to his seventeenth-century audience. The fair was where ordinary people had the opportunity to sample banqueting sweetmeats. A good 'fairing' was a paper twist filled with a collection of caraway and almond comfits, candied angelica, macaroons and gingerbread biscuits.[2] Fairs had grown out of gatherings of worshippers and pilgrims at sacred sites to celebrate saints' days, and often the biscuits were shaped to celebrate the saint in whose honour the fair was held. Thus those sold at the Grasmere rush-bearing ceremony on St Oswald's day were formed into a likeness of that saint, while at the Great Charlton fair held on St Luke's day the gingerbread was stamped with his symbol, the horned ox.[3]

For two or three days a field would be transformed into a miniature town of tents and wooden booths forming streets of shops selling cloth, books, spices, groceries, haberdashery, pottery, glassware, butter, cheese and salt fish. Merchants and farmers with bulky goods such as wool, coal, iron and grain would station their carts on the edge of the fair. Even in the sixteenth and seventeenth centuries the commercial life of towns was still limited largely to market days, and there were few permanent shops. The stewards of great houses would visit fairs to lay in supplies, and shopkeepers from the capital would travel around the country buying up goods in bulk at wholesale prices to sell on in their London shops. And as the fairs expanded and attracted entertainers, puppet shows, menageries, theatrical shows and trinket sellers, people dressed in their Sunday best would flock from miles around to buy, sell and revel in the fun.[4]

Traditionally, those visiting religious fairs bought a relic or image of the saint in whose honour the fair was held as a keepsake, but this morphed into an edible representation; hence gingerbread men became a common feature of fairs.[5] The figures offended the Puritans, however, as they were reminiscent of Catholic icons. In *Bartholomew Fair*, the character of Busy shouts out against 'this idolatrous grove of images, this flasket of idols' and throws the gingerbread men on the floor in a fit of anti-papist disgust. But by this period the figures had also begun to serve anti-Catholic purposes. At the first bonfire celebrations in November 1606, just one year after the Gunpowder Plot had been foiled, little gingerbread figures known as 'Guys' were sold.[6]

English gingerbread began life as a medical remedy. The records of Robert Montpelier, apothecary to Henry III (1216–72), refer to *gingibrati* as a medical paste made from parsnips and candied with honey, ginger, pepper, nutmeg and galingale. At some point medics appear to have taken the denomination 'brati' to mean bread and replaced the parsnips with breadcrumbs, so by the 1350s the mixture was known as *gingebrede*.[7] This blend of breadcrumbs, honey, ginger and a few other spices was boiled in the still room until it took on a thick toffee-like consistency; it was then baked and served in slices or squares at the banquet. On the Continent, gingerbread was known as *Lebkuchen*, and although it was originally made in monasteries, eventually guilds of gingerbread bakers emerged in German and Austrian towns, respectively known as *Lebküchner* and *Lebzelter*. Nuremberg became the centre for gingerbread production, as it was both at the heart of southern German honey production and served as the distribution point for goods from the east that arrived in packhorse trains from Italy.[8] Here a special form of small round gingerbread biscuits known as pepper nuts (*Pfeffernüsse*) developed, which were leavened with potash so that the biscuits-cum-cakes stayed moist even if they were stored for a long time.[9]

It would appear that the cake-like gingerbread made with flour with which we are more familiar arrived in England from France at some point in the seventeenth century. This dough could be pressed into moulds and fashioned into figures and shapes, a practice that had been developed into an art by Dutch and Belgian bakers. Covered in gilt, such figures were splendid additions to the banqueting table. Gingerbread letters also became fashionable, and it was said that Dutch schoolchildren learned their alphabet from them. In the *Expedition of Humphrey Clinker*, Tobias Smollett talks of a girl who doesn't 'yet know her letters ... but I will bring her the ABC in gingerbread' (see page 4 of the picture section).[10]

Given that it was made from a few basic ingredients, gingerbread was produced in a surprising number of variations. In Ashbourne in the Peak District, it was flavoured with rose water and red wine and studded with candied peel; in Grasmere in the Lake District, it developed into a buttery ginger shortbread; in Honiton in Devon, the fairings were brandy snaps.[11] In much of the north of England, gingerbread was made with oats rather than wheat flour and known as 'tharf cakes' or parkin. Parkin was not a creation derived from the still room but rather a fancy version of the food of ordinary people. During the feast of Martinmas, often referred to as Little Lent because it was a forty-day period of fasting from November until Christmas, people frequently added honey to their oatcakes. It may seem odd that they consumed honey in an abstemious period, but since ancient times honey had been regarded as a sacred food and was associated with regeneration. (Hence the German name for gingerbread, *Lebkuchen*, which means 'life cake'.) It was therefore thought to give a pure form of much-needed nourishment to those who were fasting. 'Tharf' seems to imply something heavy and sodden, and oatcakes made with honey would have fitted this description. The denomination 'parkin' probably came about in the same way that 'Johnny cake' became the common name for cornmeal flat breads and 'George Brown' for brown bread, affectionately associating the common surname Perkin with the rough breads of ordinary folk. Ginger spiced up the festival versions of parkin, and when ginger tharf cakes were distributed to the poor on All Saints' Day, they were known as soul-mass cakes.[12]

During the seventeenth century, treacle replaced honey in both parkin and gingerbread. Treacle is the English name for the molasses or sweet uncrystallised syrup that drains out during the production of sugar as it slowly crystallises into a solid mass. From the 1650s, raw brown muscovado sugar from Britain's new sugar colony in Barbados flooded the London sugar market, and by 1692 there were 38 sugar refineries in the capital, processing the brown sugar cones into white refined sugar. A by-product was plenty of cheap molasses.

At the time, the most common use for molasses was in a medical remedy known as *theriaca*. It was purportedly developed as a universal antidote to poison in the second century BCE by King Mithridates VI, who lived in constant fear of assassination. It was a peculiar mixture of viper's flesh, herbs, spices, turpentine resin, bitumen and opium dissolved in honey. In early-modern times several cities in Italy produced the potion; Venice *theriaca* was supposedly the best. Imports arrived in London, where the English garbled the name into 'Venice treacle'. Regarding it as the best remedy for the plague, English apothecaries soon began producing a more affordable 'London treacle' in which they substituted cheap molasses for the expensive honey.[13] Before long, the molasses sold by the English refineries became synonymous with London treacle. It is possible that the earliest recipes for gingerbread that call for treacle rather than honey actually meant the medicine rather than plain molasses.[14] Gingerbread made with treacle took on its magical aura and carried a whiff of supernatural potency (see page 1 of the picture section).[15]

Plain treacle became the poor man's sugar and now replaced expensive honey in fair offerings of gingerbread and parkin. Ginger also fell in price as England started to import this originally East Indian spice from its own colonies in the West Indies. In fact, by 1696, West Indian ginger accounted for more than 60 per cent of *all* spice imports. Its wholesale price fell to

1¾d per pound, which made it one of the most affordable and widely used spices.[16] This made gingerbread and parkin the dominant confectionery affordable to the ordinary fair-goer.

A detail from William Hogarth, 'The idle 'prentice executed at Tyburn' (1747). Hogarth included in his scene one of London's best-known street vendors, the gingerbread seller known as 'Tiddy Doll'. He is holding up a gingerbread cake in one hand while he places the other on his heart to convey his sincerity. He was known for his eccentric sales patter and would assure the crowd that his gingerbread would 'melt in your mouth like a red-hot brick bat, and rumble your inside like Punch and his wheelbarrow'. He always ended by singing the refrain from a popular ballad that ran, 'tiddy, diddy, dol-lol, ti-tiddy, ti-tiddy, ti-ti, tiddy, tiddy, dol', hence his nickname. He was renowned for dressing like a person of rank and Hogarth has depicted him in his characteristic gold lace suit with a ruffled shirt and a feather in his hat, the whole completed by a large white apron.

Although the selling of rich spiced cakes and pastries at fairs was forbidden during the Commonwealth and Protectorate, with the Restoration fairs and festivals revived and gingerbread fairings returned.[17] And as market towns developed, gingerbread stalls became a regular feature of market days.[18] Growing up in the 1860s, George Sturt still recalled that 'it was customary to buy gingerbread' at the fair, 'thick hunks... or circular disks embellished with lemon peel which had to be removed. Hunks or disks, it was none of it really nice... a trifle bitter even – yet the occasion made it palatable.'[19] Indeed, fair gingerbread had a poor reputation – witness Ben Jonson's name – Joan Trash – for his gingerbread seller. In the play, Lanton Leatherhead the hobby-horse man threatens Joan: 'Sit farther with your gingerbread progeny there, and hinder not the prospect of my shop, or I'll have it proclaimed in the Fair, what stuff they are made on.' He claims that her biscuits are made of 'stale bread, rotten eggs, musty ginger, and dead honey'.[20] Indeed, all too often the gilt decoration on gingerbread fairings was there to disguise the substandard nature of the product. Hence the expression 'to take the gilt off the gingerbread'.[21]

CORNISH FAIRINGS

Cornish fairings have been made commercially by the Furniss bakery in Truro since 1886. Their name indicates their much older origin as one of the sweet treats revellers in the south-west would have bought at a fair. These are my favourite ginger biscuits: easy to make and possessing a perfect combination of chewiness and crunch.

  225 g plain flour
  2 tsp baking powder
  2 tsp bicarbonate of soda
  2 tsp ground mixed spice
  1½ tsp ground cinnamon
  3 tsp ground ginger
  pinch of salt
  120 g butter
  120 g caster sugar
  grated zest of one lemon
  4–5 lumps of stem ginger, chopped into little pieces
  5 tbsp golden syrup

Preheat the oven to 180°C. Line two baking trays with grease-proof paper.

Sift the flour, baking powder, bicarbonate of soda, spices and salt into a large bowl. Rub in the butter until the mixture resembles fine breadcrumbs. Stir in the sugar, lemon zest and stem ginger. Warm the golden syrup over a gentle heat and add. Mix well.

Bring the mixture together into a dough with your hands. Divide the dough in half and break each half into 12 walnut-sized pieces and roll them into balls.

Place on the baking trays (allowing room for the biscuits to spread) and flatten each ball slightly with the back of a fork.

Bake for 8–10 minutes. They should be golden brown and have a crackled surface. Don't worry if they are still squishy when they come out of the oven; they harden as they cool.

Leave for five minutes on the tray then use the eighteenth-century confectioner Frederick Nutt's technique to loosen the biscuits from the greaseproof paper. Turn the biscuits out onto a cooling rack so that the paper is upmost and brush the paper with a pastry brush dipped in water. Wait a few moments and the paper will easily peel off the biscuits.

LEBKUCHEN

450 g plain flour
1 tsp baking soda
1 tsp baking powder
1 tsp powdered cinnamon
1 tsp ground cardamom
½ tsp powdered cloves
½ tsp powdered anis
½ tsp grated nutmeg
½ tsp ground ginger
225 g honey
200 g sugar
125 g butter
1 large egg, beaten

Sift the flour, baking soda and baking powder into a bowl. Sift the spices into another bowl.

Gently heat the honey, sugar and butter together, stirring all the time until the butter has melted and the sugar dissolved. Do not allow the mixture to boil.

Remove the pan from the heat and stir in the sifted spices.

Gradually stir in the sifted flour, adding as much as is needed to make the dough, when stirred, pull away from the sides of the pan. This will probably require most of the flour.

Allow the dough to cool for five minutes. Remove to a bowl if the pan is still very hot.

Beat in the egg, then knead the dough with your hands, first in the pan or bowl and then on a flat, lightly floured surface. If it is too sticky to handle, knead in a little more flour until it no longer sticks to your hands.

Divide the dough into four pieces and roll out each piece to 6 mm thickness, then cut out biscuits and place on greased baking trays. Leave them to rest for 1–2 hours at room temperature.

Heat the oven to 165°C and bake for 15–20 minutes. Do not allow to brown.

Cool on a wire rack and glaze with an icing sugar wash, or dip in melted chocolate.

5

In which Spanish fishermen make biscuit soup on the Barbary coast

For a mother to fail to prepare her daughter for what to expect on her wedding night 'is like sending her to sea with no biscuit'.[1]

In the 1590s every spring about 30 Spanish fishing vessels would set sail from the Canary Islands heading for the Barbary coast. There, the beaches for 600 miles south of the Atlas Mountains were deserted. The Moroccan king's cruisers did not venture this far south and inland was nothing but barren desert crossed only by a few nomadic tribespeople. This meant that the fishermen could go about their business undisturbed. They would spend the mornings fishing and then go ashore about midday to clean and salt their catch. By five or six in the evening they were ready to eat their only meal of the day. On a flat hearthstone they kindled a fire and suspended a kettle over the flames. While some of the catch boiled in the kettle, in another pot the cook would mix shredded onions with broken biscuit and season it with pepper and vinegar. Once the fish broth was ready, he poured it over the biscuit mixture to produce a soup.[2]

This fish soup – which was remarkably similar to the brew of onions, herbs and olive oil that the monks of the Kosmosoteira monastery poured over their bowls of crushed biscuits – was how ship's biscuit was supposed to be eaten.[3] For fishermen and sailors – and as we will see later, for soldiers too – who lacked the facilities for grinding grain and baking bread in large firewood-hungry ovens, biscuit was their substitute bread. In order for it to last, ship's biscuit needed to be baked until it contained only 10 per cent water; ideally, it was rock hard. To consume it, therefore, sailors and fishermen softened the biscuit in water or some other liquid to reconstitute it into a form of bread. The soup the Spanish fishermen prepared on the west African beaches was a timeless dish. Those dependent on biscuit for their sustenance made variations on this soup throughout the centuries and across the globe. If they only had biscuit, they cooked a simple soup of 'black biscuits', water and salt.[4] To this basic 'breadscouse' they would add whatever scraps of meat, vegetables and flavourings they had to hand. In Lapland they made *lapskuis* with walrus meat; in Germany *labskaus* might include both meat and herrings. The English normally added salt beef or pork and, crucially, vinegar.[5] They knew that the Spaniards used orange and lemon juice as an antidote to scurvy; assuming that the fruit's remedial quality was its acidity, they substituted citrus juice with cheaper vinegar.[6] This meant that although it had no medicinal value, vinegar became a ubiquitous flavouring on English ships and a standard ingredient in English lobscouse. In Liverpool, scouse was such a common meal among dockers that they – and later all the inhabitants of the city – acquired the name 'Scousers'.

In the Middle Ages the efficient production of ship's biscuit was a prerequisite for any power that wished to establish maritime dominance. In the eastern Mediterranean easy access to timber had allowed Venice to build up large merchant

CHARLES AUGUSTUS ABBEY'S RECIPE FOR SCOUSE

Abbey first went to sea on 12 April 1857, aged fourteen, in the clipper the *Surprise*, one of the first American vessels to enter the China–England tea trade.

'I have made *"scouse"* for the last two days ... by breaking up some biscuit & soaking it in water a few minutes & cutting in bits of beef, then put in some *"slush"* or grease of any sort & let the cook bake it for me. It is better than nothing though, how ever bad it may be.'[7]

The diary of Charles A. Abbey (1857)

Slush was the fat that rose to the top of a vat of boiled salt beef. The cook was not supposed to give it to the sailors to add to their duffs or puddings because it was considered unwholesome and even to cause scurvy.[8] Instead, they would save it and sell it once they went ashore to tallow makers, who would gather on the docks when ships came in. This made the cook a small profit and is the origin of the term 'slush fund'.

and naval fleets, and along with Florence and Genoa, the city state emerged as a thriving hub on the trade route that linked the Byzantine and Muslim worlds to northern Europe.[9] The city's Arsenal was the most dramatic expression of its maritime power. At the time, this great shipbuilding and repair yard was probably the biggest industrial complex in Europe. It inspired Dante's description of the deepest pits of hell. As Virgil descends into the eighth circle, he encounters sinners condemned to endlessly smear unsound vessels with boiling pitch, while others perpetually twist cordage.[10] Next door to the Arsenal, probably equally hot and hectic, was the biscuit bakery. Even in the seventeenth century, by which time Venetian power was waning, this single bakery swallowed one tenth of all the grain arriving in the city.[11]

When in the 1290s Philip IV set up the Clos des Galées at Rouen to build galleys for the French Crown, he charged the master of the new shipyard (modelled on the Venetian Arsenal) with the task of establishing an efficient bakery to provision the growing French fleet with biscuit.[12] The Ottomans initially relied on biscuit imports from Egypt to provision their navy, but as Ottoman power grew, the sultan set up bakeries in Istanbul under the charge of the *emin-i peksimad* (officer of the biscuit).[13] Naval administrators closely monitored biscuit quality to ensure that standards were maintained; from time to time samples were even sent to the sultan himself. Before long there were bakeries on Crete, the Peloponnese, Cyprus and in the Dardanelles.[14] Venetian and Spanish spies paid close attention to the level of activity at these bakeries as increased production indicated that the Ottomans were preparing for a naval campaign.[15]

In order to support maritime exploration, John I of Portugal (1357–1433) also set up a large naval biscuit bakery, next to the royal palace.[16] The Portuguese held out little hope of breaking Italian dominance over Mediterranean trade and instead focused on finding a sea route round the coast of Africa, where they hoped to discover the sources of the gold, ivory and spices that reached Europe across the Sahara. In the early fifteenth century, Europeans still had only the haziest notion of the configuration of the world's continents. Indeed, the most accurate map available to them was still based on the descriptions of the second-century BCE geographer Ptolemy. The Europeans knew that Asia was the source of the spices and silks that the Arabs traded with Venice, but the Muslims sat astride the land route to the east. Some thought it might be possible to circumvent them by travelling west across the forbidding expanse of the Atlantic. Others thought it might be possible to sail around Africa and reach the east that way, even though Ptolemy had depicted the Indian Ocean as a landlocked sea.[17]

The exploration of these alternative routes to the Indies involved leaving behind the confines of the familiar maritime world, where ships only made short passages out of sight of land. In the Mediterranean, a ship's captain navigated by using his ability to recognise coastal landmarks, his knowledge of the distance between them and the course he needed to set in order to move from one to another. In contrast, oceanic explorers had no idea how long they would have to sail out of sight of land, and any coastline they encountered would obviously have been of little help in fixing their position. Advances in astronomy made navigation on the open ocean possible. Astronomers had discovered that they could use the apparent immobility of the pole star and the movement of the sun as a means to navigate. Using a compass, astrolabe and quadrant, mariners were now able to calculate their latitude.[18] Improvements to hulls and rigging had also inadvertently created trading ships able to withstand oceanic conditions.[19]

Biscuit played a humble but equally important part in overcoming the obstacles of time and distance. Most Mediterranean and Baltic journeys took only a few weeks or days: Barcelona to Alexandria took eight weeks, Genoa to Tunis ten days. Exploratory voyages took years.[20] In the familiar world of the Mediterranean or North Sea, ships could call in at a friendly port if they ran into trouble or ran short of food supplies or water. Isolated on the open ocean, explorers were dependent on what they carried with them. Even if they did touch land, it was not always certain that they would be able to find food in the strange new worlds they encountered. Indigenous people were often unwelcoming, sometimes hostile, and frequently did not have surplus supplies of food available to trade. Importantly, it also became clear that diseases were most effectively avoided by staying at sea.[21] A good supply of biscuit and salt meat packed into the ship's hold was essential in making explorers self-sufficient for long periods of time.

Over the course of the fifteenth century, the Portuguese became leaders in maritime exploration. The records of the Lisbon bakery show that, well supplied with biscuit, they edged their way down the African coast until in 1488 Bartolomeu Dias succeeded in rounding the southern tip of Africa, confirming that the Indian Ocean was open to the Atlantic.[22] In 1492, Christopher Columbus – funded by Portugal's main competitor, the Spanish Crown – sailed west and encountered the Americas. Meanwhile the Portuguese appear to have commissioned a series of voyages to investigate Atlantic navigation. The shipping records that would verify this are missing from the chancellery, but the records of the Lisbon bakery show that it was producing far more biscuits than would have been needed for the voyages that are listed.[23] Moreover, when Vasco da Gama set sail for India in 1497, the route he took across the Atlantic was extraordinarily accurate by contemporary navigational knowledge. He sailed in a great arc, initially following a south-westerly route far out into the ocean until he almost touched Brazil before picking up westerly winds that blew him east and round the Cape of Good Hope. It is clear that the Portuguese had already worked out the winds and currents that would allow them to confidently navigate across the Atlantic and into the Indian Ocean.[24]

The food conditions on a voyage of exploration replicated those experienced during the European winter. The Scandinavian peasantry who suspended their poles of oatcakes from the roof beams knew that they had to last until the spring thaw. Across Europe animals were slaughtered in the autumn and their meat salted down, while sacks of dried peas, lentils, grain and biscuits were carefully packed into well-ventilated storerooms. When da Gama set sail from Lisbon, he carried enough biscuit, rice, salt pork, salt fish, cheese, wine and vinegar to feed his 170 men generous rations for three years.[25] By spring, most northern Europeans were pre-scorbutic, even if they were not suffering from full-blown scurvy. Da Gama's crew were the first mariners to encounter the disease. Southern Europeans, whose Mediterranean diets were rich in ascorbic acid, often had small reserves of vitamin C stored in their livers. But when da Gama's crew first sighted the African coast, they had been sailing across open ocean for thirteen weeks – the longest recorded passage any European seamen had yet made out of sight of land – and they were beginning to show symptoms of scurvy.[26] By the time they careened the ships on the east African coast in January 1498 in order to carry out repairs, they had been living on biscuit and salt meat for five months, and many of the sailors' gums had 'swelled and rotted, so that their teeth fell out, and there was such a foul smell from the mouth that no one could endure it'. Da Gama's solution was to order that each sailor 'wash his mouth with his own water [urine]'.[27]

A few months later, da Gama's sailors were able to obtain fresh food when they stopped at Melinde on the East African coast, and they soon recovered. The sailors on Ferdinand Magellan's 1519 attempt to discover a western route to the Indies were less fortunate. The expedition only succeeded in finding a passage round the tip of South America 14 months after leaving Seville. As they emerged into the Pacific in November 1520, Magellan was assured by his officers that the fleet still had three months' worth of provisions. He was confident that the crossing would take only a few days. As they sailed north up the Chilean coast, they caught a westerly wind and set out to cross an ocean that covers one third of the earth's surface. It would be three months and twenty days before they sighted land again. By that time the biscuit they had bought in the Canary Islands a year earlier had crumbled away to a powder crawling with worms and stinking of rat's urine; the penguin and seal meat the men had salted down in South America had begun to rot and was also crawling with maggots; the water had turned putrid and yellow. The crew fell sick with scurvy and 19 men died. When they finally reached the island of Guam, they were able to gather fresh food and water before continuing their search for the Spice Islands.[28] Magellan's ambitious project to circumnavigate the globe by sailing west subjected his sailors to extreme deprivation. But as scurvy was the inevitable consequence of prolonged reliance on a diet of salt meat and ship's biscuit, it remained the scourge of sea life for hundreds of years.

The consequence of maritime exploration was an explosion in global trade. Only a couple of decades after Columbus reached Haiti in 1492 and da Gama anchored off Calicut in 1498, European ships had reached as far as the isthmus of Panama and Brazil in the west and China and the Spice Islands (Moluccas) in the east. Within another 10 years, Magellan had crossed the Pacific Ocean and Spanish *conquistadores* had defeated the Aztec empire. The once-empty Atlantic and Pacific oceans were now traversed by hundreds of ships. Already by 1505 the Portuguese were sending an annual fleet of 20 vessels to the Indies, and by mid century fleets of 60 or more ships left Spain each year carrying the goods Spanish settlers required to maintain a European lifestyle and returned laden down with hides, sugar, cacao, tobacco and gold and silver bullion.[29] In contrast to the old European sea trade centred on the Mediterranean, in this new maritime world long-haul sea passages crossing vast expanses of ocean were the norm. It took six to eight weeks to sail across the Atlantic, four months to traverse the Pacific, and a return trip to the Spice Islands lasted at least eighteen months.

Long-lasting ship's biscuit was this trans-oceanic trade's essential fuel. The Lisbon bakery now churned out hundreds of thousands of tons of biscuit to supply the East India fleets. Rather than setting up its own bakery, which would have been more efficient, the Spanish Crown relied on private contractors to produce the necessary ship's stores as and when they were needed. Biscuit makers thrived in the northern port towns of Santander and Bilbao, from where many of the fleets set sail for the Americas.[30] The Europeans established a series of outposts around the globe, with dockyards to repair shipping and biscuit bakeries to resupply the fleets for their return voyages.

The Dutch and the British initially joined the Atlantic trade as smugglers and pirates, preying on Spanish and Portuguese shipping, but eventually they established their own trading companies. Within a few years of the founding of the Dutch East India Company in 1602, 150 bakeries had sprung up around the tiny village of Wormer in the waterland north of Amsterdam to supply the East India fleets. Any surplus biscuit the bakers packed into barges and sold at the markets in Amsterdam.[31]

The biscuits made at these European bakeries were no longer bread rusks. When in August 1498 da Gama's expedition sailed from East Africa, where they had rested for a few months before they set out across the Indian Ocean, the local ruler sent a parting gift of 'biscuit … rice and butter, cocoa-nuts, sheep salted whole like salt meat, and others alive … fowls and vegetables … and much sugar in powder in sacks'. He had ordered the biscuit 'to be made in the Moorish fashion, which is like mouthfuls of bread'.[32] The Muslim traders on the east African coast still relied on old-fashioned rusks, made from twice-baked slices of bread. In contrast, the Lisbon bakeries rolled the biscuit dough into sheets after it had risen and then cut it into squares. These they still baked twice, first in a hot oven and then again in a moderate one, but European ship's biscuits were now flat discs rather than hard slices of bread.[33]

From the late sixteenth century, Britain built a trading empire to rival that of its European competitors. England's North American and West Indian colonies absorbed English manufactures and supplied salt cod, tobacco, rice and sugar in exchange. A series of trading posts along the west African coast allowed them to participate in the triangular Atlantic slave trade, while the English East India Company, founded in 1601, established bases throughout the Indian Ocean and flooded the London markets with spices, textiles and tea. Between 1650 and 1815 the Dutch, Spanish, French and British were in constant conflict around the globe as they sought to undermine each other's commercial power. With each skirmish the British increased their naval strength in order to protect their maritime trade.

By the time Britain emerged victorious from the Napoleonic wars in 1815, it commanded the largest and most powerful navy in the world.[34]

Already in 1560 the Tudors had built a naval victualling yard on the site of an abandoned Cistercian monastery near the village of East Smithfield, close to St Katharine's Dock. The yard contained a large storehouse for food and a number of ovens for baking biscuit.[35] But most naval biscuit was supplied by private bakers, who had a poor reputation. In the 1560s, William Clowes, the Lord Admiral's surgeon, was dismayed by the 'rotten and unwholesome victuals' that were served to Elizabeth I's seamen: 'their bread was musty and mouldy Bisket, their beer sharp ... their water corrupt and stinking ... their beef and pork ... of a most loathsome and filthy taste ... in so much that they were constrained to stop their noses when they did eat and drink'.[36] English bakers were accused of adulterating their flour with ground peas, chalk and bone dust. Worse, provisions were kept down in the ship's damp, vermin-infested hold, and on long, warm voyages the biscuit inevitably became damp.[37] In Shakespeare's *As You Like It*, Jacques makes reference to this when he describes the fool's soggy brain as 'drie as the remainder biscuit after a voyage'.[38] Damp biscuit was liable to become infested with the black-headed larvae of the cadelle beetle. Sailors referred to the maggots as 'bargemen', for as the biscuit was distributed to each mess, they would crawl out into the wooden bread barge.[39] According to one miserable young sailor, these maggots made 'your throat cold in eating ... like calves-foot jelly or blomonge'.[40]

The cadelle beetle in its adult form was known as a weevil.[41] In *Roderick Random*, which Tobias Smollett based on his experiences as a naval surgeon on a warship in the West Indies, he describes how 'every biscuit ... like a piece of clockwork, moved by its own internal impulse, occasioned by the myriads of insects that dwelt within it'.[42] That a biscuit might well have moved under propulsion from its resident vermin does not seem quite so unlikely in the light of Joseph Banks's comment that he had frequently observed 'hundreds, nay, thousands, shaken out of a single biscuit'. Banks's position as gentleman naturalist on James

Cook's scientific expedition to the South Pacific in 1768–71 meant that he ate in the captain's cabin with Cook and the ship's officers. They solved the problem of the weevils by re-baking their biscuit 'in an oven, not too hot, which makes them all walk off'. Banks spared a thought for the rest of the crew, however, who lacked such means to rid their biscuit of weevils and 'must find the taste of these animals very disagreeable, as they...taste as strong as mustard, or rather spirits of Hartshorne'.[43]

During the War of Jenkins' Ear (1739–48), the high rate of illness and death among the sailors in the Caribbean made it apparent that poor food was affecting the navy's capacity to fight. It was this naval engagement that Smollett was drawing on when he described the weevily biscuits in *Roderick Random*. The navy introduced a number of measures to improve victualling. It was thought that the excessively salty nature of the sailors' diet was the cause of scurvy, and so salt fish was dropped from the sailors' ration and replaced by oatmeal and sugar. Lemon juice and pickled cabbage were also added, and the navy made greater efforts to resupply naval squadrons with fresh food even while they were at sea.[44]

In addition, the navy began a campaign to weed out the private contractors who cheated them by supplying poor-quality goods.[45] In the 1770s, the contract with the Portsmouth baker Christopher Potter was cancelled as he was accused of baking his biscuit in too slack an oven and on one occasion using flour so rank that the bakers themselves were forced to stop working, overcome by the stench of the steam from the ovens.[46] The naval depots at Chatham, Dover, Deptford, Portsmouth and Plymouth, which had begun life as stores, now evolved into centres of food production, with slaughterhouses, breweries and bakeries. Twelve ovens operated at Deptford, with another six at Portsmouth, eight at Plymouth, six at Dover and one at Chatham. The navy was able to ensure the quality of the biscuit from its own bakeries.[47]

In his *Universal Dictionary of the Marine*, the poet and sailor William Falconer described how the industrial principle of the division of labour pioneered by the

English factory system was applied to the work of biscuit making in the naval bakeries. Each oven was operated by a team of bakers, each of whom performed one task repeatedly, deftly coordinating their efforts so that they 'worked together like the wheels of a machine'. One baker made the dough in a vast vat, while another kneaded the great mass too unwieldy to be worked by hand by means of a pivoted beam attached to the wall. Sitting astride one end, he shuffled to and fro in a most 'uncouth' fashion, thus working the beam over the dough.[48] Next, the moulder shaped the dough into biscuits and another baker docked the biscuits, stamping holes in them to allow the steam to escape and prevent the dough from bubbling and blistering during baking. Then, with a rhythmic clack of his shovel-like peel, the peeler slid 70 biscuits a minute into the oven. When all 33 assembly lines of bakers were working at full capacity, they were capable of churning out 13 million pounds of biscuit each year, enough to supply 33,850 men. Made from stone-ground wholewheat flour, and so hard that they gained the nickname 'purser's nuts', the biscuits were a condensed form of fibre and calories. Four of them amounted to the sailor's allowance of a pound of biscuit a day.[49]

The sailors nicknamed the Deptford yard 'Old Weevil', for good reason. While the Dutch and the Americans realised that the best way to keep biscuit was to pack it into airtight boxes, the British did not follow their example until late in the nineteenth century. Instead they packed their biscuits into sacks or casks. They did, however, make efforts to keep the 'bread room' airtight by lining it with mats or planks, which were then caulked with pitch or tar.[50] But in fine weather they made the mistake of ventilating the room, filling it with warm, damp sea air and thereby creating conditions conducive to the breeding of the biscuit beetle. It was no wonder a retired sailor at Greenwich Hospital described himself 'as stanch an old blade as ever knock'd a cock-maggot out of a king's biscuit'.[51]

The stomach-churning descriptions of maggoty, weevil-ridden biscuit make us think that the food on board naval ships was always bad. In fact, for every memorable description of bad biscuit, it is possible to find hundreds of references in contemporary sources that simply describe it as a mundane item of food. Even in *Roderick Random*, biscuit features several times without adverse comment as a normal feature of a shipboard meal. The eponymous hero 'sups plentifully' on cold boiled beef and biscuit with a midshipman; eats Cheshire cheese, onions and biscuit with Mr Morgan; and is entertained to a more elaborate repast of soup, roast pullet, asparagus, biscuit and Burgundy by Monsieur d'Estrapes.[52] Sailors complained a great deal about their food, calling their salt beef 'Irish horse' and the fellow who gave out the 'purser's nuts' 'Jack Dust'. But at the same time they resisted any attempts to change or improve their diet, complaining bitterly when they were supplied with alternatives like rice, lentils or chickpeas, which were sometimes all that was available in places like Calcutta or Macau.

The naval diet of beef three or four times a week was certainly better than that of the British agricultural labourer, who was glad of a warm meat-based meal once a week. Indeed, the promise of good food was held out to young boys as a reason for joining the navy. One man who had run away to sea when he was seventeen described how two sailors fell in with him and his friend while they were wandering the Liverpool docks. They asked the boys if they were looking for a ship and praised their captain, promising that 'he'll order the purser's steward to blow your kite out with lobscouse and choke your luff with figgy-dowdy'. To a young man scraping by on bread and cheese, the prospect of meat stew and a pudding made of crushed biscuit, pork fat, plums, figs, rum and currants must have been tempting.[53]

During the French Revolutionary and Napoleonic Wars (1792–1815), naval administration and supply came under extreme pressure. By 1801, the victualling service was responsible for provisioning 400,000 sailors and soldiers, 90,000 of whom were stationed across the globe. With each of them entitled to a daily pound to a pound and a half of biscuit, this amounted to an annual requirement of 83,428 tons.[54] Double gangs of bakers were put on the ovens at Portsmouth and Plymouth so that they could work through the night. Sometimes the demand was so great that there was no time to dry out the biscuits in special repositories above the ovens; no sooner were they out than they were packed into bags and dispatched.[55] The efficient victualling system enabled the success of Britain's military campaigns.[56]

Twenty-nine victualling ships operated in the Mediterranean, while a similar number shuttled provisions from the dockyards to the fleet patrolling the English Channel.[57] Due to the sailors' dislike of substitutes, the navy went to great lengths to ensure that even the most distant supply ports could dole out biscuit. Contractors in the West Indies were able to import biscuit from America, but in India the navy brought in wheat and built flour mills and bakeries at Calcutta and Madras to ensure that the sailors received their supply.[58] At home, the drive to weed out corrupt bakers continued, and over time the Victualling Board became less and less lenient. In 1810, Thomas Hearn was reprimanded for delivering 100 bags of 'old, smelly and maggoty' biscuit to the agent victualler at Portsmouth and was given no further contracts, despite having been a major supplier to the navy since 1793.[59] After Napoleon's defeat, the navy set about encoding the lessons they had learned from the years of conflict, and warned contractors that if their biscuit failed to meet their requirement that it should be 'good, sound, sweet... [made with] dry English wheat [and] thoroughly kiln-dried', for every substandard hundredweight bag, two shillings would be docked from their payment.[60]

The pressure of wartime demand stimulated innovation in the field of food processing. In France, the government's promise of a prize for innovations in food preservation motivated Nicolas Appert to develop a technique for hermetically sealing food in glass bottles. Appert's method applied to tin cans eventually gave rise to the British meat-canning industry, which became a major supplier of tinned beef to the navy.[61] Meanwhile Thomas Grant, superintendent at the Portsmouth victualling yard, worked on a way to apply the power of steam to biscuit making. In 1832, his innovative steam-powered machinery was introduced at the depot. The mixers he invented could produce five hundredweight of dough within a couple of minutes. The unwieldy mass was now effortlessly kneaded in a drum, doing away with the bum-shuffling baker on his kneading beam. Huge rollers transformed the mass into a sheet, which passed through a printing-press-like stamping machine. This pressed the biscuit shapes into the dough, at the same time docking them with tiny holes, before the whole sheet was passed into the oven, itself heated by a steam-powered furnace. The new machinery could churn out biscuits at the rate of 7,000 tons a year. Had it been available at the time, the navy would only have needed 11 ovens to fill its needs for 1801, at about a quarter of the cost. Thomas Grant was awarded £2,000 by Parliament and a gold medal by the Society of Arts.[62]

Ship's biscuits were thus one of the first foodstuffs to be industrially produced. Grant's steam-powered machinery was introduced in the naval depots at Deptford and Plymouth and later in supply bases such as Malta, where throughout the Napoleonic Wars the flour had been ground in donkey-powered stone mills like those used in Roman times.[63] Grant put the navy at the forefront of industrial food production, and details of his biscuit-making machines were published in scientific journals. It took a few years for his innovations to have an impact on commercial biscuit making. It is unclear whether J. D. Carr knew of his machines when he introduced similar machinery to make ship's biscuits in his Carlisle bread factory five years later. Nine years after that, in 1846, Huntley & Palmers opened the first fully mechanised biscuit factory, in Reading, and made Britain the world's leading producer of industrial biscuits.

Biscuit was an indispensable tool of empire building. It was as essential to the sailors who first explored the globe as the astrolabe and the compass. The merchant marines that were the lifeblood of the European trading empires that followed and the navies that protected them were equally dependent on ship's biscuit. So too were the early colonial settlements that resulted from the European exploration of the oceans.

6

In which Joseph Banks enjoys fish and biscuit boiled for about an hour

Chowder which I believe is Peculiar to this Country…is the Chief food of the Poorer & when well made a Luxury that the rich Even in England at Least in my opinion might be fond of. It is a Soup made with a small quantity of salt Pork cut into Small Slices a good deal of fish and Biscuit Boyled for about an hour unlikely as this mixture appears to be Palatable I have Scarce met with any Body in this Country Who is not fond of it whatever it may be in England Here it is Certainly the Best method of Dressing the Cod.[1]

The chowder Joseph Banks enjoyed when he visited Newfoundland in 1766 was a reminder of the settlement's beginnings. At the end of the sixteenth century, a flotilla of fishing ships would set sail every spring from the West Country bound for the northern coast of America. Once they reached Newfoundland, the fishermen set up makeshift camps and spent the summer fishing. They cured their catch in salt and dried it on racks on the beaches. By the end of the season they would have accumulated great 'haystacks' of salt cod, which they sold to Dutch, French and Spanish merchants who arrived off the coast towards the end of the summer, their ships loaded with Spanish export wine.[2] The exchange was lucrative. Salt cod was a popular alternative to meat in the southern Mediterranean, and Spanish wines were valued in England. In Shakespeare's *Henry IV*, Falstaff devotes an entire soliloquy to the merits of a 'fertile sherrie' and attributes the valiant nature of Prince Harry to its blood-warming properties.[3] As the weather began to turn, the fishermen would pack up and set sail for home. Newfoundland offered little in the way of food resources and for the duration of their stay the men were reliant on their ship's stores. Their staple food was lobscouse – the food of fishermen throughout Europe. In the West Country, with its strong links to Brittany through the butter trade, lobscouse went by the name of chowder, derived from *chaudière*, the Breton word for the cauldron-like pot in which French fishermen prepared their biscuit soup.[4]

Even the founding of a settlement in the 1660s by groups of fishermen and Royalist noblemen fleeing the Commonwealth barely affected the diet in Newfoundland. The island's interior supported few game animals, as the indigenous Beothuk discovered to their cost when they withdrew inland away from the European invaders. The growing season was short and the settlers' kitchen gardens produced only a few hardy vegetables. For food supplies they relied on ships like the *Unicorne* of London, which arrived in Newfoundland in 1640 with a cargo of forty barrels of Irish beef, a ton of sea biscuit, three tons of French aqua vitae and one and a half tons of tobacco.[5] The West Indies supplied the settlers with rum and molasses in exchange for their spoiled cod, which the planters fed to their slaves. Ireland was the main source of Newfoundland's provisions of salt butter, beef and pork. The latter was a lucrative by-product of the Irish butter industry, as the smallholders fed the buttermilk that was left over after butter making to the pigs. Irish salt pork was the favoured meat in Newfoundland and therefore a main ingredient in the chowder, which, as Joseph Banks discovered, remained the 'chief food' of ordinary Newfoundlanders in the eighteenth century.[6] Even in the first half of the twentieth century a family living in an outport would prepare for the winter by stocking up on the same ship's stores that the first settlers had relied on: '20 or 30 barrels of flour, so many bags of bread (hard tack), a puncheon of molasses, tea, sugar, [and] beans'. A quick meal might consist of 'hardtack [biscuit] broken with a hammer or marling pick ... soaked for a few minutes in water, and then briefly heated in a pan with molasses and a bit of butter'.[7]

If he had ventured further down the North American coast, Joseph Banks would have been able to sample a New England version of chowder, made with clams. New England's cookery also betrayed the first settlers' dependence on ship's stores. The early colonists found it was far more difficult than they had expected to plant a settlement in the strange American land. The first attempt to found a colony, on Roanoke Island in 1585, failed for want of the regular arrival of food supplies from England. A second attempt funded by the Virginia Company of London at Jamestown in 1606 survived due to the efforts of Captain Christopher Newport, who sailed backwards and forwards between England and America bringing supplies of salt meat and biscuit as well as more settlers to replace those who had died of disease and starvation.

The fair allocation of the stores of salt pork, dried peas, ship's biscuit, oatmeal and beer was a constant source of conflict among the settlers. Jamestown's first governor, Edward Maria Wingfield, was accused of keeping the choicest provisions, such as oil and spirits, for himself and his close associates while denying the sick and dying even a spoonful of beer. He was eventually removed from office and sent back to England. But Wingfield's sense of entitlement paled in comparison to that of George Percy, who in 1609 became governor. He was an unlikely candidate for this role, not least because his family was in disgrace as it was implicated in the Gunpowder Plot. He fell into the role by default as the more respectable leaders of the expedition had all died. The account books of his brother, the ninth Earl of Northumberland, show that the Northumberland household spent the substantial sum of £58 in 1608, rising to £77 in 1610, on clothes, furnishings, biscuits, cheese and butter to send out to Percy in Jamestown. Meanwhile he presided over the starvation of his fellow settlers. By the end of the winter of 1609–10, only 60 out of 500 settlers were still alive. The decision had already been made to abandon the colony, when the arrival of a supply fleet in May 1610 with yet more biscuit and salt meat, livestock, and crucially a cache of tobacco seeds that one of the would-be settlers had picked up in Bermuda, turned the fortunes of the colony around. Ten years later, the profits the colonists made from growing tobacco meant that they were able to buy in their own food stores and were no longer dependent on the irregular flow of supply ships sent by the Virginia Company.[8]

Further up the coast in the 1620s and 30s, the founders of what became New England struggled to carve productive farms out of the densely forested American landscape. Even when they did manage to laboriously dig out the enormous tree stumps, plough the land and plant the fields with wheat, the grain was attacked by fungus and the wheat germ shrivelled inside the husks. The colonists depended on the willingness of the local Native Americans to trade foodstuffs and were forced to imitate their method of growing maize, squash and beans in untidy gardens. They were so hungry they took to foraging on the muddy beaches for shellfish. Roger Clap, who arrived in America in May 1630, recalled 'in the beginning ... oh the hunger that many suffered ... to be supplied only by clams, mussels and fish ... bread was with many a very scarce thing; and flesh of all kinds as scarce'.[9] Many of the colonists regarded this diet with some horror, based as it was on foodstuffs that they thought fit only for animals and the poor.

The key to New England's eventual success was not farming but fishing. Over time a community of fishermen settled on the shores of the new colony, many of them West Countrymen who had come out to work a season in Newfoundland and found their employer had no space on his ship to carry them home at the end.[10] The fishermen were shunned by the farming population as rough-and-ready, ungodly folk. But in the 1640s, the decline in the Newfoundland cod fishery caused by the English Civil War opened up new economic opportunities. The New

Englanders began to supply southern Europe, Madeira and the West Indies with salt cod, and at the same time they were able to open new markets for their timber, pitch and tar. This boosted their shipbuilding industry and carrying trade, and these along with the cod fishery became the foundation on which New England's eventual wealth and prosperity was built.[11]

In the nineteenth century, however, New Englanders cast their region as the home of America's ideals, a region populated by hardy, independent yeoman farmers who were model citizens. The corn bread and baked beans that had once been emblematic of the settlers' failure to establish English farming and the chowder that was the mainstay of the fishermen the pious had regarded as marginal lowlife were now regarded with pride as dishes made of distinctively American foods which had saved the founding fathers from starvation. Clam chowder in particular was celebrated as a New England heritage dish.[12] An entire chapter of Herman Melville's 1851 novel *Moby Dick* is devoted to chowder. When Ishmael and Queequeg call in at Nantucket, they stay at the Try Pots Inn, which Ishmael tells us serves this 'favourite fishing food' for breakfast, dinner and supper. 'Oh, sweet friends! hearken to me. It was made of small juicy clams, scarcely bigger than hazel nuts, mixed with pounded ship-biscuit, and salted pork cut up into little flakes; the whole enriched with butter, and plentifully seasoned with pepper and salt.'[13]

There is today little consensus as to the authentic recipe for New England chowder and much discussion about which fish to use, whether you should add milk or cream, tomatoes or potatoes. The confusion arises from the fact that the early colonists would have made their chowder with whatever ship's stores they had available. The only certainty is that the base would have been biscuit, the vital colonial foodstuff that enabled early settlers to gain a foothold in the strange new land uncovered by maritime exploration.

Settlers brought a range of cookbooks with them to the New World. One of the oldest is known as 'Martha Washington's Cookbook', a fair copy of a manuscript cookbook of the kind kept by gentlewomen like Elinor Fettiplace and Rebecca Price. Like Lady Elinor's manuscript it contains recipes for all the standard seventeenth-century banqueting foods, such as preserves and comfits, wafers and bisket breads.[14] These confections and biscuits quickly passed into the American colonial baking tradition. In the first American cookbook, published in 1796, Amelia Simmons includes a recipe for Shrewsbury cakes that would not have looked out of place in an English cookbook. Judging from Sarah Rutledge's collection of the recipes of the women of Charleston from the 1840s, and the recipes that were sent in to *Godey's Lady's Book*, a popular magazine with a circulation of 150,000 in the 1860s, American women baked the full range of English biscuits: Shrewsbury cakes, rout cakes, ratafias, jumbles, macaroons, sweet wafers, and various versions of the sponge finger.[15]

What confuses us today, however, is terminology: what the English would now call biscuits, the Americans call crackers or cookies; what the English think of as scones, southern Americans call biscuits. This confusion can be unravelled by tracing the introduction of Dutch bakery traditions into the Americas. The American use of 'biscuit' is related to the development of soft breads in northern Europe and, in particular, to Dutch bakery traditions.

Throughout Europe there was a vibrant tradition of making soft bread rolls, rings and loops. Often these were twice baked to form various biscuits. In Italy rings of dough were baked into bread-stick like *taralli* while in the Netherlands soft rolls made with butter-enriched dough were made into golden rusks with a hollow centre. Often these soft breads were boiled before they were baked like the *panesigli* that feature in Latini's cookbook.[16] In France the breads were formed into double loops of dough and potash was added to the water in which they were boiled. A popular fairing in France, these dark smoky breads with a brown crust and a soft centre were known as *nieules*. In Germany, rock salt rather than potash

A New York street vendor of pretzels and a customer.

was added to the water and the breads were known as *Bretzelen* – bracelets – as children wore them as amulets on All Souls' Eve. When German emigrants took them to America, *Bretzel* became pretzel.[17]

The bakery culture was particularly strong in the Low Countries. Here, the Dutch referred to pre-boiled breads as *krakeling* and a popular game was for two children to *krakeel* (quarrel) over a pretzel-shaped bread by each hooking their little finger round one side and pulling. For the pious Dutch the game conveyed the idea of man caught in the middle of a struggle between the forces of good and evil like a *krakeling* tugged on by two children.[18] After 1581, when the United

Provinces achieved independence from Spain, rising earnings encouraged the development of a vibrant consumer culture. The late-sixteenth-century Dutch had sufficient disposable income to sleep on feather beds and eat from fine plate.[19] The ready availability of New World sugar encouraged the development of an array of waffles, pancakes and sweet breads studded with candied peel or fruit, dusted in sugar and dipped in caramelised syrups (see page 4 of the picture section).[20]

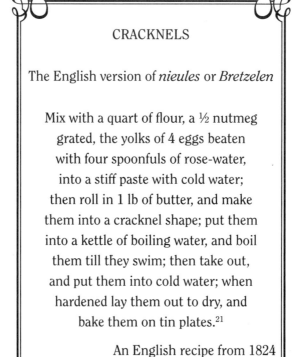

CRACKNELS

The English version of *nieules* or *Bretzelen*

Mix with a quart of flour, a ½ nutmeg
grated, the yolks of 4 eggs beaten
with four spoonfuls of rose-water,
into a stiff paste with cold water;
then roll in 1 lb of butter, and make
them into a cracknel shape; put them
into a kettle of boiling water, and boil
them till they swim; then take out,
and put them into cold water; when
hardened lay them out to dry, and
bake them on tin plates.[21]

An English recipe from 1824

The Dutch took their soft breads and sweetmeats with them to their colonies. In 1624, the Dutch West India Company established a fort at the confluence of the Mohawk and Hudson rivers as a hub from which to control the fur trade with the Iroquois. In the summer months it was visited by Native Americans bringing in packs of beaver pelts to exchange for *wampum* – a shell currency – with the Company traders. A Dutch settlement grew up outside the fort and to the annoyance of Company officials the settlers began trading with the Iroquois for furs, offering them in exchange ironware axes and kettles, cloths and beads as well as sweet breads and pastries. Just as the desire for spices, sugar, porcelain, tea, tobacco and textiles was the engine that drove European exploration of the globe and the creation of trading empires, so too the desire for European goods drew indigenous people into the global economy. The Iroquois liking for Dutch bakery goods led to so many furs being diverted from the West India Company's coffers that it was forced to prohibit the settlers from baking sweet and fruited breads during the summer. One Dutch baker was fined because 'a certain savage' was seen leaving his house 'carrying an oblong sugar bun'.[22]

Dutch baking traditions persisted long after the English takeover of New Netherland in 1664. We can see this from the recipes for rusks contained in Amelia Simmons' cookbook, which are strikingly similar to the rusks Dutch settlers made in their South African Cape colony. Simmons' dough is enriched with butter and milk; in South Africa Dutch settlers added lard or butter, sometimes milk or cream to their bread dough and slightly sweetened it with sugar.[23] The Dutch settlers at the Cape fashioned this dough into small rolls that they split in two after the first baking and dried out in the oven until they resembled toast. In South Africa, rusks became a staple food for travellers. The Boer pioneers loaded them into their wagons before they set off in search of land in the African interior beyond the reach of the British colonial administration, which took possession of the colony during the Napoleonic Wars. They were still a favourite food of the late-nineteenth-century settlers who moved further into the African interior.

Zillah Carey recalled that during her family's trek into Rhodesia in the 1890s, the toast-like rusks were 'a favourite to eat with coffee'.[24]

Simmons' instructions show that Dutch and English bakery traditions intersected. Seventeenth-century English gentlewomen used similar dough mixtures to make soft sweet breads known as simnels and hard crisp biscuits known as cracknels. In Norfolk, rusks made in the Dutch style from twice-baked soft rolls were known as hollow biscuits.[25] By the eighteenth century, both American and English bakers often dispensed with the second baking but still referred to the soft, sweet breads they made as biscuits because they were made with a bisket bread mixture. At the beginning of the twentieth century, biscuit was still the term used for a soft bap in Guernsey and for fluffy barley-meal scones in north-eastern Scotland.[26] Another of Simmons' rusk recipes probably started life as an English bisket bread of the kind Lady Fettiplace made, as it relies entirely on beaten eggs as a leavening agent. She instructs that 15 eggs to 4 lb of flour should be beaten 'into a large biscuit' and baked.[27] From her use of the term it is possible to see that American soft breads or scones, whether they were derived from Dutch rusks or English bisket breads, eventually all became known as biscuits.

Simmons' egg-leavened rusk would have required ferocious beating if it were to achieve the desired light, fluffy texture of a good biscuit. The Dutch used yeast to leaven their breads, but yeast was hard to obtain in the colonies. At the Cape, the Dutch settlers used must as a substitute. Grapes were introduced to the colony soon after it was established in 1652 as a supply post for the East Indiamen. The idea was that the ships could stock up with fresh grapes to ward off scurvy. In fact, grapes contain very little vitamin C and so they failed to fulfil their intended purpose. However, the vineyards gave rise to the South African wine industry. The natural yeasts on grape skin (the source of the bloom) makes must a good leavening agent. For the few weeks of the year after the harvest when the liquor was available, the Dutch made *mosbrood*, which became a much-loved Cape speciality. However, with the texture of brioche, it did not stay fresh for very long, and so to preserve their *mosbrood* rolls the settlers slit them in half and baked them into dry rusks.[28]

Yeast was also difficult to obtain in colonial America and bakers often had to resort to using temperamental and time-consuming sourdough starters of flour and water left to ferment overnight. They found a yeast substitute in potash. Perhaps they learned to use potash from the Native Americans, who used it to nixtamalise maize. It is made by evaporating the solution obtained by leaching wood ashes. The white residue that remains is mainly potassium carbonate. If brought into contact with a liquid – lemon juice, sour milk, honey, molasses – potash produces a chemical reaction that releases carbon dioxide and forms little air pockets within a sponge mixture. Americans learned that a pinch of potash added to a biscuit bread mixture made the bread rise quickly.[29] By the nineteenth century, baking soda – as potash was called once it was commercially produced – was the universal leavening agent for biscuits.

In the American South, quick biscuit breads became the daily staple and slow and laborious yeast breads were reserved for special occasions.[30] Edward Dale, who grew up on a Texas prairie farm in the 1870s, recalled that although 'every woman made biscuits using the same ingredients, which were flour, buttermilk, lard, a little soda, and salt, no two women's biscuits were alike. Some were large, tough, and of a bluish tinge; others light, dark brown, and flaky; some were streaked with soda, and others with too little soda were heavy and flat. They varied in size, too, but were usually of fairly generous proportions.'[31] After a hard morning's work on the farm splitting rails or chopping cotton, the men looked forward to a midday meal of 'meat, eggs, hot biscuits, gravy, and maybe pancakes!'[32]

The American use of the terms cracker and cookie are the result of a far more straightforward Americanisation of Dutch words. It is likely that the Dutch term *knäckebröd*, used to denote crisp, hard biscuits, in American English became cracker. The Dutch word *koek* and its diminutive *koekje* are the root of the American 'cookie'. It is even possible that early Dutch settlers in New Netherland

A migrant to Texas making biscuit in her makeshift tent home in the 1930s.

pronounced *koekje* as 'koekie', as is still the case in some western Dutch dialects.[33] In the Netherlands, *nieuwjaarskoeken* were wafers; in America, they were ginger-bread moulded into shapes and figures. Gingerbread cookies were a feature on 'muster days', when all men between the ages of 18 and 45, who were required to join the local militia, gathered at the local tavern for a day of drills and military practice. These occasions took on the atmosphere of a European fair. The men would bring their families, and food stalls and entertainers would set up around the tavern, selling gingerbread figures just as they did at the English fairgrounds. After independence, figures of the king were replaced with the American eagle.[34]

Just as it was in England, gingerbread was often given as a love token. The New England judge Samuel Sewall carefully wrapped up some gingerbread he was given at the home of the Massachusetts governor and presented it to the widow he was courting.[35] The Americans showed a marked preference for softer, more cake-like gingerbreads over the crisper, harder biscuits that dominated in England. Hence, the distinctive oatmeal, pecan and peanut butter biscuits, or rather cookies, American bakers invented in the nineteenth century tend to be softer and chewy.

PEANUT COOKIES

The first mention of peanuts as a possible ingredient in cookies seems to be Eliza Leslie's suggestion in her 1837 *Complete Cookery* that pounded groundnuts could be used instead of almonds to make macaroons. But in early nineteenth-century America, white southerners spurned peanuts as 'slave food'. Slaves had grown them in their garden plots to supplement their rations of cornmeal and salt fish. In the North they were seen as a vulgar snack of the poor. But during the Civil War many white Americans were forced to turn to peanuts to overcome food shortages. By the late nineteenth century they had been redefined as an American heritage food. In 1896, Fannie Farmer was probably the first cookbook writer to include a recipe specifically for peanut cookies in her *Boston Cooking-School Cookbook*. Farmer's book was a surprise success and from then on peanut cookies were established in the American cookie repertoire.[36] This is Farmer's recipe. It is not as sweet as modern cookies but if you are feeling particularly indulgent they taste good spread with jam.

2 tbsp butter

¼ cup sugar

1 egg

1 tsp baking powder

½ cup flour

¼ tsp salt

2 tbsp milk

½ cup finely chopped peanuts

½ tsp lemon juice

12 whole peanuts

Cream butter, add sugar, and egg well beaten. Mix and sift baking powder, flour and salt; add to first mixture; then add milk, peanuts, and lemon juice. Drop from a teaspoon on an unbuttered sheet of paper one-inch apart, and place one-half peanut on top of each. Bake twelve to fifteen minutes in a slow oven. This recipe will make twenty-four cookies.[37]

Use Nutt's technique to loosen the paper: turn the biscuits out onto a cooling rack so that the paper is upmost and brush the paper with a pastry brush dipped in water. Wait a few moments and the paper will peel off the cookies.

7

In which Mrs Elizabeth Raffald opens a confectionery shop in Manchester

In 1763 Elizabeth Raffald opened a confectionery shop in Fennel Street, Manchester. Here she sold elaborately iced and decorated 'bride' cakes, jars of jelly and jam, boxes of fruit paste, crystallised fruit and flowers, macaroons and sponge finger biscuits. A customer looking for an elaborate centrepiece to impress her dinner guests could choose between a glass bowl with gilded fish swimming in transparent wine jelly, a 'hen's nest' of spun sugar complete with eggs fashioned from flummery (almond cream), or silver and gold 'webs' of spun sugar for covering a dish of sweetmeats. There were plenty of such confectioner's shops in London – such as that run by the Italian Domenico Negri in Berkeley Square (later to become famous as Gunter's) and six more round the corner on Bond Street – but Raffald's was a new phenomenon in a northern city. It catered to the class of wealthy entrepreneurs and factory owners who emerged out of the Industrial Revolution.[1]

Building on the success of her business, Raffald also opened a cookery school, which she ran from her shop, and in 1769 published *The Experienced English House-Keeper*. Her school was modelled on the Hackney establishment that

This sketch of a scene inside a patisserie was made by an artist trying out ideas for a design to be painted on a china dessert service. On the sketch the artist scribbled an explanation of the scene. He tells us that the woman with her back to us in the centre is a mother giving her child a Savoy (sponge finger) biscuit while the child hiding on the left is a 'petit gourmand' stealing sponge fingers from the basket.

Rebecca Price attended in the 1670s, though Elizabeth Raffald aimed to teach confectionery skills not to the ladies but to their servants. Before her marriage Elizabeth had worked as the housekeeper for Sir and Lady Warburton of Arley Hall in Cheshire.[2] Unlike Lady Fettiplace who spent many hours in her still room, Lady Warburton would have left to her servants the hot work of boiling sugar and stirring preserves. Confectionery was no longer an art practised by gentlewomen.[3]

With the influx of West Indian sugar into England, the sweet stuff had lost its magical aura. It was no longer necessary to master the mysterious art of clarifying and refining sugar, as the refineries dotting the banks of the Thames did the work of transforming the brown muscovado shipped by the planters into sparkling white crystals. Over the course of the eighteenth century, the quantity of sugar imported to England increased from 4 lb to 20 lb per person, and its price fell accordingly.[4] By the time Raffald opened her shop, sugar had diffused throughout all levels of society. Even street sweepers and road menders could afford to heap it into their tea.[5] But if the art of sugar work no longer conferred status on its practitioner, the popularity of confections had not abated.

Fashionable households still served sweetmeats for dessert at the end of a meal. In 1783, Parson Woodeforde was enchanted by the table at a dinner given by the Bishop of Norwich. Different-coloured sugars arranged in geometrical patterns had transformed it into 'the most beautiful Artificial garden...one of the prettiest things I ever saw'.[6] Pyramids of ripe fruit often took pride of place at the centre of the dessert table, with the rest of the dishes carefully placed around them in a symmetrical pattern. Cookbooks and advice manuals provided table plans that reveal dessert to be a strange mixture of sweet and savoury dishes, with roast pheasant, stewed mushrooms and pickled smelts sitting alongside jellies and biscuits, creams and custards. Hippocras at the end of the meal had been replaced by sweet dessert wines. Ratafia flavoured with bitter apricot kernels was a popular dessert wine and shared its name with the hard little macaroons made with the same flavouring that were often served alongside it. Table plans for the dessert frequently suggest plates of biscuits and wafers as corner dishes.

Confectioners and biscuit makers often advertised that they sold a selection of wine biscuits. Biscotti, sponge fingers and langue de chats were all long and thin because they were made to fit into the small glasses of the time. It was a common practice to dip hard biscuits into wine in the manner of the Spanish king, who, the Italian visitor Giuseppe Baretti observed, 'breaks the biscuit in two, steeps it in the [Canary] wine, and eats it, but never drinks the wine'.

Toasting was a common feature of ceremonial dinners and banquets. Toasts were proposed that proclaimed the shared beliefs of the diners. Biscuit bakers and confectioners began to produce biscuits stamped with patriotic symbols that were

This boxwood stamp was made to produce biscuits to commemorate the marriage of Prince Frederick, Duke of Albany and York to Princess Frederica Charlotte of Prussia in 1790. After drinking a toast to the happy couple the diners would have dipped these York biscuits in their toasting wine.

suitable as toasting biscuits. Werrington's of Oxford Street advertised that they sold Prince of Wales biscuit which would have been stamped with the Prince's emblem of three feathers. And an unusual stamp with a central crown motif and Royal Volunteers Biscuits around its circumference must have been used to make toasting biscuits to use in the officers' messes of the volunteer militias that were raised throughout the country during the Napoleonic Wars.[8]

DUCHESS OF YORK BISCUITS

This is the Leeds confectioner and tea dealer Joseph Bell's recipe for the type of biscuits that would have been made with the York stamp. They are rather plain, dry biscuits but when dipped in sweet sherry take on a spicy flavour.

1 lb butter, 8 oz of sugar, 3 lb of flour. Rub the butter into the flour; then add the sugar, and mix it up into a stiff paste with milk; rolle the paste out about a quarter of an inch thick, they must be cut square and stamped with a proper stamp of the happy union and baked in a good oven.[9]

Joseph Bell, A Treatise of Confectionery (1817)

If the eighteenth-century dessert course was still sometimes a mix of sweet and savoury dishes, the addition of sugar to meat dishes was falling out of favour. France had taken Italy's place as Europe's culinary centre, and the proponents of *nouvelle cuisine* rejected the complex flavours arising from a mix of spices.[10] They wanted their food to reflect the classicist notions of rational order and harmony and thus emphasised simple, natural flavours.[11] In particular, *nouvelle cuisine* eschewed the Arab use of sugar, and it was relegated to the sphere of confections, creating the strict sweet–savoury divide that we are familiar with today.[12] Most importantly, the French chefs ignored humoral theory. The idea that sugar was a near-perfect food was no longer of interest to a cook.[13]

It took some time for sugar to fall entirely out of favour in English cookery. The English middle classes were reluctant to relinquish the spicy, sweet-sour flavours of the Arab world. The addition of spices and sugar was an easy and quick way to add depth of flavour to a dish, while it took hours to extract the *jus* from a chicken to create the base for a delicate soup. What was more, the apparent simplicity of *nouvelle cuisine* meant that it was immediately evident if the ingredients were not of the finest. English middle-class cooks took against finicky French food. The cookbook author Mary Kettilby protested that while a woman might be laughed at for 'sugaring a mess of Beans', the fancy French chefs concocted distasteful and expensive dishes.[14] Hannah Glasse summed up these attitudes when she dismissed those who 'would rather be impos'd on by a French Booby, than give Encouragement to a good English cook!'[15] The unfortunate result was that as spices and sugar were pushed out of savoury dishes a rather dull English style of plain cooking developed.

The one realm in which English cooks did excel was that of sweetmeats and desserts, puddings and pastries, cakes and biscuits.[16] Fear that fresh fruit caused the flux had long since abated, and the thick cooked fruit pastes and preserves of the still room were edged out by heaps of fresh apples and pears, oranges, grapes and cherries.[17] The process of enclosure meant that the poor could no longer afford to keep a cow. As dairy goods consequently began to disappear from the diet of the poor, cream became an exclusive product, and a central feature of the Georgian dessert.[18] With isinglass and West Indian arrowroot aiding the setting process, creams, flummeries, blancmanges, custards and jellies could be set into wobbly animals or ornamental shapes, the moulds for which were produced by the Staffordshire potteries. Crisp sponge biscuits, hard macaroons, and short orange and lemon biscuits all made perfect crunchy foils to these new desserts. Lady Elinor Fettiplace's wine-soaked sippets of biscuit covered with a layer of custard evolved into the trifle.[19] Elizabeth Raffald's recipe used macaroons soaked in white wine as the base, which was then covered with a layer of custard, followed by a frothy syllabub of cream, all decorated with flowers and comfits. Hannah Glasse used Naples biscuits softened in red wine and decorated the surface with ratafia biscuits, currant jelly and flowers.[20]

Chocolate and coffee had become popular as drinks in the seventeenth century; now they were used as flavourings in creams and 'puff' biscuits.[21] The French influence can be seen in the addition of lemon and orange zest, which the *nouvelle cuisine* chefs preferred as flavourings, as coriander and aniseed gradually fell out of favour. Thus Elizabeth Raffald's 'Spanish biscuits' are flavoured with only a little lemon juice. But it was the invention of the metal whisk to replace the bundle of twigs used to beat confections in the still room that marked a big step forward in biscuit making. Seventeenth-century instructions specified that at each stage of the process the biscuit dough had to be beaten for at least two hours. In the 1760s, Raffald suggested that a mere half an hour with the far more efficient metal whisk was sufficient for each stage, thus reducing the beating time from 6 to 1½ hours.[22]

Raffald refers to her sponge fingers as 'common biscuits', which suggests that when an eighteenth-century person thought of a biscuit, a sponge finger was what came to mind. Indeed, all her biscuits derive from what Lady Elinor would have called 'bisket bread': the sponge mixture of eggs, sugar and flour. Over the seventeenth and eighteenth centuries this bisket bread evolved. In the 1670s, Monsieur le Marqui Achiolier taught Rebecca Price to add cream to the biscuit mixture to produce a richer sponge. Rebecca referred to this recipe as 'shell bread', as the biscuits were baked in mussel shells. This would have caused them to take on the distinctive humped shape that we associate with madeleines.[23] If butter rather than cream was added to the bisket bread, and it was baked as a whole in a large round mould, it became a sponge cake. Eliza Acton's *Modern Cookery for Private Families* (1845) gives the first printed recipe for such a cake. It was known as Madeira cake, not because it was flavoured with Madeira but because, like the biscuits that were its ancestor, it was considered to go well with sweet wine.[24]

Biscuit dough mixtures became increasingly elaborate as they were enriched with eggs, cream or butter and various flavourings. The dough would be rolled out, cut into discs and baked for a short while to give soft cakes or for longer to make it crisp.[25] Although we would think of these creations as biscuits, Elizabeth Raffald referred to them as cakes – ratafia cakes or Shrewsbury cakes – to indicate that they were small domes or discs of dough. At the same time, other confections such as wafers, cracknels and macaroons were still thought of as specific creations rather than falling under a general heading of biscuits. In the eighteenth century, the new dough mixtures propagated a range of sweet creations. Jumbolds were the descendants of the alphabet-and-knot biscuits of the banqueting table. While still warm and malleable, the dough could be fashioned into intricate loops. The dough could also be moulded into little baskets, which were filled with sugar-paste flowers and used to decorate the dessert table. Alternatively, such biscuit baskets were filled with sweetmeats and fancy biscuits and given as gifts to the guests to take home at the end of the dinner.[26] In short, the eighteenth century saw a proliferation of fancy biscuits and the cookery books abound with recipes.

JUMBLES

Take two pound of fine flower and one pound of Sugar finely beaten, the yolks of eight eggs and a little butter and cream and a few Caraway seeds and a little Rose water. Mix all these and make it into a paste and beat it an hour or two with a Rowling pin, the more you beat it the better. Then take it and roll it into long rolls the bigness of the top of your Little finger and so make them up into what fashion you please and as fast as you make them up lay them on a pie plate, rubbed over with butter. Then just as you are going to set them in your Oven to bake, take a little Cream and wet them over with a feather. Scrape some hard sugar over them and so bake them.

The expression 'to jumble something up' is derived from these biscuits. It is probably an Anglicisation of *gemelli*, the Italian name for intricately looped biscuits. Later the caraway seeds were replaced by orange or lemon zest and rather than shaping them into intricate knots bakers shaped them into ordinary flat biscuits.[27] This recipe comes from Margaretta Acworth's manuscript cookery book, begun by her mother in the 1720s and added to throughout Margaretta's life until her death in 1794. Margaretta and her husband Abraham, who was a clerk of the Exchequer, lived in a street of new brick houses within sight of Westminster Abbey. They employed five or six servants, including a cook. Margaretta's annotations in the margins of the manuscript show that she was particular about how she liked things to be done in the kitchen.

Rout cakes were a staple offering of every eighteenth-century confectioner's. When George Gascoigne advertised the opening of his shop in the *Leeds Intelligencer* in 1795, he notified customers that he sold 'rout cakes, lemonade, milk punch and spun sugars'.[28] Parmentier's in London had a more sophisticated range of offerings: 'French brandies, comfits, lozenges, drops of every colour and flavour, superior macaroons... ices and creams' and, of course, 'rout cakes of the most fanciful forms'.[29] Rout cakes were commonplace on the dessert table. In Thackeray's *Vanity Fair* a plate of them lies neglected on the dining table after the ladies have withdrawn. Contemplating his father's warning that his sister's school friend Rebecca has 'set her cap' at him, Jos Sedley absent-mindedly eats twenty-four.[30]

Recipes for rout cakes varied but the ingredients usually included brandy or sherry wine, a flavouring of some kind – ranging from citrus zest, nutmeg or cinnamon to rose or orange water – and currants or candied peel. Indeed, they appear to be a version of what were also known as Shrewsbury cakes or Easter biscuits, and although the recipes vary, they seem to have been a short, crumbly biscuit. In 1602, Lord Herbert of Cherbury sent his guardian 'a kind of cake which our [Shrewsbury] country people use... Measure not my love by substance of it, which is brittle, but by the form of it which is circular (see page 5 of the picture section).'[31]

Rout cakes were customarily served at evening parties or 'routs' (hence the name). The fashion for evening parties arose out of the changes in the timing of meals. When Pepys was writing his diary in the 1660s, dinner – the main meal of the day – was eaten at noon. By the beginning of the eighteenth century, dinner time had shifted towards two o'clock, and as the century progressed, it became later and later. By 1750, Londoners, who usually set the trends, were dining at four o'clock. A later dinner signalled gentility; only the lower orders now ate their dinner at midday. Indeed, institutions such as workhouses insisted on serving the inmates their main meal before one o'clock to reinforce their lowly social status. Throughout the nineteenth and well into the twentieth century, the working classes ate their dinner at our lunchtime and polite society had dinner later and later until eventually it was in the evening.[32] Hence today's confusion about the naming of meals.

The ladies withdrew after dinner to leave the men to their port and claret, and after a while the gentlemen would join them in the drawing room. The arrival of the gentlemen heralded the serving of tea.[33] At tea time, fashionable households displayed their wealth and sophistication, serving a fine brew in delicate china cups. The poet Robert Dodsley, who worked as a footman before becoming a successful bookseller, described this ritual from the perspective of the servant:

> The Kettle fill'd, the Water boil'd,
> The Cream provided, Biscuits pil'd,
> And Lamp prepar'd; I strait engage
> The Lilliputian Equipage
> Of Dishes, Saucers, Spoons, and Tongs,
> And all th' *Et cetera* which thereto belongs.
> Which rang'd in order and Decorum,
> I carry in, and set before 'em;
> Then pour or Green or Bohea out,
> And, as commanded, hand about.[34]

This ritual of having tea in the drawing room replaced polite society's withdrawal for the banquet in the seventeenth century. But biscuits were not immediately transferred from the banquet to tea time: they were still thought of more as an appropriate accompaniment to wine, rather than tea. And although Dodsley's poem indicates that biscuits were sometimes served with tea, it was more usually accompanied by thin slices of bread and butter.[35]

Given that dinner was normally over by the late afternoon, it became fashionable to hold evening entertainments or routs, where ladies and gentlemen would gather to sing and play cards and sample a range of 'dainties' that the host would have ordered in from the confectioner's. In the genteel world of polite society, correctly observing the social niceties was vital to maintaining one's social position; every interaction was scrutinised, every faux pas noticed and recorded. In this claustrophobic world, even the quality of one's biscuits could reveal a host's position on the finely tuned social ladder. In Jane Austen's *Emma*, the wealthy Mrs Elton, who comes to Highbury from Bath as the new wife of the vicar, is disdainful of the provincial ladies' ways. Austen tells us that 'she was a little shocked at the want of two drawing rooms, at the poor attempt at rout-cakes, and there being no ice in the Highbury card parties'.[36]

Whether to serve biscuits or cake at an evening entertainment was a burning question for the ladies of Mrs Gaskell's *Cranford*, where their 'unacknowledged poverty, and very much acknowledged gentility' meant that it was 'considered "vulgar" to give anything expensive, in the way of eatables and drinkables, at the evening entertainments. Wafer-thin bread and butter and sponge biscuits were all that the Honourable Mrs Jamieson gave; and she was sister-in-law to the late Earl of Glenmire, although she did practise such "elegant economy".' Mrs Jamieson's evening entertainments began with the servants bringing in tea trays laid with eggshell-china teacups and the appropriate accompaniment to tea, plates of thinly sliced bread and butter. All her guests would have eaten dinner at home and were now gathering in her drawing room for their after-dinner cup of tea. After a few hours of playing cards and listening to Miss Jessie sing '*Jock of Hazledean*, a little out of tune', the end to the evening's festivities was marked punctually at a quarter to nine by the reappearance of the tea trays, this time laden with wine and its natural accompaniment – sponge biscuits.[37] The narrator fears that Mrs Baker, a newcomer to the town, may have been a little tasteless when she displayed her greater wealth by offering seed cake with the wine at her entertainments. Still, although Mrs Jamieson declares that she never keeps such a thing in the house as it reminds her of scented soap, she decides to overlook the slight and gobbles down three large pieces.[38]

The seed cake Mrs Baker served was a direct descendant of the caraway-seed-filled sponge biscuits that Elinor Fettiplace would have given her guests to aid their digestion. Thus Mrs Gaskell's biscuit-centred social drama reveals how the sponge cake gradually usurped its ancestor the biscuit's place in the hierarchy of confectionery. While Lady Elinor would have been proud to adorn her banqueting table with plates of sponge fingers, if by the early nineteenth century such biscuits were still considered an appropriate offering, they were a modest one. Biscuits had slipped to a lower rung on confectionery's ladder of prestige.

SHREWSBURY CAKES, ROUT CAKES AND EASTER BISCUITS

Shrewsbury cakes, rout cakes and Easter biscuits were all based on a rich shortbread and variously flavoured with sherry, flower waters, spices, currants, the zest of oranges or lemons or candied citrus peel. Around Bristol, Easter biscuits were traditionally flavoured with oil of cassia or Chinese cinnamon. Cassia oil was supposedly used to embalm Christ's body, hence its association with Easter food. In the run-up to Easter the chemist's in the village of Pill just outside the city still puts on a display of cassia oil for local bakers.[39]

> 100 g butter
> 75 g caster sugar
> 1 egg, separated
> 200 g plain flour
> pinch of salt
> 1 tbsp brandy or sweet sherry
> 1 tbsp double cream
> a little extra cream and caster or brown sugar for brushing over the finished biscuits

Optional flavourings: 1 tbsp rose or orange-flower water, 50 g currants, 1 tbsp mixed candied peel, the finely grated zest of

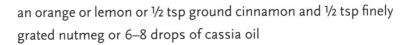

an orange or lemon or ½ tsp ground cinnamon and ½ tsp finely grated nutmeg or 6–8 drops of cassia oil

Pre-heat the oven to 180°C.

Cream the butter and sugar together in a bowl until pale and fluffy, then beat in the egg yolk and either flower water or grated zest or cassia oil.

Sift the flour, salt, and any spices you choose to add over the mixture. Stir well. Add the fruit and peel, if using, and enough brandy or sherry and cream to give a soft dough.

Knead lightly on a lightly floured surface and roll out to 5 mm thickness. Cut into rounds and place on lightly greased baking sheets.

Bake for 6 minutes. Take out of the oven and brush with the lightly beaten egg white and sprinkle with caster sugar. Alternatively mix a tablespoon of brown sugar together with a couple of tablespoons of cream and brush over the biscuits. Bake for a further 5 minutes. (Watch them carefully – one minute they are baked, the next they are overdone.)

Transfer to wire racks to cool.

MACAROONS

In the seventeenth-century the founder of *nouvelle cuisine*, La Varenne, 'modernised' the Italian macaroon by omitting the rose or orange-flower water and instead using egg whites to bind the almonds and sugar into a paste. He also gave a recipe for 'snow-sugar biskets' which we would think of as meringues. These he made by whipping egg whites together with a sugar syrup. By the eighteenth century, the two methods had been combined, and macaroons were made by first whipping the egg whites, and then adding the sugar and almonds.

It was probably the American cook Eliza Leslie who, at the same time as she suggested peanuts, first suggested using ground coconut to make macaroons. After the Civil War when imports from the West Indies increased, coconut became a fashionable addition to American confections. Now virtually all American macaroons were made with coconut. These unleavened confections became popular with America's Jewish community at Passover.[40]

In Southern India, where from the 1920s there was a thriving cashew nut industry, confectioners began making cashew

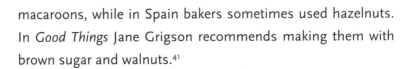

macaroons, while in Spain bakers sometimes used hazelnuts. In *Good Things* Jane Grigson recommends making them with brown sugar and walnuts.[41]

La Varenne's pistachio snow-sugar biscuits are reminiscent of the fancy macarons made in a rainbow of colours and flavours by the Parisian patisserie Ladurée.[42] There is now a world-wide craze for these but I find they look more enticing than they taste. For me there is nothing better than the macaroons that my mum used to bake: crunchy on the outside, soft and chewy in the middle. This is her recipe.

    2 egg whites
    5 oz castor sugar
    1 tsp almond essence
    5 oz ground almonds

Pre-heat oven to 180°C.

Whisk egg whites lightly, add sugar, almond essence and ground almonds. Roll into balls, place on rice paper or a well-greased baking tin, allowing room for them to spread.

Bake for about 20 minutes. Keep an eye on them that they do not burn.

Allow to cool slightly and then take off the tin and cool on a rack.

Both Shrewsbury cakes and macaroons are good served alongside Rebecca Price's 'Sillibub'.

> ¼ pint white wine
> 2 tsp grated lemon rind
> 2 tbsp lemon juice
> 3 oz caster sugar
> ½ pint double cream

Combine the wine, lemon rind and juice and sugar. Stir well and leave to stand at room temperature for three hours.

Whisk the cream to the soft peak stage and then slowly add the wine and sugar mixture while continuing to whisk the cream.

Pour into individual glasses or dishes and leave to stand in a cool place such as the stone-flagged floor of a dairy or the fridge for several hours.

This also tastes good if it is frozen and then taken out of the freezer 10–20 minutes before serving.

FUNERAL BISCUITS

Sin-eating is an old European practice. After a person's death, during the period of lying-in, a biscuit would be placed on the corpse or its coffin. Before the burial, one of the mourners would eat it in order to take on the sins of the departed and allow them to move on into the next life free of the burden of their transgressions. In the Balkans the biscuit would be made in the shape of a figure to symbolise the deceased; in the Netherlands the 'dead cake' would be inscribed with their initials. In Ireland this ritual was adapted. Here, each guest at the funeral was handed a glass of wine and a biscuit across the coffin as they filed past to pay their respects.[1] In seventeenth-century England all that was left of the practice was the custom of serving biscuits at a funeral.

In March 1664, it fell to Samuel Pepys to make the arrangements for his brother's burial. He was dismayed by the gravedigger's promise that he would 'justle' his brother into the overcrowded middle aisle of the church, and 'for my father's sake do my brother that is dead all the civility he can; which was to disturb other corps that are not quite rotten to make room for him'. Pepys became even more irritable when the guests who were supposed to arrive between one and two o'clock did not turn up until four or five, and then many more than the 120 he had invited. He had calculated for 'six biscuits a-piece and what they pleased of burnt claret' and was worried that there would not be enough sponge fingers to go round. His maid took things in her stride and served the guests 'to their great content I think'. In the end Pepys was pleased that after the wine and biscuits 'a very good company' walked with his brother's corpse to the church, where he was buried.[2]

The custom was to serve the mourners with biscuits and wine before the service. In preparation for his wife Elizabeth's funeral in June 1697, Mr Henry Currer of Kildwick Hall, near Skipton, put in an order for 30 lb of Naples biscuits with the confectioner George Fothergill in York. When the guests arrived at around ten o'clock, they were served biscuits and wine before the service was held in the church an hour later. Once Elizabeth's body had been interred, the mourners returned to the Hall for a lavish meal. It was a point of honour that the funeral meats should be generous, and the tables were often loaded with fancy banqueting stuff. Henry Currer's guests were served meat and fowls, veal pies, jellies, creams, possets and spiced funeral cakes.[3]

The practice of serving sponge finger biscuits at British funerals lasted until the Second World War. Recalling life in a Yorkshire moorland parish in the 1880s, J. Atkinson reported that glasses of wine and 'small round cakes of the crisp sponge description' were customarily handed round to funeral guests.[4] Small rounds of shortbread, often with a heart imprinted in the centre, representing the soul of the deceased, were sometimes served as an alternative to sponge fingers. Bakers also sold little parcels of funeral biscuits wrapped in black-edged paper, sometimes printed with an elegy or short poem, which were given out to mourners as a keepsake.[5]

8

In which Henry Mayhew marvels at the fabrication of fancy biscuits by a series of cog-wheels and cranks

A few years since nearly the only biscuits attainable were Captain's and Abernethy's. Over the first, there was in eating them, a very considerable risk of breaking one's teeth, unless these were adamantine; while the second, though in our opinion a very much better biscuit, necessitated the use of a toothpick to get rid of the caraway seeds which obtruded themselves into every hollow or interstice in the teeth. Within a very recent period, however, the manufacture of biscuits has become a great and increasing trade. If report is to be relied upon, the workmen in some establishments are numbered by hundreds while the variety of biscuits produced is endless, most of them having the recommendation that they do not require either extraordinary powers of mastication or digestion.[1]

'Biscuits by machinery!' declared the journalist Henry Mayhew. 'It strikes on the ear almost as funnily, at first, as chickens produced by steam.' Contemporaries were amazed by the application of steam-powered machinery to the production of a foodstuff. 'Though we can imagine our stockings and ships'-blocks, and even pins and needles, to be manufactured mechanically,' continued Mayhew, 'we repeat it *does* seem hard to believe how it can be possible to fabricate, out of a mass of puffy, unwieldy dough, "Ladies' Fingers" and "Tops and Bottoms", by a series of cog-wheels and cranks.'[2]

In the winter of 1865, Mayhew visited the Peek Frean biscuit factory at the mouth of St Saviour's Dock, Bermondsey. Just down the River Thames from the Tower of London, the factory was well placed for both rail- and water-transport links. Having inspected the factory's engine room – 'for we are always expected to admire the boilers at every factory we visit' – he emerged into the clatter of the sweet-smelling steam bakery, which he perceived to be as long as an East India-man but as lofty as a railway station. Through the misty haze of flour particles Mayhew could see row upon row of steam presses 'working away in incessant restlessness, and seeming to print [ship's] biscuits by the million'. Wheels whirled overhead, leather straps attaching the machines to the steam engines snapped, and amid the thundering machinery men and boys hurried about, their faces coated in white flour dust. Mayhew worked out that the biscuits rolled out of each cutting machine at a rate of 160 pieces a minute or '100,000 in the course of a ten hour working day … It seemed impossible to us that such an absolute infinity of biscuits could ever be consumed by the entire community of sailors over the whole globe itself.' Boys carried the trays of biscuits to the travelling oven, where they disappeared through a narrow aperture only to emerge brown and crisp at the other end twenty minutes later. Watching the baked biscuits rattling onto trays with only a single lad to collect them, Mayhew was again struck by the marvel of automation.[3]

By 1865 ship's biscuits were only a secondary trade for Peek Frean: 'fancy' biscuits made with the best flour were their real concern. In the materials room Mayhew was taken aback by hundredweight flour bins and butter cans, great piles of sugar cones, countless sacks of almonds, barrel upon barrel of currants and enough 'monster' milk churns to give the 'impression that all the cows in the world must be used dry, merely for the production of steam "fancy" biscuits'. Different combinations of ingredients were weighed into the mixing machines and then the various doughs were wheeled into the immense machine room, the size of a music hall, filled with the 'hubble-bubble of moving machinery' and the shouting of more white-coated, flour-dusted men and boys. A constant stream of busy lads hurried past him carrying metal trays dotted with spots of dough to be placed in the 'traps' that lowered them to the ovens below. Here the 'Pic-Nic' biscuit machine alone churned out 1.5 million biscuits a week. 'In Heaven's name,' Mayhew exclaimed, 'who eats all these millions of "Pic-Nics"? Why if the entire world went pic-nicking the whole of their lives, it would seem to us utterly impossible to devour such amount of dry, juiceless food.'[4]

Biscuits were one of the first foodstuffs to be produced by rational industrial production methods. In 1865 most bakeries were small-scale enterprises, using only ten sacks of flour a week to make enough bread to serve one or two villages or a district of a town.[5] The idea that the mixing, kneading and rolling of dough could be achieved by the action of steam-powered cranks and automated rollers was astonishing to contemporaries. The scale of the exercise was also extraordinary. Within the vast, noisy spaces of the factory halls a small number of men operated dozens of machines churning out millions of biscuits that would have taken thousands of artisanal bakers to produce in traditional bakeries. While ship's biscuits had enabled sailors and maritime explorers to sail across vast oceans, reaching the remotest parts of the globe, now industrial production allowed sweet biscuits to overcome time and space to reach a global market of customers spread across the world's continents.

The story of the industrial production of the biscuit begins with two Quakers: Thomas Huntley in Reading and J. D. Carr in Carlisle. The key to Huntley's success

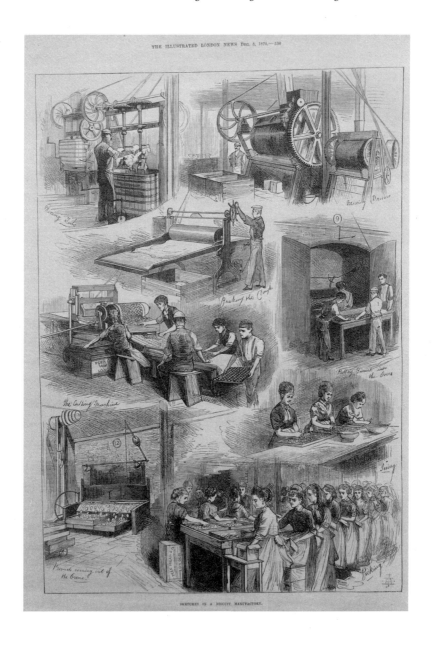

was the location of his bakery, which he opened with his father Joseph in 1822 opposite the Crown coaching inn on the London Road. Whenever one of the six daily stagecoaches stopped at the inn, Huntley's would send over a boy with a basket of biscuits.[6] While most bakeries in the 1820s only reached customers within a small radius, by this means Huntley's customer base and reputation extended all the way along the busy coach route between London and Bristol.

Parallel to the road between Bristol and the capital ran the newly opened Kennet and Avon Canal, which fed into a system of waterways that connected Reading to the whole of southern England.[7] Huntley's landlord and next-door neighbour, the fishmonger James Cocks, had made use of this new transport network to build up a successful business. In the kitchen behind his shop, Cocks made a fish sauce, and he employed a network of retail agents to sell it to grocers in London, Bath and Bristol, whom he supplied via the canals.[8] The Huntleys now took on one of Cocks's travelling representatives to persuade grocers to buy 'Reading biscuits' as well as 'Reading fish sauce'. At the same time Joseph's other son, also Joseph, who ran an ironmonger's workshop opposite the bakery, began making tins for his father. When packed tightly into these tins, the biscuits survived their journey between bakery and shop with fewer breakages. Joseph junior also produced special 7 lb shop-display tins with glass lids, which temptingly displayed the biscuits to the grocer's customers. By 1838, when Joseph senior retired, leaving the

(left) In these sketches of the Peek Frean biscuit manufactory from the *Illustrated London News* the 'cog-wheels and cranks' that worked the heavy machinery of the 'Mixing tubs' and 'Mixing drums' are clearly visible. Below, rather than shuffling on his bottom up and down a see-saw-like dough break as was common practice in the old naval bakeries, using the new machinery all the baker had to do to knead the mass of dough was turn a wheel. The dough then went through the cutting machine and men and boys collected the biscuits; they can be seen on the right, 'putting the Biscuits into the Oven'. Bottom left is a sketch of 'biscuits coming out of the ovens' that conveys the wonder of automation which Mayhew felt as he watched the biscuits rattle out of the oven – not a worker in sight, as if the 'biscuits were begotten by natural laws.' On the right, three women are shown icing the biscuits while rows of other women pack them into boxes and tins.

business to Thomas, Huntley's had grown from a tiny enterprise that took six months to get through one sack of biscuit flour to a thriving business with 117 grocers on their books.[9]

Meanwhile, in 1837 the Carlisle baker Jonathon Dodgson Carr opened a bread factory next to the canal basin in Caldewgate, already an industrial centre with several textile mills. As a Quaker, JD, as he was always known, held that the prime function of trade was to provide one's fellow man with life's essentials.[10] He lived in a city at the heart of Britain's industrial transition to the mechanised factory system and thought that if the industrial advances he saw all around him were applied to baking, he would be able to cut costs and sell cheap bread. Bread prices in the 1830s were artificially high due to the Corn Laws, which had been introduced in 1815 to prevent the import of cheap Russian and American wheat into Britain. In addition, towns in particular were plagued with 'underselling' bakers who cut their costs by adulterating coarse flours with alum. This made the bread white but was also liable to inflict 'wrenching dyspepsia' on those who ate it.[11] The 'undersellers' paid low wages to their journeymen bakers and forced night work on them so that they were able to churn out four or five batches a day to a good-quality baker's two.[12] JD campaigned against the Corn Laws, which were eventually repealed in 1846, but in the meantime he cut costs by milling his own flour and installing steam-powered bread-making machinery at his factory.[13] From 1837 the mill workers of Carlisle, reliant on shop-bought bread for at least two thirds of their calories, were able to buy cheap, unadulterated bread from his factory shop in Caldewgate.[14]

Carr also made ship's biscuits, and on a visit to a friend's printing works, it occurred to him that if steam-powered machinery could stamp out pieces of sheet metal, it would be possible to design a machine that would cut biscuits out of dough.[15] He seems to have been unaware of Thomas Grant's steam-powered machinery already producing tens of thousands of tons of ship's biscuit at the naval dockyards; instead he commissioned his biscuit-cutting machine from an

American manufacturer.[16] Carr's factory was well connected to the western ports by canal, and a new railway branch line soon linked the canal to Carlisle station, which in turn connected the factory to the port of Newcastle in the east.[17] Thus JD had access to a transport network that enabled him to reach a large and widely dispersed market. But he did not at first take advantage of this. Fancy biscuits were initially a sideline for his bread factory. In 1844, the factory only produced 350 tons of four different types: captain's, Pic-Nic, shortbread fingers and alphabet biscuits.[18]

While Carr's business had plenty of room for expansion, Huntley's dingy cellar bakehouse was soon stretched beyond capacity. Thomas Huntley supervised the baking of at least 20 different sorts of biscuit as well as cakes and bread, aided only by a dough break – the seesaw contraption naval bakers used to knead large quantities of dough – a hand-operated rolling machine and a stamp hand-roller that printed the legend *HUNTLEY* on Jamaica biscuits.[19] He struggled to meet the growing number of orders brought in by the firm's successful salesman John Cooper. Within six months of joining the firm in 1842, Cooper had added 82 grocers to Huntley's client list.[20] He had been appointed by Thomas's new partner, George Palmer, a confectioner from the West Country who had joined the firm on Joseph's retirement. It was Palmer who was the driving force in the expansion and modernisation of the business. He immediately purchased a steam-powered mixer to lighten Thomas's burden. Again it is unclear how aware Palmer was of Grant's naval biscuit-making machinery, but he was friends with a local engineer and inventor, William Exall, and the two men set about designing mixing drums for fancy biscuits, rollers and biscuit-cutting machines, as well as a mechanical squirt gun for macaroons.[21] When in 1846 Palmer installed these ingenious machines in an old silk factory conveniently located between the canal and the River Kennet, Huntley & Palmers were equipped with the most sophisticated food-processing machinery in the world. Within three years the firm achieved spectacular growth, doubling its turnover and increasing its output of biscuits fourfold.[22] By 1860 they were producing 3,200 tons of biscuits a year; by 1874 the output had increased to 12,600 tons, making them by far the largest biscuit manufacturer in Britain, let alone the world.[23] Carr's never rivalled Huntley & Palmers in size but its production also expanded. When JD died in 1884, the company was manufacturing 950 tons of 128 varieties of fancy biscuit every year.[24] It is no surprise that as the world's leading industrial country, Britain was also the birthplace of the industrial biscuit (see page 5 of the picture section).

Who was eating all these biscuits? In Reading in the 1820s, according to one contemporary account, the town's social circle was made up of 'the clergyman, the doctor, the solicitor, the banker, the brewer and the retired general and admiral who has served under Nelson and Wellington, the widower and spinster with a good income'. This apparent cast list for a Jane Austen novel socialised by playing whist at each other's houses, finishing off the evening 'with the temperate tray of sandwiches and negus' – a warm, sweetened and spiced port – and Joseph Huntley's macaroons and sponge fingers.[25] It was this group occupying the social middle ground between the aristocracy and the manual workers that comprised the new factories' customers. In the late eighteenth century they had made up only about a tenth of the population, but the wealth generated by Britain's industrial growth swelled their numbers until they accounted for about a quarter of the populace by the mid nineteenth century. Between 1850 and 1870 this social group benefited from incomes that rose faster than prices. They spent their extra wealth on the paraphernalia of gentility: servants, clothes, furniture, wallpapers and carpets, fine wines and prepared foods such as confectionery and biscuits.[26]

The machine-made biscuits that emerged from Huntley's and Carr's factories, having been 'scarcely touched by the hands of the workpeople', had an appealing aura of purity about them that was unusual in an era when foodstuffs were routinely adulterated.[27] In George Augustus Sala's spoof *Lady Chesterfield's Letters*, the noble lady warns her daughter about the grocer who would put 'chicory into my coffee...sells me sprats pounded up with Venetian red for anchovy sauce, and turmeric for mustard'. The baking trade was notoriously dishonest, and its alum-adulterated products were made in ill-ventilated, dusty cellars where rats and cockroaches scuttled across the boards that doubled as work benches and beds for the journeymen bakers.[28] Lady Chesterfield suggested that while her daughter might not wish to enter the greengrocer's shed or enquire about the price of kidneys at the butcher's, in an attempt to protect herself from such swindles she might engage in the more genteel aspects of shopping and buy her own biscuits and fancy bread.[29] In this bewildering world of deception, the Quaker biscuit manufacturers presented themselves as beacons of reliability. When customers bought Quaker-made industrial biscuits they could trust the claim that they were made in scrupulously hygienic conditions with pure ingredients and were therefore 'superior' biscuits.[30]

The biscuit makers frequently depicted their factories on their tins and posters. While nowadays warehouse buildings and smoking chimneys would have little appeal, nineteenth-century customers derived satisfaction from the technological sophistication of industrially made biscuits.[31] Foodstuffs that we would now consider mundane, even shameful, store-cupboard standbys were thought chic and modern. Few cooks today would proudly announce that their custard was made with Bird's custard powder. But when Alfred Bird first began selling his eggless dessert powder in the 1840s, it was bought with enthusiasm by middle-class households as an ingenious 'scientific' product. Indeed, industrially manufactured foods were initially too expensive to be eaten by anyone other than the middle classes.[32] Since the seventeenth century, sweet biscuits had been associated with indulgence, and by constantly emphasising their 'superiority', the biscuit manufacturers succeeded in transferring this association of fancy luxury to industrially produced biscuits. While it was seen as something of a failure for a host to serve bought cake, it was perfectly respectable, even refined, to serve factory-made biscuits.[33]

During the nineteenth century, the routine of middle-class daily life changed, as longer working days meant that the polite hour for dinner moved to six or seven in the evening. Industrial biscuits fitted into the various niches that consequently appeared in the daily routine of food consumption. The middle classes had both the means and a reason to buy industrial biscuits.[34] Now that breakfast was taken at an earlier hour in order to enable the men to leave for work, a long stretch of time opened up between meals. It became the norm for ladies to take a small midday snack. An Indian visitor to England described how at noon the ladies of the family he was staying with would interrupt their round of embroidery, drawing, walking, writing letters or playing cards to take 'a biscuit or cake with a little fruit and water'.[35] This midday sustenance became known as luncheon, after the 'nuncheon' of a mid-morning glass of ale and hunk of bread and cheese eaten by farm labourers in the fields.[36]

Many professional men considered it rather low-class to eat at such an early hour, and if they did give in to hunger they would often do so without making any concession to the act of eating.[37] If Anthony Trollope's character Mr Fidus Neverbend 'ate a biscuit in the middle of the day ... [he] did so with his eyes firmly fixed on some document'.[38] The biscuit manufacturers now presented the plain biscuit as an ideal intermediate meal to stave off hunger pangs without unnecessarily overloading the stomach during the hours of work.[39] After the move to the new factory, Huntley & Palmers' first great success was a refined version of the captain's biscuit called the Pic-Nic.[40] Carr's most popular biscuit was also a lighter, more palatable version of the ship's biscuit, the Captain's Thin. In Dickens' *Pickwick Papers*, just such a plain biscuit and a piece of cheese or sausage made a frugal lunch for the likes of Mr Solomon Pell, whom a messenger finds at the courts snacking on an 'Abernethy biscuit and saveloy'.[41]

In addition, biscuits, along with fruit, wine and preserves, were by now well established as essential ingredients for a proper dessert. Despite their straitened circumstances, the Jenkyns sisters in Mrs Gaskell's *Cranford* 'always had wine and dessert... Miss Jenkyns used to gather currants and gooseberries for it herself... We felt very genteel with our two glasses apiece and a dish of gooseberries at the top, of currants and biscuits at the sides, and two decanters at the bottom.'[42] Now, rather than having to supervise their preparation, the genteel lady could stroll to the grocer's and choose her favourites from a tin of Carr's Rich Desserts. An obliging grocer would allow his favoured customers to pick out the soft lemon-flavoured shortbreads and the Coburg biscuits with a pretty flower iced on top, in preference to the plain oblong Freyburgs, with just a sprinkling of sugar, or the knobbly Shrewsbury biscuits.[43]

Cambridge undergraduates served biscuits and oranges at the dessert parties they would hold in their rooms after dinner in hall. Charles Bristed, an American studying at Trinity College in the 1840s, pontificated that 'at such regales, one met with the three conditions of a perfect symposium: good dishes and wine, an entire absence of display and pretension, and the genial conversation of clever men'.[44] No doubt William Makepeace Thackeray would have dismissed him as a snob. Thackeray's own description of such wine parties is less pretentious: 'A parcel of lads who had been whipped three months previous, and were not allowed more than three glasses of port at home... [gathered round] a table covered with bad sweetmeats, drinking bad wines, telling bad stories, singing bad songs over and over again.'[45]

The children of the middle classes were sometimes allowed to join the adult party at the end of the meal. Charles Dickens recalled how his friend Macready's children would 'come in at dessert and have each a biscuit and a glass of water, in which last refreshment I was always convinced that they drank with the gloomiest malignity, "Destruction to the gourmandising grown-up company".'[46] Alternatively, children were allowed a biscuit for their supper. Writing in her nineties of her memories of a late-nineteenth-century Scottish childhood, Amy Fraser's mouth still watered 'for an Abernethy biscuit such as my mother issued, one at a time … with a mug of milk at bedtime. They were plain and wholesome and were almost the only biscuits we ever saw. We may have had a "ginger snap" sometimes but we had no fancy or chocolate biscuits…. They came closely packed, unwrapped, in a large, deep, square tin and *never a broken one among them* till they were grasped in our eager fingers.'[47]

From mid century it became customary to serve a 'savoury' – a small salty titbit – after dessert, to cleanse the palate of any cloying sweetness in preparation for the glass of port or Madeira the gentlemen enjoyed once the ladies had withdrawn. Typical savouries were oysters or prunes wrapped in bacon, known either as 'angels' or 'devils on horseback'. Cheese, which had traditionally been seen as the vulgar 'meat' of rustics, now became a popular savoury item too, often in the form of cheese straws – sticks of cheese-flavoured dough sprinkled with paprika that occupied a position somewhere between a biscuit and a pastry.[48] Romary's of Tunbridge Wells, a small, non-industrial but remarkably successful bakery, supplied Harrods, Fortnum and Mason, Jackson's of Piccadilly and even Macy's of New York with a two-shilling selection tin of savoury biscuits flavoured with Cheddar, celery, parmesan and onion.[49] The industrial biscuit manufacturers produced a range of thinner, crisper savoury biscuits, such as Britannia, Cabin and Table Water, whose names evoked their origins as ship's biscuits.[50] Jacob's of Dublin created Cream Crackers out of a fermented dough that was folded several times to make a flaky, multi-layered, feather-light biscuit.[51] The simplest of savouries was a cheese board, a glass of celery sticks and a selection of biscuits.

To start with, novelty and a reputation for quality sold industrial biscuits. Huntley & Palmers were initially sniffy about advertising. It went against Quaker principles of 'fair trading' and smacked of the 'puffery' associated with quack medicines such as Holloway's Pills, pastilles of a few harmless ingredients that were sold as a cure-all and saver of life.[52] Herbert Foxwell, Professor of Political Economy at University College, London, recalled that as a child he was taught never to buy anything that had been advertised.[53] Wary of introducing even a hint of unprincipled trading practices, Huntley & Palmers preferred low-key black-and-white leaflets and flyers and small notices in the good newspapers and periodicals. One of them, in the *Berkshire Directory* of 1842–3, read: 'Huntley & Palmers respectfully call attention to their celebrated biscuits ... if bought in tin cases, in which they retain their quality for a considerable time, the tins are allowed for on their return.'[54] The most ostentatious advertising they engaged in was to hand out small packets of biscuits to the first-class passengers boarding Great Western trains at Paddington station with the message printed on them that they should look out for the Huntley & Palmers factory as the train passed through Reading.[55] J. D. Carr, however, had an instinct for promotion and was the first biscuit manufacturer to secure a royal warrant. Thereafter, 'By Royal Appointment' appeared on everything associated with Carr's, from biscuit tins to their letterhead.[56] Until 1867, when they secured their own warrant, Huntley & Palmers had to make do with displaying the coats of arms of various bishops, peers and Oxbridge colleges on their tins.[57]

Always eager to find new avenues for promotion, Carr managed to obtain the contract for supplying the refreshment rooms at the Great Exhibition of 1851, and invented a sweetened milk 'Exhibition biscuit' for the occasion. Indeed, in a constant attempt to catch the attention of the public, the manufacturers were forever producing new varieties of biscuit. JD experimented in the family kitchen together with his six children. The recipes he instructed the factory to try out were often written on the back of bills and pages torn from school exercise books. Some were signed by the children and bore messages such as 'If this recipe proves successful some biscuits would be greatly appreciated when ready.'[58]

There are of course limits to how many ways flour, butter, sugar and eggs can be combined. Distinctiveness had to be manufactured, and often the 'newness' of a biscuit lay less in the flavour than in the shape or the name that awarded it character or style.[59] Continuing the tradition of patriotic toasting biscuits, a favoured tactic was to sell by association with royalty. Huntley & Palmers wanted to name the Osborne biscuit 'Victoria', but the Queen refused and the palace suggested that instead they should name it after her favourite home, on the Isle of Wight. Most of the 'royal' biscuits have disappeared today – no one produces Prince of Wales, Albert or Balmoral biscuits any more – but a few have lived on. The Marie, brought out in 1875 to celebrate the marriage of Victoria's second son Alfred to the Grand Duchess Marie of Russia, is still one of the most popular biscuits in Spain.[60]

Another ploy was to name a biscuit after a celebrity. In 1861 Peek Frean brought out the Garibaldi to celebrate the unification of Italy.[61] It was an oblong biscuit of two thin layers of dough with currants sandwiched between them. Rather than fading into obscurity like many other 'celebrity' biscuits, the Garibaldi has lived on due to the 'Garibaldi mania' that swept the country when the general paid a visit three years later. To Queen Victoria's chagrin, everywhere he went the general was greeted by cheering crowds the like of which had never been seen. In London half a million people lined the streets, waving red scarves and handkerchiefs, clapping, shouting, cheering and singing.[62] Garibaldi's appeal reached across the social spectrum. To the upper classes he was a heroic opponent of Continental despotism who had driven the Habsburgs and Bourbons out of his country; to the working classes he was an inspirational champion of universal suffrage.[63] Peek Frean were delighted by the increased sales of their biscuit, which now became firmly established in the British biscuit repertoire.

By 1865 the newcomer Peek Frean had become a serious rival to Huntley & Palmers. Originally set up in 1858 by James Peek on a wharf in the east London docks, the firm's beginnings were unpromising. As a ship's biscuit manufacturer it struggled to compete with the 15 other bakeries on the docks. After an ill-fated move in 1860 to manufacture aerated bread, the company faltered. Peek now went into partnership with his nephew, George Frean, a miller from Portsmouth, who suggested that as there were no fancy biscuit manufacturers in London, the company should branch out into this sphere of production. Yet despite installing the most up-to-date machinery and ovens, the company lacked expertise. It was only when Frean approached his old school friend, John Carr, JD's youngest brother, who had worked at the Carlisle biscuit factory for nearly twenty years, that things began to look up. In 1865 John Carr invented the Pearl biscuit. This soft domed biscuit was an innovation in industrial biscuit making because it was the first mechanically produced soft dough biscuit and did not require 'docking' – holes pierced in it to release the steam. It was a roaring success, and by the end of that year, Peek Frean's turnover was already half that of Huntley & Palmers, who responded by bringing out their own versions of Peek Frean's most successful biscuits: the Pearl, the Garibaldi and the Marie.[64]

Other biscuit makers with regional customer bases now also moved into steam-powered factories and began to challenge Huntley & Palmers' pre-eminence. Soon after he purchased the original 'Oliver and Fancy Biscuit Establishment' at 13 Green Street in Bath in 1869, James Fortt rationalised the laborious hand production of Dr Oliver's biscuits by installing biscuit-making machinery. Before long his shop was manufacturing 17,000 biscuits a year – enough to supply grocers around the country with the distinctive cylindrical tins of the biscuit that he renamed Bath Olivers, playing on the town's association with the late-eighteenth-century fashionable elite. By the early twentieth century, demand for Bath Oliver biscuits had become so great that Fortt opened a new factory on Manvers Street, with eight electrical ovens that baked Bath Olivers by day and bread by night.[65] By 1904 the biscuit was so well established in the national consciousness that one *Punch* cartoon pictured a 'dingy Bohemian' demanding 'I want a Bath Oliver.' The haughty waiter's reply was 'My name is *NOT* Oliver!' According to *The Lady*, 'You want a Bath Oliver' became a catchphrase.[66]

Naturally, Huntley & Palmers responded by producing their own line of Bath Olivers. Fortt's was never large enough to present a substantial threat to them, but in the 1880s McVitie & Price of Edinburgh and Macfarlane Lang of Glasgow moved into state-of-the art steam-powered factories in their home towns, and by the early 1900s they had opened branch factories in London.[67] In Ireland in 1851, William and Robert Jacob moved the successful bakery operation they had inherited from their father from Waterford to a factory in Dublin. In an advert in the *Waterford Mail* they declared their intention to secure for themselves 'a portion of the present demand for those imported from Carlisle and Edinburgh'.[68] Not only did Jacob's eventually corner the Irish biscuit market, but by 1903 the company had become the third largest biscuit manufacturer in Britain after Huntley & Palmers and Peek Frean.[69] In 1914 they followed up the success of their Cream Cracker in England by opening a branch factory in Liverpool.[70]

The established biscuit manufacturers reacted to this competition by increasing the variety of biscuits they sold. Their haphazard logic was that if they produced as many new biscuit lines as machines and labour would allow, a proportion would eventually succeed.[71] When J. D. Carr's sons inherited the factory in 1884, even though the company was already dangerously overstretched, their first decision was to take out a loan to add a modern, electrically lit wing to the factory, which allowed them to increase the number of biscuit lines from the 128 varieties they were already producing.[72] No sooner did one of these many biscuit lines become a bestseller than the other firms would follow by bringing out their own version. Carr's Excursion biscuits, brought out in the late 1850s, were matched by Huntley & Palmers' Travellers in 1857. In the 1880s, Jacob's competed with them by making Tramway and Tourist biscuits.[73] The result was that customers were presented with a bewildering and continuously expanding range of biscuits, most of which – such as the African Shoot, Country Life, Duchess, James, Neptune Dessert, Sarah Bernhardt, Taffy, Tennis and Whist – failed to find a permanent place in the national biscuit repertoire and have long since disappeared.[74] In this

The back of a French trade card advertising the many varieties of biscuit made by Huntley & Palmers.

commercial environment where products were easy to copy, the biscuit firms ran the risk of being just one producer among others. They therefore fought to establish themselves as *the* quality firm.

Yet this concentration on creating an image of superiority meant that the manufacturers resisted exploring ways of producing their lines more cheaply or selling them for less. They believed that in a luxury market a low price could act as a disincentive to buyers.[75] Thus Huntley & Palmers' fanciest iced rout biscuits cost two shillings a pound, more than a day's wages for most of the population. Even their cheapest ginger nuts at 6d a pound were well beyond the pocket of the working classes. It meant that workers who made the biscuits in the factories could not afford to buy them.

Bakers at Carr's and Huntley & Palmers worked at least a twelve-hour shift, from six in the morning to six in the evening, with a half-day on Saturdays, for between 16 and 18 shillings a week. As a paternalist Quaker employer, JD was proud of the light and airy working conditions in his factory, and both companies provided schoolrooms for the 'boys' from 14 to 19 who made up the majority of their workforces. More importantly, both firms set up sick funds, which the workers paid into every week to insure themselves against sickness or incapacitation. However, the employers' moral rectitude meant that at Huntley & Palmers smoking, swearing or drinking liquor at work incurred a substantial fine; at Carr's they were grounds for dismissal. Moreover, they did not feel their moral influence should stop at the factory gates: JD dismissed any of his hands seen frequenting one of Carlisle's many public houses. As an alternative, they provided their workers with reading rooms stocked with a range of newspapers and periodicals. In the style of the beneficent lord of the manor, Huntley & Palmers held celebratory factory suppers and teas for their employees to mark occasions such as George Palmer's wedding or the opening of a new factory building. The highlight of the year was the works outing, when Huntley & Palmers took its employees on a boat trip down the Thames and JD organised a visit to the Lake District.[76]

These acts of benevolent paternalism gave the biscuit factory employees a sense of belonging to a community, even if it was one in which everyone was expected to know their place and exhibit due deference. George Cadbury cynically remarked that if workers felt their labour was valued, they worked harder.[77] Yet the reality was that no matter whether the biscuit workers *felt* appreciated, in monetary terms their labour was valued at very little. On a trip to London in 1870, JD bought the foreman of his sugar biscuit department a pair of spectacles for 18 shillings: the weekly wage he paid to one of his bakers.[78] While this small act of kindness came naturally to him as a paternalistic employer, it would never have occurred to him to pay his workers sufficient wages to enable them to buy their own spectacles.

When two workers dared to approach George Palmer to request a wage rise, he kicked them down the stairs from his office.[79] And yet as a good Quaker Palmer felt obliged to pass on to his customers any fall in the price of ingredients. Indeed, throughout the nineteenth century Huntley & Palmers adjusted the price of their biscuits to reflect the fluctuating cost of flour.[80] The Quaker logic was that business should serve the customer by making the best possible goods at the cheapest prices.[81] A low wage bill was an essential part of keeping prices down and the large pool of labour in the countryside around Reading and Carlisle meant that the biscuit factories could pay low wages and still be assured of a steady supply of workers. The Quakers believed that it would not be in the interests of their customers if the manufacturers charged more for their biscuits in order to fund higher wages for their workers.

A baker living on 18 shillings a week would have had to spend at least 2s. 6d on rent for a damp, substandard house and another shilling on coal; this would have enabled the family to cook their meals but it was not enough to allow them to keep the fire going all day to keep warm. Food would have accounted for another 12 shillings. The poor used potatoes to bulk out their diet as they were cheaper than bread, and together the two staple foods would have provided about two thirds of their calories, while accounting for only 20 per cent of the food budget. Meat, on the other hand, was expensive: many families spent as much as a third of their food budget on it. They favoured bacon, because although it cost twice as much as fresh beef or mutton, it kept well and was still palatable when cold. Beef or mutton usually only featured on Sundays in a meat and vegetable stew. A few precious pennies would have bought salt, pepper and mustard, fish sauce or vinegar to liven up the stodgy food.

At least a shilling went on an ounce or two of tea and a pound and a half of sugar to sweeten it. Nothing revived flagging spirits like the 'Englishman's opium': a cup of sweet tea. 'Put the kettle on and we'll all have a nice cup of tea!' wrote George Orwell. '*That* is how your mind works when you are [poor].'[82] The soap the family needed to maintain a semblance of cleanliness and the candles to light their dingy rooms cost at least another 10d. And if the worker's sick fund contribution was 6d a week, and the children's schooling cost another 8d, this left

4d to put aside for clothes or boots for the children. There was no room in such a budget to buy fancy biscuits.[83]

The working classes might buy lemon-peel-studded discs of gingerbread at a fair, enjoy a caraway-seed biscuit with their sherry while visiting a pleasure garden with their sweetheart or dip a soft biscuit in their gin-and-peppermint at the bar of a gin shop.[84] On the streets of London, Henry Mayhew observed that 'the Jews' crisp butter biscuits rank very high' with the coster boys, who claimed that they 'slip[ped] down like soapsuds down a gully hole'.[85] Biscuits were sold by the street vendors on Petticoat Lane, where hungry Londoners could buy 'hard-bake' – ship's biscuit – or one of the 'large hard-looking biscuits' sold by youths 'crying Ha'penny biscuits, ha'penny; three a penny, biscuits' to eat 'with a morsel of cheese'.[86] But if working-class people were looking for a sweet treat they would usually choose an orange or dried dates, a halfpenny glass of ginger beer or some hard-boiled sweets.[87] It would never have occurred to them to enter a grocer's and ask for half a pound of Huntley & Palmers ginger nuts.

As Henry Mayhew watched the 'infinity of fancy biscuits' clatter out of the machines at Peek Frean, he commented that 'it seemed as though biscuits constituted the staple article of the food of the entire human race, rather than being the mere toothsome snacks of a small portion of mankind, eaten between the usual meals'.[88] It was in the nature of the factory system to become more efficient over time and produce ever more goods. But even the wealthiest middle-class customer spent only a tiny proportion of their food budget on biscuits. Although Britain's middle class expanded into the biggest in Europe as the British population doubled between 1850 and 1911, as long as industrial biscuits remained a luxury product the domestic market was simply not large enough to absorb the enormous output of the biscuit factories. Low wages meant that industrial biscuits continued to be beyond the reach of about two thirds of the British population. This was the self-defeating logic of early capitalism: workers were perceived not as potential consumers but as 'living tools … to be worked so much, and paid so much, and there ended; something to be infallibly settled by laws of supply and demand'.[89] As long as the manufacturers failed to realise that their workers were also their customers – and acknowledged that they too were entitled to the small comforts of life – they were forced to look elsewhere for markets to absorb their surplus biscuits.

GARIBALDI BISCUITS

110 g plain flour

¼ tsp baking powder

pinch of salt

25 g unsalted butter, cold

25 g caster sugar

1 large egg

3 tbsp milk

100 g dried fruit (a mixture of currants and sultanas works well)

zest of ¼ lemon

Preheat oven to 190°C. Line a baking tray with baking parchment.

Mix the flour, baking powder and salt together in a bowl.

Chop the butter into cubes then add to the bowl and rub in. Stir in the caster sugar.

Separate the egg. Whisk the egg yolk and milk together, then add to the flour mixture and gently stir until the dough comes together. Use your hands to bring it into a ball.

Dust the worktop with flour, place the dough in the middle and dust again.

Roll out to a rectangle 20 x 30 cm. Tip the fruit and lemon zest onto one half of the rectangle. Spread the fruit out so it forms an even layer over half the dough. Fold the other half over the fruit. Roll out the sandwiched dough to a 20 x 30 cm rectangle again.

Cut into two lengthways and then cut each strip into 8 so that you have 16 small rectangular biscuits. Place on the baking sheet. Brush the tops with the egg white (use only a small amount, not the whole white) and sprinkle with a little caster sugar.

Bake for 14–16 minutes until golden brown. Cool on a wire rack.

DIGESTIVE BISCUITS

On 14 September 1665, Samuel Pepys was walking home from a meeting at the Admiralty when, 'being full of wind and out of order', he stopped at 'the Bear at the Bridge-foot... and there called for a biscuit and a piece of cheese and gill of sack'.[1] In the same way that someone suffering from Pepys's affliction today might reach for a Rennie tablet, a seventeenth-century gentleman ate a biscuit. Sponge fingers had been introduced to England as 'savrous' confections that comforted the stomach. They contained sugar, that perfect foodstuff that helped the body maintain its natural equilibrium, and usually some seeds, such as caraway, coriander or aniseed, which were thought to assist in settling the stomach and suppressing the noxious fumes that could rise from a gut in the process of 'cooking', or digesting, its contents. Hannah Woolley included all three seeds in a recipe for bisket bread that she called 'diet bread', indicating that it was a health foodstuff that might be used as part of a regimen to maintain the humoral balance of the body.

TO MAKE DIET BREAD OR JUMBOLDS

Take a Quart of fine Flower, half a Pound of
fine Sugar, Caraway seeds, Coriander seeds
and Aniseeds bruised, of each one Ounce,
mingle all these together, then take the
Yolks of eight Eggs, and the Whites of three,
beat them well with four spoonfuls of Rose-
water, and so knead these all together and
no other Liquor, when it is well wrought,
lay it for one hour in a linen cloth before
the Fire, then rowl it out thin, tie them in
Knots and prick them with a Needle, lay
them upon Butter'd Plates, and bake them
in an Oven not too hot.[2]

Hannah Woolley, *The Queen-like
Closet* (1670)

In England, the belief that caraway seeds were a cure for the 'windy colic'
apples were thought to induce meant that caraway-seed biscuits and
apples were a common pairing. In Charles Dickens' *The Pickwick Papers*,
Bob Sawyer gives Arabella 'two small caraway-seed biscuits and a sweet
apple' as a love token (which she rejects as unpleasantly warm from having
been kept too long in his pockets).[3] After an evening of 'chat and backgammon',

Jane Austen's Mr Woodhouse, who fusses a great deal about his guests' digestion, serves baked apples with biscuits, which surely would have been caraway-seed sponge fingers.[4]

The process of digestion was the focus of a great deal of anxiety throughout the eighteenth and nineteenth centuries. Concerted intellectual activity was thought to divert blood from the stomach to the brain, and fretful descriptions of the torments of their guts abound in the correspondence and diaries of lettered gentlemen. Samuel Taylor Coleridge worried about his digestion to the point of distraction and attributed all troubles in his life to his stomach.[5] As the place where food was at best dissolved and at worst putrefied, the stomach was regarded with suspicion as an organ that could threaten a person's entire well-being. Moreover, the belief that nervous sympathy existed between the body's organs meant that a disordered stomach was identified as the root cause of a host of other ailments, from heart trouble to chronic anxiety.[6]

Modern urban life was identified as the cause of the wave of digestive problems that according to both medical journals and the popular press had engulfed the population. The long working day, which meant that many people crammed all their meals into just a few hours from the late afternoon, was blamed for over-stuffed, overworked and inefficient stomachs.[7] At the same time, excessive amounts of rich food and alcohol were held responsible for overloading the nation's alimentary capacities. In *Surgical Observations on the Constitutional Origin and Treatment of Local Diseases* (1809), Dr John Abernethy railed against imported foodstuffs in particular. Medical doctrine held that foods grown locally were best suited to a person's constitution. Abernethy claimed that exotic foods cultivated in tropical climates overpowered the British stomach. Excess food that the stomach was unable to digest then fermented into a rancid acid that burned the throat and mouth and filtered into the bloodstream, which carried this noxious poison to every organ in the body. No matter what his patients' ailments, from toothache to syphilis, Abernethy inevitably diagnosed a disordered stomach as the cause of their problem.[8]

Abernethy was caricatured as 'Dr My Book' in the popular press, as he was forever quoting from 'my book' in his lectures and insisted that his patients bought a copy of *Surgical Observations*.[9] But even if they were less fanatical, most physicians agreed that the stomach was central to both physical and mental health. Indigestion was portrayed as the national disease. Thomas Allbutt, a self-proclaimed 'stomach doctor', commented that if the newspapers were to be believed 'martyrs to dyspepsia' could be found on every street corner. Their pages were filled with advertisements for after-dinner pills, cordials, powders and pepsins to fight the 'demon dyspepsia'.[10] The peculiar and surprisingly popular *Memoirs of a Stomach* (1853), purportedly written by the stomach of a middle-class gentleman, disseminated the view that the nation was destroying its alimentary health by indulging cravings for inappropriate foods. 'Mr Stomach' gets off to a bad start in life when the wet nurse engaged to feed his orphaned master fills him with breast milk infused with porter. He then struggles through his youthful master's predilection for sweetmeats made with adulterated flour, his exotic breakfasts of imported foodstuffs at college, and the rich Continental foods he enjoys on his honeymoon. Finally, a well-paid job in the City compounds Mr Stomach's miseries with excessive alcoholic stimulation which induces 'horrible bouts of indigestion'.[11]

Diet was inevitably at the centre of any therapeutic regimen that identified the stomach as the key to the body's well-being. While in the seventeenth century food and drugs were used to manipulate the body's inner
functions, in the following century the emphasis shifted towards temperance. The ideal diet was light and easily digestible so as not to place too
great a strain on the system. For a disordered stomach Dr Abernethy recommended a spell in the countryside, away from the unnatural life of the city,
and a light diet of fresh milk and egg custard, rhubarb pills and boiled water
flavoured with fresh ginger.[12] Yet he made no mention of the caraway-seed
biscuits that share his name. The doctor is supposed to have suggested to a
baker near St Bartholomew's Hospital in London that the Captain's biscuits
he bought for his lunch would be improved by the addition of a little sugar
and some caraway seeds. This just-so story of 'how the Abernethy got its
caraways', was however, a later invention of nineteenth-century journalism.
Abernethy's obsessive campaign to improve the nation's alimentary health
led to the association of the doctor with this 'digestive' biscuit, which happened to hail from the same Scottish town as the doctor's ancestors.[13]

Biscuits were, however, usually part of the diet recommended to soothe a
dyspeptic stomach. In 1796, the local clergyman in Billericay was so moved
by the plight of one of his parishioners, an obese miller called Thomas
Wood, that he gave him a copy of the Venetian nobleman Louis Cornaro's
Discourses on the Sober Life (1583–95). Wood had eaten himself into a terrible
state and suffered from heartburn, stomach pains, headaches, gout and
the sensation that he was suffocating after eating. Cornaro had been an
early proponent of temperance, who attributed his good health well into his
nineties to the fact that he had renounced his dissipated ways in his forties

and followed an abstemious regimen. Wood took Cornaro's advice to avoid all foods that disagreed with him and eat only what his stomach could easily digest. He gave up meat and cheese and lived on a pudding made of sea biscuit. This diet, accompanied by a regime of cold baths and dumb-bell exercises, restored the miller to excellent health.[14]

Biscuits also featured in the regimen recommended at the end of Mr Stomach's memoirs. He proposed taking a brisk early-morning walk and, if hungry, to 'munch a dry biscuit on your way rejoicing'.[15] After a day of frugal meals, supper should be avoided, but it was a good idea to keep 'a little reserve of biscuit by the bedside' in case of wakefulness.[16] In the summer of 1838, the incorrigibly greedy Queen Victoria was trying to slim down and complained of being hungry when out riding with Prime Minister Lord Melbourne, who responded that she should 'try a hard biscuit'. A few months later she was again complaining of being hungry, exacerbated by watching Lord Melbourne tuck into some cold partridge for breakfast. Her petulant response to his suggestion that she 'eat a dry biscuit' was, 'No, that I didn't like.' 'Then you are not very hungry,' was the prime minister's response.[17]

No doubt a hundred years earlier Dr William Oliver had given similar advice to his fashionable patients when they came to Bath to take the waters and rest their stomachs from the excesses of their overly rich diets. The nineteenth-century just-so story of 'how the Bath Oliver was made' claimed that the doctor invented the light but nourishing biscuit for his patients and on his death in 1764 bequeathed the recipe to his coachman, together with 10 sacks of flour and £100 to enable him to set up a bakery. The recipe was then passed down through a succession of the bakery's owners until in 1869 James Fortt bought the 'Oliver and Fancy Biscuit Establishment' at 13

Green Street. Oliver biscuits were, in fact, made by bakers throughout Bath, but Fortt claimed that his were made using 'the original recipe'. He hung a picture of Dr Oliver in his shop and began selling them beyond the city, rebranded as Bath Oliver biscuits. By 1909 he had acquired the technology to enable him to print an image of the doctor on every biscuit he manufactured.[18]

In his advertising, Fortt played heavily on the health benefits of his biscuits. Bath Olivers were presented as 'the only fermented biscuit in the world', and the yeast in the dough was said to make them 'good for invalids suffering from acidity of the stomach'.[19] In the eighteenth century, as humoral theory's grip on medical thought lessened, digestion was re-envisaged as a chemical process of fermentation. David MacBride, an experimentalist proponent of this chemical view of digestion, warned that if food was detained in the stomach rather than passing on into the digestive tract, the later stages of fermentation, which took place safely in the intestines, occurred instead in the stomach, and the acid this produced caused the burning pain of dyspepsia.[20] Bath Olivers were supposed to be particularly easy to digest because the overnight fermentation of the biscuit dough did some of the work of digestion even before the food entered the stomach.

From the early nineteenth century, however, there was something of a debate about the safety of yeast. The German scientist Justus von Liebig argued that the process of fermentation it brought about was itself a form of putrefaction, and that leavened bakery products were in effect in a state of decay.[21] In his search for an alternative, he invented baking powder, a means of raising bread by inorganic chemicals such as phosphate. This, he argued, produced a pure loaf of bread. Commercial baking powders were soon pro-

This Roman fresco almost certainly depicts a charitable distribution of free bread rather than a conventional bread stall. But the loaves are the same circular breads divided into wedges that would have been sold on the streets of Pompeii and which the slaves had just put into the oven at the Modestus bakery on the morning of 24 August 79 CE.

In this illustration in the *Tacuinum Sanitatis*, a medieval handbook on health, a customer is buying theriaca at an apothecary's. The book exemplifies the process by which classical learning was re-introduced into medieval Europe from the Islamic world. It was a Latin translation of the eleventh-century treatise the Taqwim al-siha (Maintenance of Health) by the Baghdadi physician Ibn Butlan.

In this painting of *The Circumcision* of Christ by Mantegna the young boy in red is holding a ring-shaped biscuit in his hand, probably bought from one of the biscuit vendors who would have plied their wares on the streets of the Italian town of Mantua where the artist was employed in the early 1460s.

In this nineteenth-century Dutch painting a maid bakes waffles over a fire in a brazier, the thick, probably yeast-based dough in the bowl next to her.

A reconstruction of an English Renaissance sugar banquet. The bacon and eggs, playing cards and pair of gloves are all made from sugar paste, as are the blue and white 'china' plates. Amid the comfits, fruit and nuts are elaborate knot and alphabet jumbles (biscuits), gingerbread figures and wafers.

A detail from the sugar banquet of a gingerbread lady, neatly docked Shrewsbury biscuits, biscuits stamped with a flower design, gilded alphabet and iced and plain knot biscuits (jumbles).

A detail from the sugar banquet of rolled wafers and a sugar paste ace of hearts.

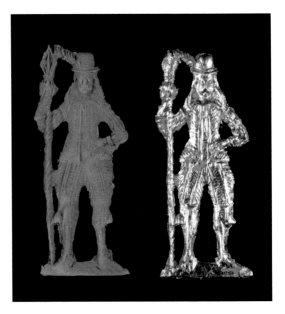

A plain and a gilded gingerbread figure of a militiaman holding a pike made using this seventeenth-century wooden gingerbread mould. In the evening scene from William Hogarth's series of four times of the day (below), the little boy squabbling with his sister is clutching a gingerbread man that would have been made in just such mould.

Hanging in the doorway of their house in this seventeenth-century painting of a Dutch baker and his wife are the soft pre-boiled breads that in Dutch were known as *krakeling* and in America became known as pretzels.

The centrepiece of this nineteenth-century illustration of the dessert is the dish of sweet biscuits.

A utilitarian biscuit tin from the first half of the twentieth century.

Postcard depicting Huntley & Palmers' Reading biscuit factory.

Huntley & Palmers trade cards peopled by fashionable ladies and gentlemen in a variety of bourgeois settings implied that not only did the company make 'superior' biscuits, they were chosen by a superior class of people.

(*left* and *right*) Trade cards from a series showing children around the world enjoying Huntley & Palmers biscuits.

Huntley & Palmers trade cards pressed home the message that the company's biscuits reached every corner of the globe.

INDIA—FORT ON THE INDUS.

CHINA—STREET MARKET.

A CANADIAN LOG STORE.

RUSSIA—OVERTAKEN BY WOLVES.

HINDOOS.　　HINDOUS.　　HINDUS.

An advert from 1936 for McVities Digestives showing how biscuits were now considered suitable to be eaten at any time of day with any meal or snack.

moted as a 'scientific' alternative to yeast that induced a clean and healthy form of fermentation in the stomach. Endorsements from doctors and scientists appended to baking powder advertisements assured customers that bakery products made with baking soda helped guard against indigestion.[22]

In the 1860s, the Aerated Bread Company began manufacturing 'pure and unadulterated, scientifically manufactured, healthy...bread' by pumping gas or aerated water into the dough.[23] *Punch* lampooned their product in a cartoon that showed the Cocker family 'floating about the ceiling of the Parlour in an utterly Helpless Condition' after eating aerated bread.[24] J. D. Carr's interest was piqued, and in 1864 he bought a machine to make 'aerated' biscuits that would be 'absolutely pure', as the dough was raised without recourse to yeast.[25] Aerated bread and biscuits both proved a failure, however. Louis Pasteur's theory of fermentation as a natural microbial process gained ground over the last half of the nineteenth century, and in the light of his research, Liebig's view of fermentation as a dangerous form of putrefaction began to seem like misguided scaremongering.[26] Besides, people preferred the flavour of yeast-leavened bread and bakery goods. They did, however, continue to have faith in baking soda as a remedy for dyspepsia.

Alexander Grant is usually credited with having invented the Digestive biscuit, so named because it was made with large quantities of baking soda. Grant began his career as a humble journeyman baker. On arriving in Edinburgh to search for work, he is said to have responded to Robert McVitie's claim that there was no job available at his Queensferry Street bakery by declaring that this was a shame as he was 'a fell fine baker'. And as he left the shop he picked up a scone and remarked, 'Well, anyway, ye canna make scones in Edinburgh.' His impudence is said to have secured him a job. By

1892, when McVitie & Price launched their Digestive biscuit, Grant had risen to the position of factory manager. Grant's Digestives were made according to a special formula, which he kept secret. He insisted that he should always be present to mix the essential ingredients whenever his biscuits were made. When in 1901 McVitie & Price opened a branch factory in Harlesden, Grant would travel between Edinburgh and London so that he could supervise the preparation of his Digestives at both factories.[27] This was characteristic of a man who had a reputation for absolute domination and for needing to 'always be supreme – the first and last word in McVitie & Price'.[28]

Long before McVitie & Price began manufacturing Grant's Digestives, bakers and biscuit manufacturers had been selling their own Digestive biscuits with the promise that they would 'keep the body in a regular state'.[29] Huntley & Palmers launched a Digestive biscuit in 1876 made with coarse sweetmeal flour. The benefits of wholemeal flour had been extolled by temperance campaigners like Sylvester Graham since the 1830s.[30] In addition, sweetmeal was made with malted grain. Malt releases enzymes that break down starch into fermentable sugar. This meant the biscuits tasted slightly sweet, and as with Bath Oliver biscuits, here too the process of fermentation was perceived to have begun even before the biscuit was consumed. Grant's addition of baking soda to sweetmeal biscuits merely improved on their ability to aid digestion.

In the nineteenth century, biscuits were seen as the perfect vehicle for a range of digestive aids. In the 1860s, a Mr Bragg of Wigmore Street, London, concocted charcoal biscuits as an 'unsightly but not unpleasant' way of administering the charcoal that was given to sufferers of indigestion, flatulence and foul breath.[31] Thereafter charcoal biscuits routinely featured

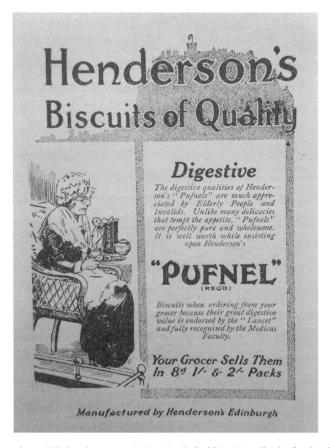

This advert for an Edinburgh company's Digestive Pufnel biscuits walks the fine line between promoting its product as a medical remedy suitable for the frail and yet at the same time a refined addition to any well-to-do tea table.

in frugal diet plans. In 1906, Ronnie Knox, up in London to visit his brother, was disappointed by his choice of a vegetarian restaurant where all they served was 'charcoal biscuits, grass and raisin salads'.[32] Arrowroot was introduced to England from Jamaica at the end of the eighteenth century. It was believed to be a wholesome food that was 'less apt to become sour during digestion than any other farinaceous food', and arrowroot gruel or jelly was fed to infants, the sick and the delicate.[33] William and David Arnott became acquainted with the starchy root on their voyage out to New South Wales in 1847. When the brothers expanded their Sydney ship's biscuit bakery into a biscuit manufactory in 1880, one of the first products they launched was milk arrowroot biscuits, which they marketed as particularly suitable for children's delicate digestions. They ran one of the first ever advertising campaigns that solicited feedback from customers, by encouraging parents to send in photographs of their healthy children who had been fed on the biscuits. Over the next 60 years, the company received tens of thousands of baby photographs. The winning entrants were regularly featured in Arnott's newspaper advertisements.[34]

Huntley & Palmers biscuits were routinely stocked by druggists alongside indigestion powders and rhubarb pills.[35] And yet despite the association of their biscuits with unpleasant ailments such as flatulence and the gross workings of the stomach, manufacturers managed to surround them with an aura of bourgeois elegance. In 1888, James Fortt claimed in an advertising pamphlet that 'it is difficult to find a more welcome present...for a person at a distance, than a tin of Fortt's "Oliver Biscuits"'.[36] Sarah Brydges Willyams echoed the sentiment when she wrote to thank Benjamin Disraeli in March 1862 for 'the most delicate [Oliver] biscuits' he had sent to her along with a leash of golden plovers.[37] In the 1930s, another of Fortt's adverts successfully combined elegance and health concerns, smoothly reassuring consumers that even 'the most fickle digestion can welcome Bath Olivers without a qualm' and promoting the biscuits with cheese as the perfect end to a meal for people who had 'to consider their digestions'.[38] Having worked so hard to promote his brand as the quality biscuit for the 'discerning' customer, Fortt would have been delighted by the way in which Evelyn Waugh wove Bath Olivers into his wartime elegy for the aristocracy. When in *Brideshead Revisited* Sebastian and Charles taste their way through the wine cellars of Brideshead, it is Bath Oliver biscuits they nibble on between bottles:

> Sebastian had found a book on wine-tasting, and we followed its instructions in detail. We warmed the glass slightly at a candle, filled it a third high, swirled the wine round, nursed it in our hands, held it to the light, breathed it, sipped it, filled our mouths with it, and rolled it over the tongue, ringing it on the palate like a coin on a counter, tilted our heads back and let it trickle down the throat. Then we talked of it and nibbled Bath Oliver biscuits, and passed on to another wine.[39]

9

In which the English drown the
French market with cataracts
of plain and fancy biscuits

The French have come frankly to acknowledge our pre-eminence as biscuit manufacturers. It is the machinery some say, that enables les Anglais to excel in this particular branch of production.[1]

At the Paris Exhibition of 1878, the journalist George Augustus Sala described how a 'biscuit scramble' would erupt around the Huntley & Palmers kiosk every afternoon when there was a distribution of free samples. Sala complimented the firm's Continental agent, Mr Joseph Leete, for 'sparing no pains to make the display of the renowned Reading firm attractive and complete'. In a glass-fronted wooden display case an 'astonishingly varied assortment of biscuits' were exhibited 'in tins, square and round, long and short, thick and thin'.[2]

Huntley & Palmers had been unsuccessfully attempting to break into the European biscuit market for some time before the inspired appointment of Leete in 1865 breathed new life into the campaign.[3] To curry favour with their French and Belgian customers, the company began producing Napoleon and Leopold

The Peek Frean display stands at the International Health Exhibition, held in London in 1884.

biscuits. At the Universal Exhibition in Paris in 1867 these were displayed in tins with specially designed labels featuring the French and Belgian tricolours. In an attempt to demonstrate that their products were compatible with Continental modes of consumption, they advertised their 'sponge rusks' as particularly suitable for stirring champagne. But Edmé Guillot, the owner of Huntley & Palmers' only biscuit-manufacturing rival in France, was head of the judges and made sure his own firm carried off the gold medal.[4] Huntley & Palmers triumphed, however, at the Exhibition of 1878, where they won gold.[5] Sala crowed that the French had been forced to acknowledge that 'eminent and even illustrious as they are as pastry cooks and confectioners, [they] are incompetent to make biscuits that will keep. French biscuits are sweet and showy, and succulent; but after a day or two, *c'en est fini avec eux*. They lose their gloss, their flavour, and their crispness, and become limp, sour, dry and tasteless.'[6]

Huntley & Palmers succeeded in acquiring the same reputation for excellence on the Continent as they had already won for themselves at home. By conducting a blind test, Leete persuaded the proprietor of an illustrious Parisian food emporium on the Boulevard Malesherbes to stock Huntley & Palmers biscuits over Peek Frean.[7] As the first industrial nation, Britain was at the forefront of the production of processed foodstuffs. The British middle classes had embraced these as novel symbols of the country's material progress. Now that northern Europe was experiencing its own industrial revolution, British food manufacturers targeted the Continent's growing middle-class market. Sala was proud that while 40 years ago the only place 'in Paris where one could procure English groceries, wines and spirits was at Cuvillier's', now the English were drowning the French market 'with cataracts of plain and fancy biscuits, pickles, sauces, condiments, and even with preserved fruits, jams, and jellies'.[8]

In 1870 the first English biscuit warehouse outside Paris opened in Bordeaux. Meanwhile Carr's were making headway in Belgium and the Netherlands. When JD died in 1884, export had become Carr's busiest department.[9] While Belgium, France and the Netherlands absorbed nearly three quarters of all Britain's biscuit exports, Leete also ventured into Spain, Portugal, Scandinavia, Russia and Turkey. On a visit to St Petersburg, Sala discovered that it was possible to buy 'Reading biscuits' at the Anglisky Magasin, although customs duties made them prohibitively expensive.[10] European nations, of course, had their own biscuit-baking traditions, but the advent of the English biscuit companies awakened a taste among European consumers for Britain's industrial biscuits. Within ten years of Leete's appointment, Continental sales accounted for nearly half of Huntley & Palmers' total sales.[11]

Once the English biscuit companies had laid the foundations for a Continental industrial biscuit market, European bakers stepped in to capitalise on their success.[12] In the first wave of industrialisation Europe had imported British steam locomotives and heavy machinery; now Huntley & Palmers' European rivals bought steam-powered mechanical mixers, kneading and stamping machines and travelling ovens from British engineering companies like T. and T. Vicars and Joseph Baker. In the 1860s Jean-Honoré Olibet, a baker from Bordeaux, sent his son Eugène to England to study the art of biscuit making. Eugène returned having placed orders for machinery with British engineering companies, and in 1872 Olibet opened a steam-powered biscuit factory on the outskirts of Bordeaux.[13]

Others soon followed his example. Jean-Romain Lefèvre and his wife Pauline Utile ran a patisserie in Nantes. Their best-selling biscuits were Rose de Reims – pink sponge fingers that had acquired their distinctive colouring when a seventeenth-century baker added cochineal to his bisket bread to disguise the unsightly brown streaks left by the vanilla he used as a flavouring. Lefèvre sent his son Louis to investigate English machinery for making sponge finger biscuits. This was installed at their bakery in 1882, and that year their Rose de Reims won a gold medal at the Nantes Exhibition. Three years later, Lefèvre-Utile (LU) opened a steam-powered biscuit factory, and in partnership with his brother-in-law Ernest, Louis grew the company into one of France's leading fancy biscuit manufacturers.[14]

Just as it had been in Britain, in Europe too, biscuit manufacture was at the cutting edge of industrial food production. Biscuit manufacture was one of Spain's first ventures into factory food processing. In 1876, Viñas y Asociados of Barcelona opened a fully automated biscuit factory, equipped with English-made mechanical mixers, blenders, stampers, two ovens and its own tin-box workshop. They even recruited Englishmen to train their management team.[15] Likewise, one of Italy's first ventures into industrial food production was the fancy biscuit factory – again complete with English biscuit-making machinery – set up by the Lazzaroni family of confectioners and coffee-house owners in their home town of Saronno in 1888.[16] In both Spain and Italy biscuit manufacture only made a minuscule contribution to the national economy – Viñas y Asociados employed just 150 people – but the factories were innovatory in their management and marketing methods and became models for subsequent agri-businesses.[17]

European biscuit manufacturers not only imported British equipment but mimicked the British firms' biscuits. Viñas y Asociados specialised in English cinnamon- and vanilla-flavoured sugar wafers. Olibet made the full range of cracknels, ginger nuts, Nic-Nacs, Maries and Alberts that Huntley & Palmers had worked so hard to insinuate into French tastes. They even named the first biscuit they invented the Saint Georges to give it an English aura.[18] For the Belgian baker Eduard De Beukelaer too, success lay in copying the English. His tight finances meant that on his fact-finding trip to England he was only able to afford a dilapidated biscuit-cutting and printing machine, but he nevertheless opened a steam-powered factory in Antwerp in 1875. In 1884, his decorating department began producing imitations of the popular English iced biscuits known in Belgium as *Engels lekkers* (English treats). By 1888 De Beukelaer's four ovens were working eleven hours a day to produce 1,500 kilos of English-style fancy biscuits.[19]

In Germany H. Schmuckler advertised the fact that his small biscuit-making enterprise on Friesenstrasse in Hanover made English-style products by naming it Fabrikgeschäft Englische Cakes und Biscuits (English Cakes and Biscuits Factory). When Hermann Bahlsen bought the company in 1889, he renamed it the Hannoversche Cakes Fabrik H. Bahlsen, and thus began the German confusion over the terminology for biscuits. In imitation of the English strategy of naming biscuits after celebrities, Bahlsen named the thin buttery biscuit that he began producing in 1891 the Leibniz, after the philosopher – Hanover's most celebrated past inhabitant. It was marketed not as a biscuit but as *'Der Beste Butter-Cakes'*. It was an instant hit. The Leibniz won a gold medal at the Chicago World Fair in 1893 and Bahlsen opened a distribution warehouse that dispatched tins of Leibniz 'butter cakes' all over Germany. Germans pronounced 'cakes' as 'keks', and the misnomer was enshrined in the language in 1912 when Bahlsen renamed his company H. Bahlsen's Keksfabrik.[20]

By the 1880s the European companies felt sufficiently sure of themselves to innovate without reference to the English. In 1886 LU launched the Petit Beurre, a rich buttery square whose superiority, according to Louis Lefèvre, lay in the Nantes-based firm's easy access to Brittany's high-quality butter.[21] Not to be outdone, two years later Olibet introduced their own Petit Beurre and, in a sure sign that the biscuit economy was now Europe-wide, in 1891 Huntley & Palmers launched theirs.[22] By the early twentieth century, European biscuit manufacturers were even beginning to challenge the British on their home turf. In typically jingoistic fashion, the Conservative candidate for the 1904 Reading by-election complained in the *Daily Mail* that the French biscuit firm Guillot was undercutting Huntley & Palmers by selling its sugar wafers in the town for nearly a penny a pound less.[23]

French deference towards the English as the premier biscuit manufacturers had evaporated. In 1914 Lefèvre likened the British Petit Beurre to the bland 'boiled turnip which is loved by our neighbours beyond the Channel', and went on to claim that it was 'as insipid as a foggy day on the Thames'. His own Petit Beurre, on the other hand, was 'a really French biscuit, really Breton, with a hint of salt, a drop of milk, a knob of the delicious butter that has earned our Armorican region such universal renown'.[24] England might well have been the home of the industrial biscuit, but Olibet's adoption of the French national icon, the rooster crowing at dawn, reminded their customers that they were the first European industrial biscuit manufacturer to challenge the English.[25]

At the beginning of the twentieth century, Huntley & Palmers' fortunes were flagging. Having begun as the most sophisticated food-processing plant in the world, by the early 1900s their machinery was obsolete and their marketing strategies outdated. Rather than investing in the up-to-date machinery that T. and T. Vicars and Joseph Baker (later Baker Perkins) were supplying to their competitors, they continued to make their machinery in their own engineering department. While Peek Frean had dropped the practice of making as many biscuit varieties as possible and kept a blacklist of slow sellers that they then phased out of production, Huntley & Palmers clung on to their dilapidated South Factory in which they produced small batches of their slow-selling biscuits. They also rejected proposals that they should follow their competitors and start wrapping biscuits in paper packages rather than selling them loose in tins.[26] Ironically, they were saved by their imitation of a European biscuit.

After George Palmer's death in 1897, his three sons took over the running of the firm. Walter Palmer travelled a great deal in search of new biscuit varieties and was said to be able after just one bite of a strange biscuit to 'accurately and rapidly describe all the materials which had gone in to its makeup'.[27] He came home from one of these trips with the idea for the Breakfast Biscuit, and collaborated with his brother Alfred in building the complex machinery needed to manufacture a small square rusk with rounded edges that, according to one nostalgic consumer, tasted like dense but crunchy sponge.[28]

The inspiration for Walter's Breakfast Biscuit was almost certainly *Zwieback*. *Zweybacken* was the sixteenth-century Swiss term for twice-baked, and at that time would have been more akin to the hard, dark barley-bread rusks eaten on the Greek island of Santorini than the lighter, friable rusks that the Swiss chef Joseph Favre described in his *Dictionnaire universel de cuisine pratique* in 1895. Favre reported that *Zwieback*, made from toasted slices of a slightly sweet bread, was eaten throughout Switzerland and Germany. While the sixteenth-century Swiss dipped it in their morning soup, the nineteenth-century recipe book of Catharina Fehr suggests that it was considered a suitable accompaniment to coffee, chocolate or wine.[29] Schiller's wife sent Goethe a package of home-made *Zwieback* in 1796 to dip in his breakfast chocolate.[30]

Today Germans associate *Zwieback* with the biscuit-making firm set up by the baker Friedrich Brandt in the north German town of Hagen in 1912. In fact, Brandt learned the art of making these brittle twice-baked rusks in Friedrichsdorf, just north of Frankfurt, where he served his apprenticeship.[31] Here two bakers, Christoph Sternler and Jean Georg Frederic Seidel, were the first to sell *Zwieback*, in the late eighteenth century. Sternler had served on Dutch warships, and as *Zwieback* is similar to the rusks the Dutch took to South Africa and America, it seems possible that he learned the art of baking it in the Netherlands. In the mid nineteenth century the neighbouring town of Homburg developed into a fashionable spa frequented by Europe's wealthy, and this gave the Friedrichsdorf *Zwieback* bakers a boost. Like Bath's Oliver biscuit, *Zwieback* was considered a light, easily digestible food, kind to the stomachs of those recovering from dyspepsia, such as Edward VII, who often visited Bad Homburg to undergo a fasting cure. Several bakers now set up *Zwieback* factories, and tins of the biscuits could be found not only in high-end department stores in Berlin and Vienna but as far afield as Constantinople and Russia, whose nobility frequented the Bad Homburg spa.[32]

Walter Palmer must have been aware of *Zwieback*'s supposedly medicinal qualities. He seems to have invented the Breakfast Biscuit for the benefit of his wife's friend, the author George Meredith, who, like so many gentlemen of the period, suffered from indigestion; thus among the Palmers it was known as 'Meredith's biscuit'.[33] The Breakfast Biscuit was advertised as a perfect, light, nutritious food for the overtaxed modern digestive system, responding to contemporary calls for a simpler dietary regimen in which breakfast was 'reduced to health food and

One of the adverts Huntley & Palmers placed in magazines and periodicals to advertise their new Breakfast Biscuits.

hot water'.[34] Huntley & Palmers marketed their biscuit as an 'elegant' alternative to a baker's roll at breakfast time.[35] This is how it is still eaten in Switzerland today, spread with butter and/or honey and eaten with a cup of coffee or chocolate.

Strangely, given the good quality of French bread, this biscuit, which was essentially desiccated toast, was a hit in France. The Breakfast Biscuit revived Huntley & Palmers' flagging sales on the Continent.[36] Joseph Leete managed to persuade the French customs authorities to charge lower duties for this particular variety because it was a form of bread rather than a conventional biscuit. Its affordability, combined with the testimonials of a number of French doctors who praised it for its digestive properties, seems to have secured its success.[37]

In Britain, by 1904, the Breakfast Biscuit ranked seventh in popularity behind the Petit Beurre, Fancy, Thin Lunch, Marie, Osborne and ginger nut. It helped that no other biscuit manufacturer brought out their own version, probably because a twice-baked biscuit made from a yeast-based dough was too complicated and costly to produce. Huntley & Palmers even began a targeted advertising campaign, characteristically taking out space opposite what they considered to be 'interesting' articles in the quality press. It seems to have made an impact: sales increased by 40 per cent in one year. When the company began selling Breakfast Biscuits in paper packages, demand more than trebled, and by the outbreak of war in 1914 they were selling 5.5 million packets a year.[38] Thus the most ancient form of biscuit – the twice-baked substitute for fresh bread – temporarily halted the decline of one of the first industrial biscuit firms.

Until the 1850s most advertisements were small black-and-white print announcements. But in 1853 the government abolished advertising duties, just as a plethora of newspapers and periodicals aimed at a middle-class readership were being launched. These were the perfect medium for attractively illustrated advertisements. Just as biscuits led the way in industrial food production, they were also at the forefront of the nineteenth-century branding and advertising revolution. Rather than marketing each and every variety they produced, the biscuit manufacturers concentrated on promoting their company names. This was an innovative step, because for most products at mid century, the name of the place where they were made guaranteed quality – Nottingham stockings, Florence oil, Carolina rice, Lübeck marzipan. Indeed, Huntley & Palmers initially sold their lines as 'Reading biscuits'. But with an increasing number of manufacturers all producing similar varieties, the brand name of the company became more important.[39] The biscuit makers worked hard to turn their firm's name into a promise of stability and reliability. Then, the company's hope was that, whichever biscuit variety they preferred, the customer would nevertheless remain loyal to his or her chosen brand.[40]

Advertising targeted that ever-expanding middle-class section of the population benefiting from industrialisation and urbanisation. 'The man and woman in good or fairly well-to-do circumstances', one trade magazine reminded biscuit manufacturers, were 'the buyers of the world'.[41] This middle section of society was by no means a cohesive group. Its members were divided by varied financial circumstances; whether they belonged to rural or urban communities; and in their politics and religion, which ranged from Tory to radical and High Anglican to nonconformist. They were, however, bound together by their idealisation of a 'genteel' lifestyle, which recast the home as a sphere separate from the world of work, in which middle-class values were both cultivated and displayed.[42] As their disposable incomes increased, they surrounded themselves with the paraphernalia of gentility: elegant furniture, expensive clothes, ornate tableware, cosmetics, soaps and scents, good food and wines.

The elitist tone of the advertising for firms such as Huntley & Palmers and Olibet suggested that biscuits were an essential part of this world. Advertising posters and postcards were peopled by ladies and gentlemen in fashionable outfits with coiffed hair eating their biscuits in a variety of bourgeois settings: manicured gardens with large houses in the background; interiors replete with oriental carpets, patterned wallpaper, clocks, candlesticks and fresh flowers, with uniformed servants hovering in the background; playing polo and golf, skating, fishing, shooting and hunting. 'Life in a chateau or on board a pleasure yacht requires foresight when it comes to provisions,' one advert for Olibet proclaimed. 'The mistress of the house never forgets to lay on a large supply of Olibet biscuits, prized for their finesse, their conservation and their variety.'[43] This elitist style of promotion trod a fine line between trust and exploitation, as it suggested that the biscuits were expensive simply for the sake of exclusivity. But because biscuit advertising played on 'the narcissism of little differences', it worked.[44] It succeeded in transforming mundane industrial biscuits into markers of distinction. Only discerning customers looking for 'dainty' and 'elegant' biscuits would choose Huntley & Palmers or Olibet.[45] What's more, these messages appealed not only to those who could afford a luxurious lifestyle, but also to the growing raft of clerks and schoolteachers, shopkeepers and artisans who aspired to such gentility. The right biscuits could breathe luxury and good account into even a modest household (see page 6 of the picture section).

As we have seen, while most of the biscuit manufacturers produced enough fine-quality fancy biscuits to supply a mass market, they stubbornly refused to do so at mass-market prices. In 1911 Louis Lefèvre acknowledged that LU could not expect to sell more biscuits in France unless it compromised on ingredients and made cheaper biscuits. Still, he spoke for the majority of quality biscuit manufacturers when he stated that, regardless, his company would not make anything other than 'very fine, but also relatively expensive biscuits'.[46] As the century wore on, a new generation of biscuit makers less squeamish about catering to the working classes began the process of democratising the biscuit. In the meantime, faced with European competition, the English biscuit manufacturers looked to the Empire to absorb the rest of their surplus production.

PIPPIN'S DOG BISCUITS

Traditionally stale, hard or burned bread was thrown to dogs. The French priest François Richard, who lived on the Greek island of Santorini in the last half of the seventeenth century, remarked that the hard biscuits the islanders lived on were 'so black that when I showed a piece to one of our monks in Naxos, he sincerely told me that in France it would be bread to give to the dogs, but he doubted that even the dogs would eat it'.[47] The Cincinnati electrician James Spratt is supposed to have had the idea to make dog biscuits in the 1860s after seeing dogs eating discarded ship's biscuits at the Liverpool docks. He marketed his 'Meat Fibrine Dog Cakes' made of wheat meal, vegetables, beetroot and meat to English country gentlemen as a nutritious supplement to a sporting dog's diet. Like Huntley & Palmers biscuits, industrially manufactured dog biscuits soon became part of the paraphernalia of the genteel lifestyle. These are my dog Pippin's favourite biscuits; mint is the magic ingredient.[48]

250 g wholewheat flour
200 g oatmeal (or rolled oats)
150 g cornmeal
50 g wheat germ

50 g flax meal, can be combined with ground pumpkin and sunflower seeds

1 tbsp baking powder

25 g finely chopped mint

1 egg, beaten

300 ml chicken or beef stock

1 tbsp coconut oil or lard or dripping (dissolve in the stock)

Combine the dry ingredients and the mint.

Add the egg and pour in the stock/oil mixture and mix well.

Put the dough in a plastic bag and let it rest overnight in the fridge.

Roll out as thin as possible and lay flat on a lightly greased baking sheet. Score into small squares with a blunt knife.

Bake at 180°C for 25 minutes.

10

In which King Mwanga puts the lid on one of John Roscoe's last tins of Osborne biscuits and carries them home

The English biscuit scrupulously prepared and as scrupulously packed, will defy time and climate. That is why scarcely a ship sails from England without a consignment of Reading biscuits in its hold, and this is why you will find Huntley & Palmers' biscuits, just as you will find Elkington's spoons and forks, and Allsopp's pale ale ... the whole world over, not only in the great centres of civilisation, but in the remotest and most barbarous regions.[1]

'Only men who have been reduced to native food can tell how delightful it is to sit down in the afternoon and enjoy tea with cow's milk and a cabin biscuit or, as an extra treat, an Osborne biscuit added.'[2] This heartfelt appreciation was penned by John Roscoe, a missionary living in the Ugandan capital Kampala in the 1890s. He and his fellow missionary, Mr Millar, lived on a monotonous diet of goat mutton with mashed plantain for breakfast, lunch and dinner. English provisions were scarce and expensive as they were carried up from the coast by an annual caravan of porters. To the two men, therefore, 'even ship's biscuits were a luxury'.[3] They were down to their last two tins of Osborne biscuits, with no news of new consignments of stores having been dispatched, when the local ruler, King Mwanga, announced that he intended to visit them for tea.

Flutes and drums heralded the king's approach on the shoulders of a bearer, who knelt at the doorstep to allow him to step into the room, while a retinue of followers crowded in behind him. The missionaries had only enamelware cups in which to serve tea, but they did place on the table one of the two precious tins of Osborne biscuits. King Mwanga helped himself to several and asked, 'Who made these biscuits?' On learning that they were from Messrs Huntley and Palmer he announced that in future 'they shall be my bakers', and as the missionaries looked on in dismay, he doled out more of the biscuits to his favourite followers so that they could verify their quality. When, after an hour of pleasant conversation, the king finally rose to leave, he 'took the tin of biscuits, put the lid on it, and handed it to one of the pages, saying: "Take this home for me."' The missionaries could do nothing but watch as the precious tin was carried away.[4]

From its inception the British saw their empire as a market for its manufactured goods. The early American colonies absorbed English weapons and gunpowder, printing presses and saw mills, axes and hoes, saddles, stockings, soap and starch, boots and shoes, feather beds, clocks, spectacles, playing cards, parrot cages and even tombstones.[5] In the last quarter of the seventeenth century, the colonial trade fuelled England's growth and laid the economic and technological foundations for the Industrial Revolution. Now, with the mechanisation of production, factories produced goods according to an internal logic based on economies of scale rather than to meet an unfilled demand. Britain's early textile factories soon churned out far more cloth than could be absorbed by the limited domestic market, especially as home-produced cottons had to compete with high-quality textiles from India. The response was to shut out Indian goods by imposing prohibitive tariffs on imports of Indian cloth and offload the British surplus onto the Empire. India was flooded with cheap Manchester cottons. As a result, the Indian artisanal textile industry collapsed.[6]

Like cloth, biscuits packed in airtight tins could be mass-produced in Britain and consumed thousands of miles away; and like the Manchester cotton magnates, the biscuit manufacturers looked to Britain's trading empire to absorb their surplus.[7] Since many biscuit factories were in prime locations to take advantage of the country's transport infrastructure, they were able to access Britain's global web of trade with ease. In 1872 Samuel Palmer declared in a speech that it was the company's intention to distribute their biscuits to every corner of the world. If anyone should ever encounter an obscure place where Reading biscuits were unobtainable, he told his audience, they should let the firm know so that it could address the deficit.[8] Advertising posters and trade cards pressed home the message that the company's biscuits reached every corner of the globe: tins of Huntley & Palmers biscuits feature being loaded into an American wagon, carried on the backs of yaks crossing the Mongolian steppes, pulled on a sledge through the Russian tundra, and dangling from a pole slung across the shoulders of a Chinese street vendor (see page 7 of the picture section).

After France, India was Huntley & Palmers' biggest overseas customer.[9] Peek Frean initially captured the United States, but after the appointment of an energetic salesman, by the turn of the century Huntley & Palmers had routed their competitor and by 1906 had captured 94 per cent of the American import market.[10] Competition between the biscuit firms was fierce. A passenger on a voyage to the Cape in 1898 noted in her diary that the traveller for Peek Frean was on board and had complained to the steward about the quality of biscuits served for afternoon tea, which she agreed 'certainly were very horrid'. It turned out they were South African biscuits and the shipping company had broken its contract with the two rival firms, which stated that the line should serve Huntley & Palmers biscuits one voyage and Peek Frean the next.[11]

By the time King Mwanga was sampling their biscuits with approval, Huntley & Palmers dominated the global biscuit market. They boasted that a ship 'seldom … sails from England that does not bear within his [sic] ribs a Reading biscuit en route for virtually every port around the globe'.[12] Industrial biscuits packed in airtight tins were a godsend for the explorers, surveyors, prospectors, scientists and ethnographers who travelled into the remotest parts of the globe, mapping and marking out territory, identifying and mining exploitable resources, and describing the people, flora and fauna. 'Biscuits and chocolate are about the most portable articles of sustenance that a traveller in strange lands can carry with him,' pontificated George Augustus Sala in 1879. Indeed, 'many a wanderer in distant climes may have been able to stave off starvation by means of a tin of Huntley & Palmers "Sponge Rusks", "Diets", "Abernethy's" or "Yachts"'.[13] They were certainly delightful in comparison with the weevil- and maggot-ridden ship's biscuits that the early maritime explorers had to endure. Robert Scott ordered special glucose-enriched biscuits from Huntley & Palmers for his ill-fated expedition to the South Pole. In a letter of recommendation from Antarctica on 20 October 1911 he declared that 'After further full experience of the Antarctic and Emergency biscuits supplied by you to this expedition I am of opinion that no better biscuits could be made for travelling purposes. I consider that they especially meet the requirements of Polar work in their hardness, food value and palatability.'[14] Tins of these biscuits can still be seen on the shelves in Scott's hut on Ross Island. According to the Norwegian explorer and ethnographer Carl Lumholtz, 'the right kind of provisions is as important in the equatorial regions as in the arctic'. Having experienced the swollen ankles and racing heart that were the unpleasant symptoms of beriberi, Lumholtz made green peas part of his daily diet on his expedition through Borneo in 1914. With his pea stew he drank tinned condensed milk and ate wholewheat biscuits, his favourites being Huntley & Palmers unsweetened College Brown.[15]

Biscuits were not just practical supplies for explorers and other, less adventurous travellers. Throughout the Empire they allowed colonial administrators to keep up standards in difficult circumstances. In 1842 the political agent Thomas Postans claimed – rather disingenuously given that the remark was made in a handbook of advice to military cadets – that 'we govern millions in India by means of a high moral estimation of us as a nation by the natives of the country'.[16] The logic of the argument that the British held India by virtue of integrity rather than force was that every British official needed to be seen to embody British moral superiority. He was expected to do so by maintaining standards of dress, deportment and cleanliness at all times. One handbook for the colonial administrator advised that in his dining room he should replicate the rituals of 'the best regulated establishments of England'.[17] To the despair of viceroy Lord Elgin's daughter, this included serving 'even when the heat had increased to a trying degree … roast beef and boiled puddings like on a day temperature 0° at home'.[18]

This insistence that the food they consumed should be British extended to the cakes and sweetmeats that a memsahib might serve for afternoon tea. Books such as Flora Annie Steel's *The Complete Indian Housekeeper and Cook* included recipes for traditional British bakery goods such as seed cake and almond wafers, jumbles and orange biscuits.[19] Indian cooks and bakers were quick to learn new skills. Just as Goan and Pondicherry bakers began to make Portuguese curd tarts and French croissants, an array of English cakes and biscuits were soon on display in bakeries in the British presidency towns of Calcutta, Madras and Bombay. But out in the mofussil, where the kitchen was often a small room equipped with a charcoal brazier, baking was not a common activity in British Indian households. A plate of Huntley & Palmers ginger nuts allowed British women to preserve standards by observing the ritual of teatime without the stress of struggling to upgrade the kitchen. Thus the biscuit tin in the bungalow store cupboard was part of the paraphernalia of British officialdom. Huntley & Palmers biscuits, Crosse & Blackwell pickles and jams, Staffordshire china, crystal glassware, well-pressed safari suits and solar topis were all props that allowed the colonial administrator to act the part of an upright Englishman, a conscientious agent of civilisation.[20]

All over the Empire there were specialist shops like Spinney's, located at the top of Ledra Street in Cyprus's capital Nicosia. Run by a Palestinian entrepreneur, it stocked the imported foods colonials craved: 'English hams, Huntley and Palmers biscuits, Camp coffee, potted meats, Gorgonzola cheese ... Customers were given a chair, "a glass of lemonade or a chocolate according to the temperature", and their attention drawn to "a newly opened barrel of caviar".'[21] No matter where these expensive imported products came from – whether they were sardines caught by Breton fishermen or soup made with turtles from the Caribbean – they carried a symbolic value as the foods of 'home'.[22] While in Britain Huntley & Palmers biscuits were associated with bourgeois gentility, in the colonial context they gained added resonance as the food of the racially superior.

Thus the biscuit was introduced to the rest of the world as a quintessentially British foodstuff. In 1875, Huntley & Palmers proudly claimed that 'every civilized race under the sun' had encountered their biscuits.[23] Just as the desire for Dutch bakery goods had drawn the Iroquois into the Dutch trading economy in the seventeenth century, in the 1770s the botanist Henry Smeathman listed biscuits as one of the European goods for which west African chiefs were willing to exchange slaves. He described how they would sell 20 or 30 slaves in order to lay in supplies of salt beef, pork, hams, butter, flour, biscuits, sugar and spices and 'affect ... to live in the European manner' for several weeks before their supplies ran out and they were obliged to return to living on rice and cassava.[24] When industrial biscuits were introduced into the Empire, the effect was similar; like King Mwanga, after tasting them, many resolved in future to make Huntley & Palmers their bakers. In the 1880s, medical officer Austine Waddell observed that Huntley & Palmers

Huntley & Palmers liked to boast that their biscuits were sold all over the world. Ranged on the back shelves of this confectionery shop in Wanganui, New Zealand, are tins of Huntley & Palmers Carmencita, Café Noir, Dessert and Breakfast Biscuits.

biscuits were for sale in the Darjeeling bazaar alongside Japanese matches, Manchester silks, cotton and broadcloths, soap and tobacco.[25]

In 1835 Thomas Macaulay argued in his *Minute on Indian Education* that educating Indians in English would foster the growth of a class of Indians with English tastes, opinions and morals. Similarly, other colonialists argued that by fostering a desire for European goods among indigenous peoples, not only would they adopt the white man's habits such as drinking tea and eating biscuits, but also his values. Thus, in the colonial context biscuits were politically charged as tools of imperialism.

By the early twentieth century a substantial class of westernised Indians existed who spoke excellent English, wore European suits and shoes and furnished their homes with the British paraphernalia of gentility: mirrors, chairs and tables, clocks, Venetian blinds and pictures. This was not a matter of mere mimicry.[26] The well-educated westernised Indian elite, versed in British rhetoric, dressed as well as any sahib, living in homes indistinguishable from those the British inhabited, blurred the distinction between coloniser and colonised. The very existence of the westernised Indians questioned the British assertion that their right to rule rested on their moral and cultural superiority.[27]

In order to demonstrate that they were conversant with British cuisine and culinary etiquette the Indian elite often employed European chefs and served Italian and French alongside Indian dishes. However, the spread of British eating habits among the westernised middle classes was fraught with difficulty. Just as genteel English men and women scrutinised one another's every move, assessing their host's social status according to the quality of their rout cakes, so India's elites judged and ranked each other according to the extent to which they observed caste rules and restrictions. In England, respectability was the benchmark against which every action was measured; in India, it was purity. The Brahmins laid claim to their position at the pinnacle of the social hierarchy by leading lives that distanced them from the polluting life cycle of birth, death and manual labour; a powerful demonstration of their superiority was their refusal to accept food or drink from anyone belonging to a lower caste. Indeed, individuals wishing to improve their social standing might exaggerate their purity by adopting strict vegetarianism or taking excessive care in accepting food or drink from others.

Adopting the manners of the British ruling classes was another means to make a bid for social status, but many drew the line at eating British food. The meat-eating habits of the British were considered polluting, and quite apart from the damage it would do to their reputations, many Indians felt positively squeamish at the thought of eating sausages in batter or suet pudding. However,

Huntley & Palmers biscuits, and tea – foodstuffs that appeared to have an almost magical significance as symbols of Britishness – were accepted. As a 'foreign' food-stuff, tea was outside Ayurvedic classification; it was therefore possible to choose to regard it as a neutral substance. Even after the 1860s, by which time the East India Company had established tea plantations in India, tea drinking was not widespread among the general population. However, westernised Indians began to pick up the habit. In 1891 Gandhi noticed that 'so-called educated Indians, chiefly due to British rule' now drank tea or coffee for breakfast.[28] Like tea, industrially manufactured biscuits appeared to exist outside the rules and rituals of purity. The idea that industrial biscuits were made in hygienic conditions untouched by human hands appealed not only to nineteenth-century Britons, but also to purity-conscious Indians. Even if they did not adopt British eating habits, Indian middle-class homes began adding a packet of Lipton's tea and a tin of Huntley & Palmers biscuits to their store cupboards.[29]

Prakash Tandon observed how this process occurred in his own home in Pun-jab in the 1920s. When he was young, his mother was so strict in her orthodoxy that she did not allow the meat and fish that the rest of the family ate to enter the kitchen where her vegetarian food was prepared. When she visited a Muslim household they would fetch her a glass of water from a neighbouring Hindu fam-ily.[30] She objected to her husband's Muslim colleagues eating from the family's metal plates and cups. But with the advent of English chinaware, her attitude changed. In her mind their 'gleaming white smooth surface, from which grease slipped so easily, somehow immunised them from contamination'. At first she reserved the china for her husband's Muslim guests, but so beguiling were the shiny plates that she weakened to the point where she began using the china for the family's meals, and eventually for herself. 'This led to the next stage, that of accepting unpeeled fruit in non-Hindu homes. Then followed the acceptance of tea and manufactured biscuits and the English bottled lime cordial.'[31]

To most Indians, tea drinking was an expensive elite habit, but in 1900 the Tea Association woke up to the fact that their plantations were surrounded by a sea of potential customers and set about converting India's population into consumers. Their most successful strategy was to set up tea stalls at offices, factories and railway stations, and tea shops in large towns and the port cities. The Indian labouring classes appreciated the energy-giving value of sweet tea as much as the industrial working classes of Britain. In fact, tea became so popular that street hawkers and tea stalls soon began to be set up without the Association's encouragement.[32] In the 1890s, when the young Mannathu Padmanabhan travelled through Kerala's interior to his first teaching post, he saw only an occasional roadside stall offering bread, bananas and coffee. Fifty years later, Padmanabhan complained that small dirty tea shops could be found in even the remotest corners of the state, where villagers wasted a considerable portion of their earnings on tea and coffee.[33] By now Indians had made the beverage their own, boiling the leaves together with sugar and milk and adding cardamom and cinnamon to create sweet, thick, smoky *chai*.

Tea shops facilitated inter-caste mixing as well as raising political consciousness. Their spread coincided with the flowering of Indian nationalism, and most of these places stocked a range of newspapers. Here, men who would have felt uncomfortable about visiting each other's homes, let alone sharing meals, read the papers, discussed politics and drank tea together in comfortable communal anonymity.[34] They would not have been able to afford imported English biscuits, but by the 1890s, India had its own biscuit factories in Delhi and Calcutta, which supplied cheap biscuits to the tea shops. Surprisingly perhaps, even Indian-made biscuits appear to have elided purity and pollution concerns. In Bibhutibhushan Bandyopadhyay's novel *Adarsha Hindu Hotel*, the main character stays in a Calcutta hostel where the men are forbidden to bring in any foods that might offend Hindu sensibilities but are allowed to bring in manufactured bread and biscuits.[35] That they were machine made shrouded them in an aura of purity.

Cleverly, the Calcutta factory of Gupta and Company marketed its product as 'Hindu biscuits' and its Delhi branch called itself the Hindu Biscuit Company.[36] In 1905, the nationalist Bal Gangadhar Tilak had called on Indians to boycott British-made goods in response to the colonial government's plan to partition Bengal. The Sri Lankan campaigner for independence, Anagarika Dharmapala, complained that 'we purchase Pears soap, and eat coconut biscuits manufactured by Huntley and Palmer, and … drink the putrefied liquid known as tinned milk … while our cows are dying for want of fodder … Our own weavers are starving and we are purchasing cloth manufactured elsewhere.'[37] 'Hindu biscuits' made by a Hindu company, therefore, appealed to patriotic Indians looking to support indigenous industries. Still, even though the biscuits were Indian-made, some Indian nationalists railed against the dissemination of the English tea-and-biscuit habit. Swami Vivekananda blamed the new urban diet of tea and biscuits for the 'emasculation of the Bengali youth'. While the middle-class commentator Hemantabala Debi declared, 'I do not like this tea-drinking life. Why do we need to imitate another culture, sacrificing Indian culture altogether?'[38]

In 1949, all imports of foreign biscuits into India were banned as part of Jawaharlal Nehru's post-Independence policy of import substitution. Nevertheless, the biscuit-eating culture was firmly entrenched in India as it was throughout Britain's remaining colonies. Abdul Paliwala recalled that in the small town on Zanzibar where he grew up in the 1950s, the different varieties of biscuits it was possible to buy reflected the history of the island as a trading place where African, Arab, Persian, Indian and European cultures had converged. The Persian bakers sold soft Iranian biscuits; the Greeks made hard rusks, often containing fennel seeds, that were referred to as 'toast'; and the Indian sweet-makers offered cardamom-, vanilla- and saffron-flavoured shortbread. His family's grocery store sold African-made biscuits imported from the factory Madatally Manji had set up in Nairobi after the Second World War with up-to-date biscuit-making machinery from Baker Perkins in England.[39] But the superior biscuits – served only on special occasions such as weddings and parties – were of course Huntley & Palmers, the 'white man's biscuits'.[40] Even the most ardent anti-imperialist could not resist indulging in a British biscuit. When he was in exile in Guinea in the late 1960s, Kwame Nkrumah, the independence campaigner and former president of Ghana, habitually ate a Cadbury's chocolate biscuit with his evening cup of powdered skimmed milk.[41]

BISCUIT TINS

In 1867, to celebrate their appointment as Purveyors to the Queen, Huntley and Palmer commissioned one of their best designers, Owen Jones, to create a tin that was so attractive, customers would want to keep it long after the biscuits had been finished. Until then biscuit tins had been decorated with paper labels, but Jones now approached the printer Ben George, who had just developed a process for transferring decorative patterns onto metal surfaces. George printed Jones's design onto metal sheets and sent them on to Huntley & Boorne, the company that had grown out of Joseph Huntley's ironmonger's shop across the street from the original bakery. Here women and girls soldered the pieces together to create a long rectangular tin decorated with the lion-and-unicorn coat of arms surrounded by a floral design. 'Huntley & Palmers Reading Biscuit Factory' was printed on the side. A few years later, Carr's and Peak Frean followed suit and ordered their own decorated tins from Huntley & Boorne. Then, in 1877, the company acquired the rights to the Barclay offset lithographic process, which made it possible to print coloured designs directly onto tin, even when surfaces were curved. This technological advance now unleashed the creativity of the designers.[1]

Early tins were decorated with pictures of flowers and colourful geometric patterns; later tins featured hunting scenes, winter landscapes or turbaned figures with elephants or camels to evoke 'the Orient'. When in 1885 Gilbert and Sullivan's *Mikado* sparked a Japanese craze, the biscuit firms immediately issued tins decorated in 'Japanese' designs. From 1900, the popular art deco style led to the creation of some of the most attractive. The upper classes, who still bought their biscuits in paper-labelled tins, looked down on these garish creations. When Lewis Carroll was approached by Barringer, Wallis & Manners for permission to print the illustrations from *Through the Looking Glass* onto a set of biscuit tins, his initial response was dismissive: 'The biscuit boxes I buy are covered with paper, which of course might be decorated with pictures, but I think it would be degrading to Art to do so.'[2] However he eventually relented. Biscuit tins were so attractive that they were often kept on the mantelpiece as decorative objects, thereby serving as discreet forms of product promotion.

The appearance of these decorated containers coincided with the Victorian revival of Christmas, and it quickly became part of the tradition to give tins of biscuits as presents.[3] Tin and biscuit manufacturers would take on hundreds of extra workers for the two or three months before Christmas in order to meet the spike in demand, and every year they would produce special novelty Christmas tins. Around the turn of the century they began fashioning them into various objects: delivery vans – of course painted with the particular biscuit firm's logo – buses, houseboats, garden rollers, handbags, globes, rows of books, suitcases and postboxes. These made suitable presents for children, who could convert them into toys once the biscuits inside had been eaten.[4] The variety of shapes and elaborate decoration characteristic of biscuit tins explains Amanda's question in Noël Coward's *Private Lives*, when she asks Elyot whether the Taj Mahal looked like a biscuit tin.[5] It was only with the outbreak of the Second World War that these decorative tins fell out of fashion, as tin manufacturers turned to making containers for rations, medical supplies and ammunition. By 1945, the fanciful Christmas biscuit tin had become a thing of the past.[6]

Biscuit manufacturers delivered their varieties to wholesalers, grocers and export dealers in large square tins. These tins too were put to good use after they had served their original purpose. The *Reading Standard* claimed that Himalayan shepherds would trade a week's supply of sheep's milk for a Huntley & Palmers biscuit tin.[7] In the 1860s, Lord Redesdale met a grubby Mongolian chieftainess who was as proud of her Huntley & Palmers tin 'as a duchess of her strawberry leaves'. She used the tin – which Redesdale claimed was the only 'visible sign of her high position' – as a portable garden, in which 'she was growing a few heads of garlic wherewith to flavour the mess of mutton and millet, with chunks of brick tea and salt, which was stewing in her gypsy kettle'.[8] The Reverend John Lloyd, a missionary in Nigeria in the early 1900s, also used biscuit tins as miniature gardens. He nurtured his own flower seedlings in them because if he planted the tender shoots out too soon they would be devoured by ants.[9]

In Uganda, bibles and prayer books were purposely sized so that they fitted into Huntley & Palmers 2 lb biscuit tins, which protected them from the depredations of white ants, which could chomp their way through wood and paper at an alarming rate.[10] On a visit to his son's tea plantations in Ceylon in 1898, Lord Redesdale came across a 'small Roman Catholic chapel...no more than a tiny plaster hut...with an altar, and on the altar two candlesticks, on either side of the Figure on the Cross, to which some humble pious soul had added as ornaments his two most precious treasures: two empty Huntley & Palmer biscuit-tins. It was a most touching offering.'[11]

Biscuit tins provided useful material for African craftsmen. In the Sudan, after the Battle of Omdurman in 1898, a sword was recovered from the battlefield with a scabbard bound with bands of metal cut from the base of a biscuit tin, artfully arranged so that the name 'Huntley & Palmers' was predominantly displayed.[12] Huntley & Palmers' art deco tins of the 1930s were the inspiration for a Nubian decorator who adorned the facades of houses in the Wadi Halfa region of northern Sudan with mud-pargeting reliefs patterned in concentric circles, chevrons, zigzags, vines and flowers that he copied from the tins.[13] Biscuit tins were turned into musical instruments, such as an African thumb piano where the sound box was made with a small tin of Huntley & Palmers' 'Superior Biscuits'.[14] In Trinidad, some of the first steel pans were dustbin lids, gasoline drums and biscuit tins.[15]

Perhaps the most common use for a biscuit tin was as a money box. When in the early 1900s Anselm Guise, a young mining engineer in Bolivia, left La Paz after a fortnight's leave to return to the construction camp at Maquiqui, he carried with him the wages for the men. He had packed £1,000 in Bolivian notes into a Huntley & Palmers biscuit tin and soldered on the lid so that the tin would float in case of a mishap. He then had it sewn into a hessian bag, 'a method usually adopted in the case of packages consigned to the interior, to prevent theft of the contents'. Setting out, he entrusted the tin to his Indian servant José, who, 'quite unaware of its value, slung it, together with his own goods and chattels, in his carrying-shawl, across his shoulders'. Their journey to the camp was diverted over a 'rob-ber-infested' mountain pass. As José snored through the night with the biscuit tin beside his head, Guise reflected that nothing would have induced his servant to sleep on the mountain if he had been aware of how much money he was carrying. When they reached the bridge over the Coroico river, they discovered that it was in need of extensive repair. Guise was faced with the problem of what to do with the biscuit tin. He decided that the 'safest method was to leave it about as though it were of no particular value. For a fortnight it lay, unguarded, on the top of a pile of cases of foodstuffs des-tined for Maquiqui.' At last the bridge was repaired and, Guise recalled, 'followed by José bearing the biscuit tin – which was now to me what the albatross had been to the Ancient Mariner – I rode into Coroico, there to pay off the men'.[16]

Then there are the more unusual uses for biscuit tins. In January 1896, on board HMS *Blonde*, Prince Henry of Battenberg, Queen Victoria's son-in-law, died of malaria, which he had contracted during an expedition against the Ashanti in west Africa. As the ship had just left Sierra Leone, its captain was faced with the problem of how to preserve the body in the equatorial heat, as he was expected to take it back to Britain for a proper burial. He solved the problem by constructing a makeshift coffin out of biscuit tins and filling it with rum.[17] On a similarly macabre note, Thomas Hardy's heart is supposed to have been temporarily stored in a biscuit tin by the surgeon who excised it from his body. There was some confusion over where to bury Hardy when the writer died in 1928. His will stipulated that he wished to be interred alongside his first wife Emma in a country graveyard, but some insisted that as a great man of literature he should be buried in Westminster Abbey. A compromise was hastily reached: his body would be cremated and the ashes buried in Westminster Abbey but his heart was to be interred with Emma at Stinsford in Dorset. But when the surgeon came to perform the ghoulish act of cutting out the heart, he had failed to bring a suitable receptacle with him and a biscuit tin was fetched from the kitchen.[18]

Armies were, of course, well supplied with biscuit tins and soldiers found myriad uses for them. One of the most common was as a building material. In 1846, the French provision dump at Aumale in Algeria was known as 'Biscuitville' because most of the huts in the temporary encampment were constructed out of old biscuit tins filled with sand.[19] Even the corral at the centre of the camp, where prisoners were held, was made out of biscuit tins and sacks of barley.[20] At Rorke's Drift in October 1879, the small garrison defending the hospital and supply depot from an attack by Zulu warriors built a hasty barricade using 'mealy bags & biscuit boxes'.[21]

The soldiers of the First World War used biscuit tins to assemble stoves to warm their tents. They would place the tin on a base of clay on the wooden floor and rig up a stove pipe made of tin and lagged with clay that stuck out of the tent to make a chimney. Often the tent would scorch a little, but

These British soldiers on the Gallipoli Peninsula in 1915 have built themselves a shelter using Huntley & Palmers biscuit boxes.

the men did not mind as there was no shortage of rainwater to put out fires and they were able to cook up some comforting porridge oats.[22] Sergeant William Allen Rigden wrote home with a description of his first meal in a new position in Belgium, in which a biscuit tin made a handy seat in the muddy trench: 'Imagine me then, in an overcoat splashed with mud from collar to hem; boots thickly covered with mud; puttees invisible under it, sitting on an upturned biscuit tin with a large hot potato in one hand and a big greasy hunk of hot, fat mutton in the other, biting alternatively at each, occasionally putting one or the other down on a none-too-clean sandbag in order to have a drink of some mahogany coloured stuff the cook called tea.'[23] Biscuit tins became washbasins, and in the front line they even served as latrines. Once it was dark, the poor 'shit wallahs' had to carry them back from the front to be emptied.[24]

During the Second World War, military transport lorries resembled tinkers' carts with their array of pots, pans and biscuit tins hanging from the back and sides. As in the earlier war, soldiers used biscuit tins as makeshift stoves. 'The best way to make a cup of tea was to put some sandy soil in one biscuit tin and pour in liberal quantities of petrol. Fill another biscuit tin with water, place this on top and put a lighted match to the petrol. These field stoves didn't take long to boil up sufficient water for a "tea powder" mashing.'[25] In North Africa, R. L. Crimp described how once the water was set to boil over a biscuit-tin stove, British soldiers would line up their mugs on the ground. 'Spoonfuls of tinned milk and sugar [are] put in each...then they're filled with tea, straight out of the brew can. The Result is "Desert-Char"...as long as there's no lack of char or fags everyone's happy. When there's a shortage of either, morale slumps.'[26]

The inhabitants of the German-occupied Channel Islands, who suffered from shortages of gas to power their conventional cookers, converted biscuit tins into ovens by placing them on a fire. A one-pot meal could be cooked inside the tin while the lid could be used like the hob of a stove. But the islanders also used biscuit tins as hiding places for home-made crystal radio sets.[27] Indeed, the British Special Operations Executive, set up to infiltrate occupied Europe, developed the 'biscuit tin receiver', a miniature radio receiver packed into an unmarked biscuit tin along with a power supply and coil pack. These were dropped by parachute over France to be used by the Resistance.[28] While Allied soldiers regarded the hardtack biscuits originally contained in the tins with contempt, Japanese troops relished them. Often Japanese commanders would issue their men with only nine days' worth of food, even when they were about to embark on a campaign that would last for weeks. The soldiers were encouraged to capture enemy food supplies, or 'Churchill's rations', as they called them.[29] Used to a meagre diet of rice and miso soup, Tsuchikane Tominosuke, who took part in the Japanese campaign to capture Singapore, recalled how he savoured the tins of cheese and biscuits left behind by the fleeing British troops. He kept a biscuit tin that he picked up during this time all through the subsequent years of his captivity by the Allies, and eventually took it back to Japan with him as a precious souvenir of his wartime experiences.[30]

11

In which May Hanaphy gives every penny of the 11s. 6d she earned at Jacob's to her mother

In 1922 May Hanaphy went to work as one of 'Jacob's mice' at the Dublin biscuit factory. She was 14 and straight out of school.[1] 'You wrote an application saying you would be grateful to be given a trial,' she recalled later at the age of 90. At the interview, the lady supervisor ran a pencil through her hair to check that it was clean of nits. 'Oh, you were [treated] just like little animals,' May remembered. 'They wouldn't touch you.' The supervisor checked her nails and feet and she was made to walk across the room; a doctor examined her chest, ears and eyes; and a dentist inspected her teeth. If the dentist deemed that you needed a tooth out, you had to have it pulled before you could start work.

Jacob's were strict about timekeeping. The first factory whistle sounded at 7.50 a.m.. Harry Brierton, who joined Jacob's straight out of school in 1931, described how the workers would gather outside the gates. 'At ten to eight you'd be standing outside having a smoke and at three minutes to eight you'd start rambling in.'[2] At 8 a.m. the second whistle sounded and the gates were closed. As they filed in, the men would hang their 'checks' on a hook with the corresponding number. The checks were small brass discs about the size of a ten-penny piece on which each worker's personal number was engraved. The timekeeper would follow behind, and anyone whose check was not hanging on their hook was marked as absent and docked a day's wages. May and the rest of the girls would place their checks in a large bowl on the supervisor's desk. Mrs Gill 'was very bossy and very tall and you were afraid of your life of her'. She had a big clock in her office and kept saying that she would 'tolerate bad workers, slow workers, dirty workers, but we will *not* tolerate bad timekeepers'. If you were consistently late, you were 'gone'. Mrs Gill would not hand you your check at the end of the day and that would be that.

The first thing the girls did on getting into work was to tuck their plaits into hairnets and put on their blue linen overalls. These were pocketless, to prevent the workers from squirrelling away the odd biscuit. Harry and the other boys changed into khaki smocks and trousers held up by a red canvas belt. The men in the bakehouse wore slippers to protect their feet from the heat of the steel floors. The supervisors did not like them to open the windows, as birds would fly in and peck at the dough. The men must often have disobeyed, for as May remembered, the bakehouse was 'like an aviary' with the birds 'singing all day up in the roofs. *Always* birds in the bake house.' On occasion bakers would collapse from heat exhaustion, and until he got used to it, Harry recalled, he 'faded away and got very thin from the heat'.

When May started at Jacob's, the 1,300 workers included 'only a sprinkle of men'. Men and boys were employed in the carpentry shops, the mixing house and the bakehouse. The men operated the deafeningly noisy mixing machines and supervised the ovens. The boys did the lighter jobs, greasing the steel pans and rolling out the dough for more fragile biscuits such as shortbread. Once they reached the age of 16, reliable boys were put to work on the cutting machines. The dough ran in a big strip under the cutting presses. 'The machines used to work very fast,' Harry remembered. 'You'd have to be very alert.'

When Huntley & Palmers opened their first factory in 1846, most of their 41 employees were boys between the ages of 14 and 19.[3] They were paid the low wages of an apprentice rather than a qualified baker's 18 shillings a week. As female labour was even cheaper, from the 1850s the company began to take on women and girls. The Factory Acts, brought in to protect women and children from early industrial exploitation, had the unfortunate effect of relegating them to the role of secondary, unskilled workers.[4] Often they received less than half the men's wages. Most were young girls working for a few years after leaving school and before getting married. Between 1898 and 1911, Huntley & Palmers saved on its wage bill by quadrupling the number of women it employed from 8 to 23 per cent of its total workforce.[5] At Jacob's in the 1930s, Harry thought that for every man there were probably three women.

As the biscuits came out of the oven they fell onto a conveyor belt, which moved them into the women's part of the factory. Here they were iced and decorated, wrapped in greased-paper packages and loaded into tins. Harry thought the girls 'had the hardest jobs in the factory'. There were opportunities in the bakehouse for the boys to lark about and engage in impromptu pranks.[6] There was no room for such tomfoolery in the decorating and packing departments. Finished biscuits were fragile and needed to be handled with care; if they crumbled or the icing or sugar fell off, they were spoiled. At most biscuit factories a control ticket was placed in every tin, which meant that if it was sent back by an unsatisfied customer, it could be traced back to the packager.[7] The forewoman ran a tight ship: laughter, nudging or even animated chatter was counted as 'silly' behaviour and admonished. May recalled that 'you watched yourself and wouldn't incur their wrath'. The forewoman could sack a girl at a moment's notice.

The work of packing biscuits was relentless. The taller girls took the biscuits off the conveyor belt, stacked them along the length of their inner arm until the pile reached the elbow, then lifted their arm and deftly slid the stack of biscuits into the tin. Harry was full of admiration. 'You'd want to see their fingers going! ... Ah, it took some doing and they were going all day.' May was put on wrapping packets of six Cream Crackers for the England and Dominions export

The packing room at the Olibet Biscuit Factory in Talence, France.

trade. 'You wrapped very slow because you had to be very careful with your folds in ... If you wrapped fifty for the morning that was very good and that was marked down on your sheet. Some people were on piece-work and some on standard wage.' The girls had to examine each biscuit and put aside those that were broken, burned, speckled or under-baked. In the icing and decorating rooms they stood over trays of biscuits, squeezing and releasing a muslin funnel full of icing. It was important to stop squeezing at just the right moment, as otherwise threads of icing were carried over from one biscuit to another and the entire batch was considered ruined.[8] After a long day standing on the hard steel floors gazing continuously at the biscuits moving down the conveyor belt, the girls' legs ached and their heads swam.[9]

'Everyone *dreaded* the wash house,' May recalled. Here girls clad in heavy-duty rubber aprons and gloves washed out the tins that came back from the shops. Harry, who used to collect the empties from the shops, told how many of them would come back in a 'disgraceful' state, full of grease and filth. And the poor girls had 'to have them spotless to be used again'. May was adamant that 'if I was ever sent up there I would have left'. Another unenviable position was in the tin room, where the biscuit tins were assembled. 'The noise was *absolutely* cruel,' May remembered, 'and the women all had cut hands.' One of May's friends worked on a machine to straighten out crooked lids. One day she lost concentration, and when she put her hand in to fit the lid into place she forgot that she had her foot on the lever and the spikes came down. 'They couldn't save her hand. God love her, it had to be amputated from the wrist. They fixed her up with a glove and she was given a nice little job going around.'

The tin room was staffed almost entirely by women. In the biscuit factories, women were used for any task, no matter how dangerous or unpleasant, as long as it was unskilled. As baking was a skilled occupation, it was reserved for men, although women could be employed to perform menial tasks in the bakehouses: in the early 1900s, 287 of the 2,085 women at Jacob's were working alongside the men in the bakery.[10] The skilled men earned 28s. 7d, the less skilled 12s. 12d, but the women earned as little as 8s. 2d.

When she first began work at Jacob's, May gave 'every penny' of the 11s. 6d she earned to her mother. '*Every* penny. I was delighted to give it to her. And she'd give you back sixpence or a shilling.' As a young girl she did not need money and was proud to make a significant contribution to her family's income. Jacob's girls who got pregnant were immediately sacked. 'Quite often the parents did not want them to get married as they wanted their wage,' May remembered, so they would hide their pregnancy for as long as possible. Some managed for as much as six or seven months. When a girl got married, 'Jacob's gave you a cake and £3 ... and you had to leave … Actually, you were delighted to get married and get out. You took a load off your back.'

To keep down the wages bill, Jacob's sacked the boys in the bakehouses as soon as they reached the age of 19. 'See, they were coming to men's wages,' Harry explained. Carr's of Carlisle did the same thing. In 1896, four apprentices at Carr's attempted to challenge this practice. They handed the much-feared and aptly named foreman Mr Tremble a note saying that they would strike if those apprentices who had just been 'let go' were not reinstated. The boys complained that an apprenticeship was worth little if it did not hold out the promise of future employment. In the days of J.D. Carr, good workers could be fairly sure of a job for life. JD's son Henry, in charge of the Carlisle factory since his father's death in 1884, was conscientious about maintaining the good working conditions JD had established but felt none of his father's personal responsibility towards his workers. He took the four apprentices to court for breach of their employment contract. Although their punishment was lenient – Henry magnanimously accepted a shilling from each of them in recompense – his action damaged the firm's reputation for fairness.[11]

In the early twentieth century, Jacob's biscuit factory became a focus of the labour left's campaign against social injustice. The *Irish Worker*, the mouthpiece of the Irish Transport and General Workers' Union, railed against the hollowness of the paternalist contract and mocked the Jacobs' portrayal of themselves as good Quaker employers. George Jacob took pride in his firm's welfare arrangements. A doctor and dentist were in attendance at the factory and a convalescent home reserved a certain number of beds for employees. Workers were provided with a canteen on the fifth floor, which had a veranda where May used to love spending a few minutes in the sun. Harry recalled that there was a football ground, a recreation hall where the boys and men could play billiards, and a temperance club that organised excursions in summer. But the *Irish Worker* held up these welfare arrangements as a cynical attempt to distract the workers from the exploitation inherent in the factory system. The employers might well provide canteens and sports clubs but they still did not pay a living wage, while they themselves grew rich on the back of their employees' hard work.

The paper ridiculed George Jacob's claims that he ran the biscuit factory not for profit but in order to provide work for the poor.[12] In an article in June 1911, Delia Larkin, founder of the Irish Women's Workers Union, denounced Jacob's as 'out to make a profit, and make it they will, even though it be at the cost of ill-health and disablement to the girls, women, and men of Dublin'. While the average male biscuit factory worker earned about £50 a year and women about £25, Larkin wrote, a biscuit manufacturer's annual income was in the region of £50,000. She was outraged that female workers who had no money to spare had been pressurised into making a financial contribution to a wedding present for George's daughter. Then there was the draconian discipline at Jacob's. If a worker was caught eating a biscuit, they were dismissed. Any worker who was late was locked out and not only lost a day's pay but was also fined; and if they were late on more than three occasions in one month, they were dismissed.

George Jacob attracted the particular ire of the *Irish Worker* as he was vehemently opposed to the unionisation of his workers. Girls who refused to take off the union's Red Hand badge were dismissed, and Jacob refused to discuss wage rates with the union representatives. When the First World War broke out, the antagonism reached new heights. Jacob was seen to be colluding with the British army's recruitment drive. The *Workers' Republic* accused Dublin's capitalists of dismissing radical elements in their workforce in the hope that they would then be forced to enlist. Jacob's was said to be refusing to hire men unless they could show their army rejection papers to prove they had been willing to volunteer but found unfit to serve. An enraged James Connolly wrote in the *Irish Worker* that Jacob's had used 'their power over the means of livelihood of their employees to coerce them out of the trade union of their choice on the pain of starvation' and were now using that same power 'to coerce them into an army that stood ready to shoot them down in 1913–14', when Dublin had been gripped by a wave of strikes.[13]

Given that Connolly equated the firm's exploitation of its workforce with Britain's exploitation of Ireland, it is not surprising that the leaders of the Irish Republican Army chose Jacob's biscuit factory as one of the buildings they occupied during the Easter Rising in 1916.[14] A contingent of about 150 IRA volunteers spent six days in the factory waiting for an attack that never came. The young Vincent Byrne was given the job of throwing empty biscuit tins out of a window so that the sound of British soldiers stumbling over them would alert the men inside to a night-time attack. When he had finished, he gorged on a sack of biscuits and chocolates. At night the men crouched behind a barricade of flour sacks, with their rifles pointing towards the factory gates; by day they watched with foreboding from the factory tower as the fighting raged across the city. When the IRA were forced to surrender and the biscuit factory contingent prepared to face the British retribution, the older men helped Vincent and other younger volunteers escape by hoisting them out of the windows at the back of the factory. When she saw them fleeing through the Dublin streets, a kindly woman took them into her house to dust off the flour in which they were coated so that they could blend into the crowd.[15]

When May joined Jacob's, six years after the Easter Rising, the disciplinary regime had not changed. 'You couldn't walk around the place or leave your bench. Very strict, very disciplined rules ... Each foreman had a whistle, like a policeman.' Harry heard that in the past men had been sacked if they were caught making tea; but in the interwar years they were allowed ten minutes in the morning and evening for a break. 'If you were seen taking biscuits out you were sacked,' May remembered. 'There was a saying, "Eat all, pocket none, if you do, you'll get the run" ... We'd take a few biscuits and put them in our pockets and we'd eat them. You wouldn't go *out* with them, because there was often searches on.' By now the workers were allowed to buy rejected biscuits that were burned or underdone, broken or speckled. 'You bought them at the end of the week for two pence a bag,' May recalled. A bag of broken chocolate biscuits cost four pence. May thought it 'was a good idea because it kept you from stealing anything', but other biscuit factories gave the broken biscuits to their workers for free. Indeed, there was a saying at Huntley & Palmers that the biscuit factory employees were paid 'a pound in cash and a pound in biscuits' (although in fact most received less than a pound for their wages).[16]

Despite the repetitive work, persistent surveillance and harsh discipline, May 'loved the factory, loved my work'. She enjoyed the camaraderie among the girls and claimed that 'it was fun all the time. Oh, the girls would sing at their work ... The old songs. All the songs of that period, the grand old songs. We knew *every* song that was going.' Harry remembered that 'the girls would be as happy as Larry, all singing when they'd be working, whatever the latest songs would be. They'd all be singing together. Breaks the monotony.'

The old-school paternalism of early biscuit manufacturer J. D. Carr, who knew the names of all his employees and would don a white apron and work alongside them, had long since vanished when May and Harry joined Jacob's. To May, George and Charles Jacob were remote figures who looked down on the workers. 'We were always the peasants.' In Ireland there was the added sting of the religious divide. 'The managers and manageresses were Protestant but the workers was mostly all Catholic ... we got no key jobs. There was no promotion for you.' The Jacobs were 'tight where wages was concerned', Harry recalled: 'You were there to make them rich, that's all. Anyone that got employment there had to earn what he got.' After 49 years' service, Harry received a measly pension of £10.33 a week. 'They never treated the workers fair,' he concluded. 'You never got a fair deal ... You'd think they'd show more appreciation to workers.'

The early biscuit factories needed only a few skilled bakers to supervise the mixing and baking of the biscuits, as well as a handful of engineers to run the machines.

As most of the jobs were unskilled, the overall effect of the factories was to cheapen labour. From the early twentieth century the practice of paying workers piece rates began to dominate and replaced the paying of standard weekly wages. Betty Wallace recalled that in the 1940s and 1950s she and the other girls at Crawford's Biscuits on Elbe Street in Leith 'were on piece work and had to go hard at it to make a decent wage'.[17]

Developments after the Second World War further reduced the cost of labour. In 1954, a hundred years after Henry Mayhew had marvelled that the biscuits made in Peek Frean's Bermondsey factory were 'scarcely touched by human hand', the chairman of McVitie & Price, Hector Laing, introduced innovations in McVitie's Harlesden factory that did away with human hands altogether. He persuaded the company's suppliers to deliver their goods in specially designed lorries that either blew or pumped flour, sugar, fats and syrups down pipes into bulk storage spaces within the factory. From the storage tanks the ingredients were mechanically channelled into the dough mixer.[18] And so it continued, with the biscuit dough passing through new rolling machines, rotary moulders rather than cutters, through the ovens and on into the packaging area without once being handled by workers. These innovations were revolutionary. Automation reduced costs without compromising the quality of the ingredients. Even though McVitie's paid twice as much as many of its competitors for quality ingredients, the savings in time and labour allowed them to make twice the profit. Other biscuit manufacturers soon followed suit. Before long, processes at Peek Frean's Bermondsey factory were also automated. By 1968, the number of workers needed to produce a ton of biscuits had been cut by a third, yet the factory still produced twice as many biscuits as in 1939.[19] By the 1970s, the rows of girls merrily singing music hall songs, their fingers flying as they packed biscuits into boxes, tins and paper packages, had been replaced by noisy machines.

Laing dreamed of creating a factory where 'one day you'll be able to wake up and push a button by your bed and start up the whole factory'.[20] By the turn of the millennium, his vision had been realised as biscuit factories were fully computerised. When Alain de Botton visited a McVitie's factory in Belgium in the first decade of the twenty-first century, his reaction was strikingly reminiscent of Henry Mayhew's impressions at Peek Frean in 1865. He found it peculiar to watch 'modestly sized domestic objects emerge from the jaws of colossal machines housed in hangars large enough for airships…Biscuits which I had until then seen only in packets of nine were here rolling down the conveyor belt at a rate of eleven hundred a minute.' Mayhew had been astonished by the idea that food could be manufactured by machines; de Botton was struck by the sophistication of the technology. The biscuits were sprayed with chocolate and stuck with shards of nuts by 'machinery [that] had been borrowed from applications as disparate as the machine gun, the stapler, the space shuttle's robotic arm and the loom'.[21]

Five thousand people were employed at the biscuit factory and the work of the majority of them had nothing to do with 'anything one might eat'. The division of labour introduced in the early biscuit factories had by now divided and subdivided the manufacturing process into a myriad of specialist tasks. Each came with its own esoteric job title: 'Packaging Technologist, Branding Executive, Learning Centre Manager, Strategic Projects Evaluator'.[22] Employees focused on fine-tuning the ovens; reducing the friction between biscuits placed in a package; designing the lettering on packaging; analysing supermarket sales data; or ensuring that forklift lorries moved boxes in the warehouse with maximum efficiency. The biscuit factory appeared to have realised the 'utopian' vision of the Italian economist Vilfredo Pareto, in which each person in a society would 'forfeit general knowledge in favour of fostering individual ability in narrowly constricted fields'. While each highly specialised individual would be incapable of performing another person's task, they would all work together in a perfectly functioning whole.[23]

Biscuit factory workers no longer suffered from aching backs and legs after standing all day at their jobs; and for the most part they had escaped the tedium of performing the same action repeatedly for hours on end. Computers were now so well integrated that no one was reduced to the deadening role of a mere but-ton pusher. But what had once been an everyday domestic activity, producing a batch of biscuits, now involved a wide range of people, each of whom performed such a narrowly defined task that their focus was as fixed as that of the girls who never lifted their eyes off the conveyor belt as they iced biscuits for an entire shift. And if factory workers were now sufficiently well remunerated to be able to buy a packet of the biscuits they made, as he drove away de Botton wondered whether the modern biscuit-factory employee, with their narrow focus on a specific task, might well experience a form of the alienation felt by the nineteenth-century factory worker who had lost their economic stake in their daily activity; and whether the lack of inherent meaning in their work might cause a person to feel the kind of dissatisfaction that advertisers suggest a chocolate-coated, nut-studded biscuit would alleviate.[24]

FIG ROLL

In 1903 Jacob's brought out the Fig Roll. Bakers had been making fig biscuits since at least the eleventh century when Baghdadi physician Ibn Butlan advised the consumption of 'hot' fig and nut confections when the weather was cold. The Sicilians who bought *biscotti al fico* from the convent of San Carlo at Christmastime were still (albeit unconsciously) following this advice. But until the late nineteenth century the feat of manufacturing a biscuit with a pastry shell and a jam filling had defeated the biscuit industry. Then in 1893 the Philadelphia engineer James Henry Mitchell succeeded in devising a machine which could simultaneously create a hollow tube of cookie dough and fill it with jam. He persuaded the Massachusetts-based Kennedy Biscuit Company to trial it. Although the company did settle on a fig jam filling for the new biscuits, 'fig' was not initially part of their name. It was the Kennedy Biscuit Company's practice to name its products after nearby towns and the new confection was named after the Boston suburb of Newton. But the fig filling was so popular, that they soon became known as Fig Newtons.[25] Jacob's Fig Rolls were a copy of these best-selling American biscuits.

I use an Italian recipe for the filling and a Linzer cookie dough for the pastry shell. If you do not like fig, you can use the dough to make Linzer cookies. Both make festive biscuits for Christmas.

For the dough:
150 g whole blanched almonds
150 g sugar
250 g plain flour
½ tsp ground cinnamon
¼ tsp salt
230 g unsalted butter
2 egg yolks
1 tsp vanilla essence
grated zest of 1 lemon
(if you want to make Linzer cookies you also need raspberry jam and icing sugar)

For the filling:
200 g dried figs (hard tips discarded)
75 g raisins
3–4 tbsp brandy or sherry

1 heaped tsp finely grated orange zest

1 tsp finely grated lemon zest

½ tsp ground cinnamon*

¼ tsp ground cloves*

¼ tsp finely ground nutmeg*

*or 1–2 tsp mixed spice

3–4 tbsp runny honey

100 g finely chopped roasted almonds

100 g finely chopped walnuts

(I put the nuts in a plastic bag and bash them with a rolling pin .)

To make the dough:

Prepare the nuts: Heat the oven to 180°C. Spread the almonds on a baking sheet and bake for 8–10 minutes until lightly browned. Cool completely and grind with 50 g of the sugar.

Mix the ground almonds, flour, spices and salt in a bowl.

Beat the butter until pale, add the remaining sugar and beat until fluffy. Add the egg yolks, vanilla essence and lemon zest.

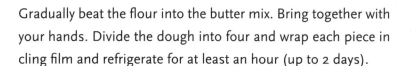

Gradually beat the flour into the butter mix. Bring together with your hands. Divide the dough into four and wrap each piece in cling film and refrigerate for at least an hour (up to 2 days).

To make the filling:

Soak the figs and raisins for 30 minutes in hot water. Chop them and add to a blender with all the filling ingredients except the honey and nuts. Blend until a smooth paste (you may need to add some of the water the figs were soaked in to aid the blending process).

Empty into a bowl and add the nuts and as much of the honey as is needed to create a thick paste (not too runny). Cover and chill for 30 minutes.

Preheat the oven to 180°C and line a baking tray with greaseproof paper.

Roll out the dough between two floured sheets of greaseproof paper. Cut into a rectangle about 10 cm by 20 cm. Place a 2 cm wide line of the fig filling down one side of the rectangle about 2 cm in from the edge. Use the paper to help roll the dough over the filling and place the roll on the greaseproof

paper. The filling will probably be sufficient to make two rolls. Bake for 15–20 minutes. Allow to cool. Carefully remove from the baking tray and roll off the paper onto a wooden board and cut into bite-size pieces.

Alternatively to make Linzer cookies: roll out the dough between two sheets of greaseproof paper and cut out heart-shaped biscuits. Cut a hole in the centre of half the biscuits to make the top biscuits. Place on greaseproof paper on a baking tray and bake for 7–9 minutes.

When cooled sandwich the top and bottom biscuits together with raspberry jam and dust with icing sugar.

12

In which Private G. L. Verney has
fried corned beef and biscuit for
breakfast, cold bully beef and biscuit
for lunch and bully beef and biscuit
stew for supper

'You don't realise how nice bread is till you've lived on biscuits for a while,' Paul
Teesdale Smith of the Australian Light Horse Regiment wrote to his sister from
the Dardanelles in November 1915.[1] Throughout the centuries soldiers have
always preferred fresh bread, or at least porridge, but the circumstances of war
have forced them to make do with biscuit as a substitute.

Roman soldiers were given 2 lb of wheat a day, which they were expected to
grind themselves. For this purpose each squad or *contubernium* of eight men was
issued with a portable hand mill. Made of two stone discs about 30 cm in diameter
and weighing around 47 kg (60 lb), it was one of their most substantial pieces
of equipment.[2] The quickest way to prepare the coarse flour that the hand mill
produced was to boil it in water to make a porridge. This could be enriched with
olive oil and flavoured with onions; Galen commented that soldier's backpacks
reeked of onions.[3] Alternatively, the flour could be made into bread and baked in
the ashes of the campfire.[4] It would probably have taken a couple of hours to first
grind the 16 lb of wheat that made up the men's daily ration and then turn it into
either bread or porridge: after a day's march and the hard work of preparing camp,

the soldiers cannot have relished the wearisome task. An easier alternative was to sell their grain to the bakers who followed in the army's wake and leave them to do the hard work of turning it into flour and baking it into bread. But this did not meet with the approval of their commanders. Most generals banned the sale of bread in camp, and soldiers were warned that they would be punished if they were found eating fancy food bought from sutlers.[5]

In the second century CE, Pescennius Niger expressly forbade bakers from following behind his army.[6] Such measures were intended to reduce the number of hangers-on. An ancient army had a long enough baggage train as it was: a force of 10,000 men needed at least 520 wagons to carry their armour, weapons, missiles, portable fortifications and rudimentary medical supplies as well as food, fuel and animal fodder. In addition, each *contubernium* had a couple of mules onto which they loaded the tent that the eight men shared at night, their arms, equipment, tools, several days' worth of rations and, of course, their hefty hand mill. Roman generals referred to the baggage train as the *impedimenta*. The lumbering carts, often breaking down on the rough roads, not only slowed down the army's advance but made the force vulnerable to attack.

Gaius Marius is often credited with reducing the baggage train even further by doing away with the mules and training his soldiers to carry most of their equipment and provisions on their person. In his biography of Marius, Plutarch tells us that on an expedition to North Africa in the late second century BCE, the general 'laboured to perfect his army as it went along, practising with his men in all kinds of running and in long marches, and compelling them to carry their own baggage, and to prepare their own food. Hence, in after times, men who were fond of toil and did whatever was enjoined upon them completely and without a murmur were called Marian Mules.'[7] The Roman soldier hung his equipment from a cross-shaped carrying pole, which he rested against his shoulder. In his pack he would carry his clothes, mess kit and his share of the *contubernium*'s tools and cooking equipment, which the eight men divided up between them. Along with his sword and shield, this would have weighed between 20 and 30 kilos.

It is unclear how many days' worth of rations the soldiers were expected to carry. The first-century CE historian Josephus tells us that legionaries carried three days' worth of food, but Livy's histories, written in the preceding century, mention soldiers carrying as much as thirty days' worth of provisions.[8] In these circumstances the men would surely have chosen to carry their grain in the form of twice-baked bread: thirty days' worth of biscuit would have been about five kilos lighter than unground wheat.[9] What's more, it meant there was no need for carrying heavy hand mills. Biscuit could be crushed and added to boiling water to make porridge, softened in a cauldron with a mess of vegetables and oil, or simply dipped in the mixture of sour wine and water that was the legionnaire's staple drink.

Biscuit was part of the Roman military arsenal. It was issued to troops when an operation called for speed and flexibility, with the lumbering baggage train left to follow at a slower pace. In some cases biscuit provisions allowed the army to dispense with the baggage train altogether, particularly when they had to move through difficult terrain. During the Nabataean campaign in 26 BCE, Aelius Gallus issued his troops with just biscuit and water so that they could march quickly through the Syrian desert.[10] When the second-century CE general Avidius Cassius ordered his soldiers to carry only essentials, he listed them as *laridum*, *bucellatum* and *acetum* – bacon, biscuit and sour wine. This was the Roman army's basic 'iron ration'. By the end of the fourth century it had become standard to keep supplies of biscuit in readiness in storage magazines at the Empire's borders, so they could be sent to troops when and where they were needed.[11]

After the collapse of the Roman Empire, throughout the medieval and early-modern period biscuit continued to function as the basis of a soldier's iron ration. Jean Froissart's chronicle of the Hundred Years War tells us that during the summer of 1386 'there was a continual milling of flour and baking of biscuits' all along the coast of northern France and Flanders, as Charles VI amassed an enormous army in preparation for an attack on England.[12] The French knew that the English would try to repel the invaders by denying them access to food, but plentiful supplies of biscuit would make them independent of local resources.[13] Froissart admired the advantage that self-sufficiency afforded Scottish horsemen, who were encumbered by neither pots and pans nor by bakeries following in their train. They cooked any beast they caught in its own skin and carried a small bag of oatmeal and a metal plate under the flap of their saddle, which they used to bake themselves oat biscuits. 'It is therefore no wonder,' the chronicler concluded, 'that they perform a longer day's march than other soldiers.'[14]

Medieval military organisation had changed significantly from Roman times. The medieval soldier carried only his arms and personal belongings. For bread he relied on the bakers who straggled along among the great tail of servants, washerwomen, prostitutes, sutlers, carpenters, smiths and fletchers that followed behind an army's baggage train.[15] Medieval and early-modern armies survived on a mixture of provisions they carried or were sent from home along extended supply lines, as well as on requisitioning, plunder and forage in the territory they occupied.[16]

From the sixteenth century, absolute monarchs at the head of efficient state administrations were able to substantially increase their armies. By the beginning of the seventeenth century, the average military force had grown from 10,000 to at least 100,000 men. Neither agricultural productivity nor transport infrastructure had improved apace, so it became increasingly difficult to feed these vast forces. As mercenary armies moved through the central European countryside during the Thirty Years War (1618–48), local populations collapsed under the strain of providing vast numbers of men and animals with food and fodder.[17] In Hans Jakob Christoffel von Grimmelshausen's novel about the war, *The Adventures of Simplicius Simplicissimus*, the rustic hero describes how soldiers plundered farms, destroyed everything that could not be taken away, raped the women and tortured the men to extract from them where they had hidden money and goods.[18] By the end of the war, 30 per cent of Germany's population had perished.

Even before the horrors of the Thirty Years War were visited on the European peasantry, it had become apparent to both the Dutch and French that they needed to organise more efficient supply lines. The responsibilities of the quartermaster were now extended to include not only reconnaissance and surveying, route planning and cartography, but also the logistics of supply and provision.[19] In the late sixteenth century, the Dutch introduced daily rations of bread or biscuit, butter, peas, bacon, cheese and salt cod or beef.[20] At the same time, the Roman institution of storage magazines was revived by French quartermasters, who began setting up stores where biscuit and salt meat could be stockpiled before a campaign.

Sir Thomas Fairfax, the commander-in-chief of Cromwell's New Model Army, and his major general Philip Skippon had both served on the Continent and were thus aware of the new quartermaster system.[21] The needs of the New Model Army in the 1640s were sufficiently large that if they were stationed anywhere for a sufficient length of time, they placed a significant strain on the long-term resources of the local population: in just 9 days they were capable of consuming enough grain to supply a parish of 300 people for a year.[22] Fairfax therefore established a commissariat to organise the army's provisions. This tapped into the sophisticated supply system that was already in place to feed the nation's capital. London's wholesale merchants drew in foodstuffs from a wide area, buying goods in bulk in the provinces and then transporting them into the city, where they were sold on to shopkeepers and pedlars. By buying its supplies on the London market, the commissariat ensured that any strain the New Model Army's demand for foodstuffs placed on English agriculture was diffused throughout the country.[23]

While Continental soldiers were willing to consume their grain as porridge, English soldiers preferred it to be baked into bread or biscuit.[24] By 1645, the army's commissariat had turned the dilapidated royal palace at Greenwich into a biscuit bakery and magazine. From here, 90 tons of cheese and biscuit were shipped down the Thames to the army's bases at Windsor and Reading every week.[25] The London market continued to feed the soldiers even when they moved out on campaign, with commercial carriers bringing a steady stream of supplies out from the capital.[26] When in 1649 the Model Army moved into Scotland and Ireland, its commanders set up a long-distance supply system, which ensured that strategically positioned magazines received regular shipments of supplies that were then sent out to the army in the field.[27] 'Nothing is more certain than this,' one of Cromwell's officers would reminisce. 'In the later wars both Scotland and Ireland were conquered by timely provisions of Cheshire cheese and biscuit.'[28]

By the middle of the eighteenth century, the French had established a sophisticated 'five-march system'. Bakeries were set up at a distance of five days' march from a supply magazine, and a convoy of carts brought flour to the bakeries. Another convoy then made the 2–3-day journey to take the bread to the troops at the front.[29] The French army that moved along the Rhine in the Seven Years War (1756–63) was described as 'leap-frogging from one set of ovens to another'.[30] According to Elzéar Blaze, who fought in Napoleon's army in Austria 50 years later, when the army marched too rapidly and moved beyond the reach of the supply depots, the soldiers had to rely on forage and plunder. Thoughtless of those who followed behind and wasteful in their excess, the French troops would slaughter whatever livestock they could lay their hands on, and, 'after marching all day, spent a great part of the night ... in making fricassees, pancakes, and fritters'.[31] Once supplies caught up with them, the soldiers were strictly enjoined to desist from plunder.[32]

During the French Revolutionary and Napoleonic Wars, British soldiers were more likely to receive biscuit than their Continental counterparts. The Navy Victualling Board now took on responsibility for provisioning the army as well as the navy. The bakers at the naval dockyards worked day and night to supply the 400,000 soldiers and sailors scattered across the globe with their daily pound of bread or biscuit.[33] The pressure these wars placed on military provisioning resulted in new food preservation and production technologies. Nicolas Appert perfected the art of hermetically sealing food in glass bottles, while Thomas Grant revolutionised British biscuit production by introducing steam-powered machinery to the naval bakeries. But these innovations arrived too late to benefit the forces who fought in the Napoleonic Wars. Even during the Crimean War (1853–6), the British army failed to draw on these new resources. It lacked a central body responsible for sustenance, and food supply therefore varied from regiment to regiment. For the most part, it was abysmal. Much of the 'fresh' meat delivered to soldiers was in such a state of putrefaction they were forced to bury it rather than eat it. Bread supplies had often run out by the evening, leaving the men with only a cup of tea for supper. The Army Sanitary Commission of 1857, set up to investigate the failures of the Crimean War – in which 19,000 soldiers died of disease while only 5,000 were killed in action – reminded the army authorities that it was their duty to supply the troops with enough food to keep them in good health. The army now responded by setting up a supply corps, which was made responsible for the sufficient provision of clothing, ordnance, stores, fuel, water and food.[34]

The first real test of the new Army Service Corps came with the Boer War in 1899. Here the British army discovered the usefulness of canned meat and biscuit.[35] The London canning factories that had adapted Appert's bottling method to tin cans received an influx of orders for mutton stew and beef bouillon. American and Argentinian corned-beef factories shipped hundreds of thousands of cans of 'bully beef' to South Africa. Canned meat was heralded as a great boon to land warfare, as it was easily transported and facilitated rapid troop movement.[36] Even though corned beef was made from the trimmings of better cuts of beef compressed into a tin, it was still more palatable than the stringy 'carrion' made from bullocks that had been kept for too long on the hoof, which had been the lot of Wellington's army in Spain, or the putrid flesh the soldiers in the Crimea received.[37] At the same time, Huntley & Palmers filled army contracts for several thousand tons of hard army biscuit.[38] But the eternal diet of bully beef and biscuit was hated by the troops. In a letter home from the Boer War in May 1900, one sergeant joked: 'We are still on bully beef, biscuits and jam, but there is a rumour afloat that we are to have bread by next Christmas.'[39]

Biscuit had its heyday as a military provision during the First World War. If industrial biscuit and bully beef were heralded as foodstuffs that facilitated the speed and flexibility of troops, it is ironic that they became the staple foods of a war that was renowned for stasis. New military technology was so heavily weighted in favour of the defensive that once the front lines were established in 1914, millions of lives were expended in futile attacks without either side making any significant territorial progress.[40]

Within a year of entering the war, Britain had an army of nearly one million men fighting on the Western Front; by 1918 this had increased to two million. The war consumed resources at a frightening rate.[41] Every day huge quantities of guns, ammunition, animal fodder and food had to be shipped to the Continent to sustain the army. The resources of the entire nation were redirected towards feeding this insatiable war machine. It had taken Huntley & Palmers only a couple of weeks to fill the orders they received for military biscuit during the Boer War.[42] Now they reduced their production of fancy biscuits and switched to 24-hour production of military hardtack. They were joined by other biscuit manufacturers. Even Chiltonian's, producers of dog biscuits, converted to making army biscuits – which is perhaps apt given that the troops referred to the military issue as 'dog biscuits'.[43] Wartime demand for biscuits was so high that in 1917–18, Huntley & Palmers produced the largest tonnage of biscuit in their history. Much of this was supplied to government bodies to stock their canteens, but thousands of tons of the military standard issue No. 4 high-fat biscuits were shipped overseas to feed the troops.[44]

The troops, however, wanted bread. By 1914, bread was the staple food of the working classes and supplied them with three quarters of their calories. Meat featured on Sundays, with perhaps some bacon or a few sausages during the week, but most meals consisted of bread and a little cheese, margarine or jam. Bread was thus the staff of life. Luckily for the troops, the mostly static nature of the war meant that the Army Service Corps was able to establish permanent bakeries at the base depots, which fed fresh bread into the supply line. Provisions and ordnance were transported from these depots at the ports by train to railheads 10–15 miles behind the front line. A poem by the soldier Gilbert Waterhouse describes the railhead at Someville as 'full of noisy din', where 'bully beef and tea, matches and candles, and (good for you and me) cocoa, coffee and biscuits by the tin, sardines, condensed milk, petrol and paraffin' were loaded on to trucks to be taken to a refilling point.[45] Here the provisions were divided up and hauled by a convoy of wagons and carts to the regimental quartermaster's stores, where they would be subdivided again into allocations for each platoon. From here they had to be transported to the trenches. If conditions were favourable, they could be pulled in handcarts over duckboards, but more often than not the men had to wade through mud and deep water with the heavy bags on their backs. This was a dangerous task. Fred Wood recalled receiving bread splattered with the blood of one unfortunate ration carrier. But the men were hungry and they 'scraped the worst off and ate it'.[46]

Official army records claim that the depot bakeries were able to send the troops 'a regular supply of bread'. But even during 1918, its most productive year, when each month the bakery in Boulogne sent out more than 15 million pounds of bread to the front line, this would still have amounted to less than half the men's ration of a pound of bread a day. The rest had to be made up with biscuit. What was more, bread and other desirable items like the 'apricots and peaches-a-la-tin' also mentioned in Waterhouse's poem tended to disappear as they travelled along the supply line. George Herbert Hill noted that ration parties 'could easily sneak a couple of loaves buckshee on the way back, or a wedge of cheese, without anyone being a bit the wiser'.[47] Much to their dissatisfaction, the food that reached the men in the trenches was mainly bully beef and biscuit.[48]

The soldier who took this photograph of a farmyard in France in 1918 wrote on the back
'The gleanings of the modern battlefield. All is fish that comes in the net: – ammunition, shell cases,
equipment, biscuit tins, in fact everything is saved.'

Soldiers complained that military biscuits were as 'hard as the hubs of hell'. They called them 'hardtack' (tack being slang for food), 'teeth-dullers' and 'jaw-breakers'; Australian and New Zealand troops referred to them as 'Anzac tiles' or, more sarcastically, 'Anzac wafers'. These names indicate that packaging the biscuits in tins was at least effective in preventing them from getting damp and mouldy: thus the soldiers were not faced with the weevily or maggot-infested biscuit that had confronted sailors in the past. But for men with poor teeth or dentures, eating the biscuits was a trial. And as sailors had known for centuries, a diet of mainly salt meat and biscuit inevitably led to scurvy. Many of the men at the Western Front were suffering from scorbutic swollen gums and constantly complained of sore mouths and loose teeth.[49]

Of course, biscuits were not supposed to be eaten just as they were, but there was not always the opportunity to cook, so soldiers often had little option but to gnaw on their hardtack. When they did have cooking facilities, like sailors the world over they crushed them and added them to stews to make lobscouse. Still, crushed biscuit added to a stew of bully beef resulted in an oleaginous and unappetising mess that made the men thirsty and constipated. In a letter home, the Australian infantryman Paul Teesdale described how the Turkish villagers who came to the army camps in search of bully beef and biscuits were the 'first people I've seen eat b & b with any show of enjoyment'.[50] The soldiers preferred to make 'burgoo' by mixing crushed biscuit with water and jam to create a sticky porridge.

The men in the trenches rarely received the standard ration as specified in army regulations. It was common practice to substitute missing items with whatever was available. On occasion this led to peculiar allocations, such as the 56 pounds of cheese, one tin of biscuits and few tins of jam given to Cavalryman Ben Clouting's unit of eight men to last them for two days. Tins of sardines sometimes replaced bully beef, and while they may have been a welcome change for some, they made for an odd meal when accompanied only by tins of plum and apple jam. 'Jam and herrings! How about that for a diet?' Private George Hewins wrote. 'I thought: It's better'n *nothing*!' But Hewins' good-natured acceptance of the army's failure to supply the troops with foodstuffs that could produce wholesome (and recognisable) meals was far from typical. For most men this cavalier distribution of random foodstuffs confirmed their sense that to the army commanders they were not humans entitled to civilised meals but cogs in the war machine to be stoked with energy and then expended in battle.[51] It is fitting that for soldiers who experienced such a powerful sense of alienation during the most industrial war the world had yet seen, their main foodstuff was fabricated by workers who also experienced the alienation of becoming nothing more than a moving part

A SOLDIER'S RECIPE FROM FRANCE –
HOW TO MAKE 'TRENCH PORRIDGE'

Take ½ lb Anzac wafers, commonly known
as whole meal biscuits or jaw breakers,
powder up, and soak overnight in about 1
pint of water – shell hole water if procur-
able. Care must be taken in the soaking
stage, or the biscuits may get too soft (I
don't think). Next day boil for about 20
minutes, then add quarter lb raisins, and
boil for another 10 minutes. Then add milk
and sugar to taste. If prepared in this way a
most nourishing and tasty dish will be the
result.[52]

Private Victor Offe, Machine Gun
Company, *The Barossa Cookery
Book* (1917)

in an industrial process. This feeling was reinforced by the fact that the officers ate separately from the men and many received a stream of good-quality food in thousands of hampers sent out to them from Fortnum & Mason.

At the beginning of the Second World War the Allies still relied on biscuit and bully beef to feed the troops. The biscuit factories once again began producing army issue. One soldier recalled that Peak Frean and Jacob's made 'light palatable ones' but the biscuits made in Australia were 'dry, solid, soap-tasting slabs'.[53] It was not uncommon for biscuit and bully beef to feature in all three meals of the day. Fighting in the North African desert, G. L. Verney had fried corned beef and biscuit for breakfast, cold bully beef and biscuit for lunch and bully beef and biscuit stew for supper.[54] Early in the war, soldiers stationed in France and Belgium were able to supplement their rations at local eateries. R. P. Evans recalled what a tremendous relief it was 'to return to the village in the evening [and] ... consume vast quantities of egg and chips'.[55] But the troops in the desert had no recourse to local cafés to supplement their diet.

British conscripts serving in the Second World War were better educated than the farmhands and servants who made up the ranks in 1914. At the same time, the deference that marked nineteenth-century paternal class relations was fast evaporating. The soldiers of the Second World War saw themselves as civilians in uniform, and the army now acknowledged that the men who had been called up to fight for their country had a right to a decent level of care. Perhaps even more importantly, the commanders realised that men fed on bully beef and biscuit were badly prepared for the task of mobile warfare that characterised this war. In January 1942, after seven weeks of fighting around Benghazi, a worrying number of British soldiers were incapacitated by scurvy, jaundice and dysentery. Gerald Page, a nursing orderly, believed that 'what Rommel failed to do, jaundice could so easily have accomplished'.[56] As an interim measure the supply corps shipped in vitamin tablets and salt pills, as well as margarine, bacon, oatmeal, onions and chutney, to add some flavour and nutrients to the soldiers' diet. But it was obvious that long-term the army would have to find a better solution.[57]

The quartermaster's department now came up with the composite ration. A box of 'compo' or C-rations contained a variety of tinned meats as well as enough biscuits, sugar and coffee to last 14 men for a day. Page's division first received C-rations in Sicily in 1943. 'We all thought they were very good compared to what we had been having in North Africa,' he recalled. 'Tinned Steak and Kidney

A soldier eating his meal of bully beef, beans and biscuit in the North African desert in December 1942.

Puddings, Steam Puddings, Soup, Chocolate, Sweets and English Brand Cigarettes and Tobacco were luxuries we had forgotten about in the desert.'[58] Nutritional science had advanced by the 1940s, and the new ration packs attempted to supply the soldiers with nutritionally balanced meals. C-rations became standard British issue for the rest of the war. While corned beef and biscuit did not disappear altogether – both were frequently contained in the compo ration boxes – they were mitigated by a greater variety of tinned meats and more supplementary foodstuffs.

Biscuits were still an important element in the K-ration survival kits issued to soldiers as they went into combat. These usually consisted of tins of veal, Spam or sausage, biscuits, cheese, a fruit bar and lemon crystals. The soldiers rarely consumed them in the way the ration designers had intended, though. One private issued with K-rations in Burma recalled that the men mixed the processed cheese with crushed biscuits, bouillon powder and water and heated it over the fire to make 'cheese bouillon'; or mixed crushed biscuits, fruit bars and chocolate with the lemon crystals to make a 'cake' that could be eaten while they were on the march.[59]

Army nutritionists understood that even the improved rations were no substitute for fresh food. Gerald Page recalled receiving issues of grapes in Italy, and as the troops fought their way north, the British army went to great lengths to supply the men with fresh bread, setting up temporary bakeries in a variety of locations ranging from churchyards to abandoned soap factories. The British mobile bakeries were the envy of the Americans, who were aware that 'soldiers probably resented [bread's] absence from a meal more than that of any other food'.[60] The British supplied the Americans with bakery equipment, and at Monte Cassino the Allies conducted an experiment, stationing a mobile bakery as close to the front line as possible. From here they shuttled freshly prepared ham and cheese sandwiches as well as hamburgers up to the troops on the front line. The soldiers' enthusiastic response to fresh food led the Americans to prioritise field kitchens in north-western Europe. In the end, ration packs with biscuit as a bread substitute accounted for under a quarter of the food provided to US troops during the European campaign; most of it was prepared in field kitchens.[61]

Today army cooks would not dare to serve bully beef and biscuit stew at virtually every meal –and neither would they get away with claiming that rissoles made with bully beef mixed with tinned herring were 'fish cakes'.[62] During the Gulf War, the majority of British forces lived inside fortified bases, where they were served a variety of dishes as part of their three cooked meals a day, including tasty curries and creamy cheesecakes. In Iraq and Afghanistan it was only those soldiers who were stationed in forward operating bases and reliant on 24-hour ration packs who suffered from 'menu fatigue'. But rather than complaining about bully beef, for many soldiers the army was now far too generous with beans. 'Beans again. Beans for breakfast, beans for lunch and beans for supper,' complained Lance-Corporal Sarah Close, a medic in Helmand Province, as she opened her breakfast pouch in December 2007.[63]

The modern British army's equivalent of Second World War compo rations are individual 24-hour ration packs, which contain three bean-heavy meals in silver pouches, a dessert such as sticky toffee or rice pudding, as well as a chocolate bar and cocoa. Packets of foil-wrapped 'Biscuits-Brown' or 'Biscuits-Fruit' are also included. 'Biscuits-Brown' are regarded as a stand-in for bread and are often accompanied by a tube of pâté. However, with most British people no longer relying on it as the main component of their diet, soldiers today do not miss bread as much as it was missed by the men who fought in the First World War. And although they joke about their hardness, biscuits are not the focus of soldiers' opprobrium, because they are regarded no longer as substitutes for a staple food but as what they have become in Britain today – snacks.[64]

ANZAC BISCUITS

In the 1950s, Sadie Davis, a bank manager's wife in Wollongong in New South Wales, had a dedicated baking day when she would make lamingtons and sponges, jam roly-poly and biscuits to last her family for the week. Even by the 1970s, when her big baking days were over, her granddaughter recalled that she 'always had a jar of homemade Anzac biscuits in the cupboard' and her veteran husband always 'had an Anzac biscuit with his morning tea or coffee'.[1]

Anzac biscuits are no longer the store-cupboard staple they used to be, but many Australians still bake a batch on Anzac Day.[2] Every year on 25 April a dawn ceremony commemorates the members of the Australian and New Zealand Army Corps (the Anzacs) who lost their lives during the ill-fated amphibious landings on the Gallipoli peninsula on that day in 1915 and over the disastrous eight-month campaign that followed. Anzac Day holds a special place in the Antipodean national psyche. When Australia and New

Zealand sent their servicemen to participate in the First World War, they were acting as nations on the international stage for the first time since achieving Dominion status. Thus in Australia (and to a lesser extent New Zealand) the beaches at Gallipoli are still remembered as the place where national consciousness was born. Here the troops were said to have exhibited a distinctive Anzac spirit: a mixture of loyalty and bravery, practicality and ingenuity, endurance and – in contrast to their class-ridden British allies – egalitarianism. This spirit, heralded for taking the mateship of the bush onto the battlefield, is still celebrated on Anzac Day and promoted as the core of Australian national identity.[3]

It is part of the Anzac mythology that the biscuits the troops were sent from Australia were made with plenty of sugar and syrup, because this would have preserved them during the two or three months it took for parcels to reach their destination. Biscuits were certainly included in the parcels that were sent out to service personnel by the Red Cross and various other charitable organisations. On 20 December 1915, nurse Irene Bonnin recorded in her diary: 'Had *another* parcel!... got a boot box tied up with R W & B ribbon given by the Australian Women's League... such jolly nice things – soap, scent, iodine and brush, boracic acid, stockings, book, chocolates, biscuits, Red Cross brooch with 1915 on the back, block of postcards etc. Really such a very nice parcel. So awfully good of them to think of us.'[4] The men at the front rarely recorded what kind of biscuit they received. On 14 January 1917, infantryman Norman McLeod Bethune wrote to his sister from the Egyptian desert to thank her for the cheese and 'delicious' biscuits she had sent, while in an undated letter Paul Teesdale Smith wrote to his girlfriend from Gallipoli to tell her that he had eaten her sister's 'tasty' biscuits with 'chicken and ham paste, raspberry jam ... and ... a flowing bowl of cocoa' with which he drank the toast 'Hell to the Kaiser'.[5]

It seems unlikely that rolled-oat biscuits were the only kind sent out to the Anzac servicemen. In fact, the 'Anzac' prefix seems at first not to have been attached to a particular type but to those biscuits and cakes women made for the bake sales that were held to raise money for the various charities and comfort funds. 'Anzac' was attached to recipes for the first time in the 1915 edition of the St Andrew's fund-raising cookery book published by the inhabitants of Dunedin, New Zealand. Newspapers and fund-raising cookery books also appended 'Soldiers' or 'Red Cross' to various recipes to indicate their suitability for these events. Eventually the prefix attached itself exclusively to the rolled-oat biscuits or crispies which are now thought of as Anzac biscuits.[6]

Enthusiasm for the Anzac myth waned after the Second World War, when Australians and New Zealanders began to take less pride in their role as defenders of the British Empire. By the 1960s and 1970s, Anzac Day had become a focus for peace protesters who decried Australia's participation in the Vietnam War and women's groups who used the day to draw attention to the many women raped during conflicts. What was more, the narrow definition of Australian identity, which viewed the ur-Australians as white soldiers and their nurturing womenfolk, not only ignored the country's original Aborigine inhabitants but also excluded the numerous immigrants from a wide variety of cultures who had made Australia their home since 1945. By the 1960s, Anzac biscuits had virtually disappeared from published recipe books, and cookbook authors had reverted to calling them 'rolled-oat biscuits'. But with the resurgence of Australian nationalism in the 1990s,

Anzac Day was revived and Anzac biscuits reappeared in cookbooks and store cupboards.[7]

Nowadays, Anzac biscuits must contain coconut, but it was not until 1925 that the ingredient was included in the recipes.[8] Coconut was particularly popular in South Australia, which Lady Victoria Buxton, the governor's wife in the 1890s, described as the 'Land of Cakes'. Desiccated coconut from Fiji and Ceylon was first imported in the 1880s, and 20 years later the state was enjoying – or suffering from – a coconut craze. In 1909, South Australia imported 100,000 pounds of desiccated coconut, which was added to virtually every imaginable sweet bake. In particular, it became the signature ingredient of the Lamington, a sponge cake coated in chocolate sauce and then rolled in desiccated coconut, which was named after the state's governor.[9] Given its ubiquity in Australian baking, it was inevitable that coconut would eventually find its way into the Anzac biscuit.

ANZAC BISCUITS

After her marriage to Gilbert Blytham in 1912, Caroline Sarah Warner began to note down recipes in a little black notebook. In the back she kept a record of the butter she made and the eggs she collected from the hens on their farm. In 1916, Gilbert enlisted, and the following year he was killed. Caroline stopped making entries in her notebook and did not resume until three years had passed. The very last recipe recorded in the notebook, dating from 1919 or 1920, was for Anzac biscuits.[10]

100 g plain flour
100 g rolled oats
100 g dessicated coconut
200 g sugar
100 g butter
2 tbsp golden syrup
1 tsp bicarbonate of soda
2 tbsp boiling water

Heat oven to 160°C.

Grease baking tray.

Mix together the flour, oats, coconut and sugar in a bowl.

Melt butter and golden syrup over a gentle flame. Mix the bicarbonate of soda with the boiling water and stir into the melted butter and syrup mixture. It will foam.

Pour into the dry ingredients and mix well so that there are no dry patches. Roll into walnut-sized balls. Place on the greased baking tray, leaving space in between the balls for spreading. Press down lightly with a fork. Bake for 10–15 minutes until golden.

Allow to cool. Remove from tray.

13

In which Pam Ashford anxiously stockpiles biscuits

When he was a young boy in the late 1930s, Ian Dunbar recalled that every after-noon at four o'clock the maid brought afternoon tea into the drawing room. On the tray were thin slices of bread and butter, Huntley & Palmers biscuits, home-made cake and home-made jam or honey. Ian was the son of a doctor who ran his practice out of the family home in Gillingham. Moderation was the watch-word of the genteel professional household, and therefore 'biscuits and cake were regarded as luxuries'. Ian was allowed only one biscuit and one piece of cake. If he was still hungry, he could have bread and butter.[1]

Before the First World War, biscuits rarely appeared at tea time. They would have been considered a poor second to home-made cake. But the First World War had established the biscuit as an alternative to cake. From 1916, sugar restrictions and butter shortages made it increasingly difficult to bake at home, and biscuits were often the only sweet products available.[2] Even though manufacturers were forced to make their Osbornes and Maries with wholemeal flour, demand was strong for the small amount of fancy biscuits they were able to produce for the civilian market.[3] After the war, cakes pushed biscuits aside again, but they had established a place on the tea table, especially at nursery teas. A survey of 5,000 households across six British cities, conducted by the biscuit manufacturers William Crawford in 1938, found that even though cake was usually served for afternoon tea in well-to-do households, about 10 to 15 per cent now also consumed biscuits.[4]

Although the availability of biscuits to civilians had been reduced during the First World War, the biscuit factories had boomed. They not only profited from contracts for tons of plain army issue, but also produced fancy biscuits to supply army canteens, the YMCA, the War Office and the Prisoners of War Committee. Theodore Carr used the profits of wartime to invest in a cutting and embossing machine, an electric lift for the confectionery department and a refrigerating plant for cold cream.[5] As soon as restrictions were lifted, the manufacturers sprang back into production and biscuits resumed their position as one of the trappings of a genteel life. In *The Light Years*, the first of Elizabeth Jane Howard's quintet of novels evoking the life of a bourgeois family, Rachel, the eldest daughter, who has remained at home to look after her ageing parents, is preparing the house for the annual summer visit of her siblings and their children. In the 'grown-ups' rooms' she checks 'that the drawers had clean lining paper, that the quilted biscuit boxes by the bedside tables contained Marie biscuits, that the bottles of Malvern water were full...The biscuits had become quite silent, crumbly and unappetising. She collected the boxes and took them down to the pantry to be refilled where she spoke to the cook who remarked that the old biscuits would do for the maids' "middle mornings".'[6] Fresh biscuits with the morning cup of tea brought to you in bed by a maid were as normal a part of the genteel daily routine as the evening bath, changing for dinner – and the belief that stale biscuits were still good enough for the maids.

Biscuits found new niches in the hedonistic world of the 1920s, with its whirl of jazz clubs, dance crazes and cocktail parties. Manufacturers brought out ranges of 'cocktail' biscuits to serve at fashionable parties, such as Romary's assorted cocktail range of Cheese Gaufrets, onion-flavoured Amadoes and celery Sticklets.

Carr's sales of Club Cheese and Table Water biscuits boomed.[7] Huntley & Palmers appointed a special representative to canvas the milk bars, which were a new phenomenon, and just as biscuits had earlier been advertised as the perfect snack to pack for a bicycling trip, now they were presented as the ideal picnic staple on a motoring jaunt.[8] The Ryvita cracker, introduced to Britain by the Toronto biscuit maker W. Garfield Weston in 1934, was eagerly taken up by women attempting to diet their way to a fashionably boyish, flat-chested, slim-hipped figure.

It was in the interwar period that the chocolate biscuit made its appearance. The first company to produce a chocolate biscuit appears to have been

THICK PARMESAN BISCUITS

For a dozen biscuits: ¼ lb plain flour, 2 oz each of butter and grated Parmesan, the yolk of one egg, salt, cayenne pepper.
Rub the butter into the flour, add the cheese, egg and seasonings. Moisten with a little water if necessary. Roll out the dough to the thickness of half an inch. Cut into 1 inch diameter rounds. Arrange on a baking sheet. Bake in the centre or lower centre of a very moderate oven, gas No. 3 or 160–70 °C for just on 20 minutes. Serve hot.[9]

Lady Clark, *The Cookery Book of Lady Clark of Tillypronie* (1909)

Cadbury's. In 1891, they filed a patent for a biscuit made out of two cocoa-flavoured rectangles sandwiched together with cream and covered in a layer of chocolate. But Cadbury's do not appear to have made any effort to market their innovation and the biscuit eventually disappeared from their list.[10] Now biscuit makers began making chocolate-flavoured biscuits or coating them in chocolate, keen to cash in on the growing popularity of confectionery, sales of which doubled in the interwar period.[11] In 1910, Peek Frean launched the Creola. Like Cadbury's earlier creation it consisted of two cocoa-flavoured biscuits sandwiched together with a chocolate-flavoured buttercream. As with the already very popular Custard Cream, the secret to the distinctive taste of the biscuit dough was that it was flavoured with custard powder. Relaunched as the Bourbon biscuit in the 1930s, it became one of Peek Frean's bestsellers.[12]

Already before the war Fortt's had begun producing chocolate Bath Olivers, which they now advertised as a perfect accompaniment to morning coffee. Given that Bath Olivers were supposed to be suitable for those with even 'the most fickle digestion', chocolate was hardly an appropriate addition, but Fortt's advertising assured their customers that even the 'weakest [invalids] can digest them'.[13] In 1925, McVitie & Price began coating their digestives in chocolate. Even more popular than chocolate-coated were chocolate-encased biscuits: Jacob's launched their Club biscuit in 1919, and Macdonald's countered with the Penguin biscuit in 1932. But the most successful of them all was Rowntree's Chocolate Crisp, launched in 1935. This winning combination of two fingers of wafer biscuit encased in chocolate was so popular that, even without any initial advertising, production had reached 80 tons a week after just a few months. Rowntree's renamed their invention Kit Kat, as they worried that other firms were beginning to make their own Chocolate Crisps.[14]

The company promoted the Kit Kat as the 'best companion to a cup of tea'. Crawford's 1938 survey found that among the well-to-do, a new habit of taking a mid-morning break was forming. The post-war shortage of servants meant that many middle-class women found themselves spending their mornings doing housework. They now began to integrate into their routine a break for a cup of tea or coffee and a biscuit. Hence Fortt's suggestion that their chocolate Olivers were good with coffee and Rowntree's slogan of 'Have a break, have a Kit Kat'.[15] Thus, besides finding a place on the tea table, biscuits now strengthened their association with tea through the insinuation that they were an appropriate snack for a tea break.

Between 1920 and 1938, the amount spent on biscuits by British households doubled.[16] Crawford's survey showed that biscuits were still predominantly eaten by the middling sort but that the skilled working classes were also becoming a biscuit-eating section of society. It calculated that families of skilled workers were spending around 1s. 8d a week on biscuits.[17] Most of these would have belonged to the 13.5 million Britons who were registered to do their shopping at the Co-op.[18] The Co-operative Wholesale Society had been founded in 1868 to purchase goods from wholesalers that could then be distributed to the hundreds of Co-op stores around Britain. In 1873, the society set up its own biscuit works at Crumpsall, on the outskirts of Manchester, to supply its stores with affordable biscuits, cakes, jams and sweets.[19]

In the last quarter of the nineteenth century, the development of railways, steamships, refrigeration and freezing technology meant that cheap food imports were flooding into Britain. To go shopping became a geography lesson: rice came from Patna, tea from Ceylon and sugar from Mauritius; lamb, mutton and butter from New Zealand; beef from Argentina and cheese, bacon and wheat from Canada and the United States.[20] Food prices dropped by about 40 per cent and this greatly increased the spending power of the working classes.[21] Shops like the Co-operative stores, Lipton's and the Maypole Dairy catered for the new kind of working-class customer, selling working-class staples such as flour, bacon, ham, cheese, eggs, sugar and tea. The rapid turnover of large quantities of just a few lines allowed them to cut their profit margins to just 10 to 15 per cent rather than the 30 to 50 per cent aimed at by traditional grocers.[22]

Moreover, Lipton's found that the more they controlled the collection, storage and distribution of goods, the more the economies of scale benefited the company and the consumer. They set up an egg-packing station in Ireland, their own tea plantations in Ceylon and a biscuit factory in Glasgow where the biscuits were pre-packaged into small, affordable packets.[23] An advertisement from 1896 announced that 'LIPTON, the People's Food Provider, Has now commenced Manufacturing Biscuits on an extensive scale in his own Factories' and that they were now available 'at price hitherto unknown', urging people to 'try them!'[24] A Board of Trade survey in 1904 found that families whose income amounted to more than 40 shillings a week were spending between 5 and 7 pence a week on biscuits and cakes.[25]

By the 1920s, Lipton's and the Co-op had been joined by Serpell's, Palmer Bros of Bristol and the International Stores, all selling a range of cheaper biscuits. A price war began as the companies competed for the custom of the growing number of 'respectable' working-class families, who shaded into a group of lower-middle-class non-manual workers. Real wages increased by 15 per cent in the interwar period and aspirations to gentility among the skilled mechanics, factory foremen, bank clerks, board school teachers, county council clerks, sanitary and police inspectors and commercial travellers on small salaries made them incorporate bourgeois rituals such as afternoon tea into their daily routines.[26] The price of budget-range biscuits came down to a shilling per pound in 1921, and 10 years later, Kemp's and Betta Biscuits reduced their prices to 6d. After Garfield Weston arrived from Toronto, he brought biscuit prices down to 5d a pound. By 1939, Weston's and Betta Biscuits, under the umbrella firm of Meredith & Drew, had increased their market share to one third. Their lines were so cheap they did not even bother to advertise: the biscuits just sold themselves.[27]

Genteel biscuit-consuming habits were spreading to all levels of society. Growing up in Kent during the First World War, Sarah Shears recalled annual visits to her grandmother and five aunts, who lived in straitened but genteel circumstances in a large house in Brighton. Every morning her grandmother had a cup of tea and a biscuit brought to her in bed and Sarah and her sister were allowed to join her for this when they visited. 'It was the biscuit that was the real highlight of early morning tea with Grandmother – a plain petit-beurre biscuit. This, to me, was the very essence of extravagant living – early morning tea and a biscuit.'[28] Even the lowly family of a Devon fisherman that Stephen Reynolds lodged with in the early 1900s started their day at sunrise with 'biscuits and a cup of tea which I make and take up myself'.[29] By the 1950s, half of the British population took an early morning cup of tea in bed and for many of them this was the 'most cherished' moment of refreshment in the day.[30]

Slab cake and biscuits were now added to the working-class spread of bread and jam, macaroni and cheese or anchovy toast that were put out for 'tea'.[31] Lower-income families also began to add supper to their daily meals.[32] While well-to-do families were rounding off their evening meal with a savoury course of crackers and cheese, for the respectable working and lower-middle classes, biscuits and cheese were their supper.[33] In Devon the fisherman's family would send the children off to bed at supper time 'with a biscuit or a small chunk of cheese' and the adults would eat the same with pickles or some fried or boiled fish and 'a pint of stout and bitter from the Alexandra'.[34] At his Wigan lodgings over a tripe shop, George Orwell recalled that his hosts would serve 'Pale flabby Lancashire cheese and biscuits... The Brookers never called these biscuits, biscuits. They always referred to them reverentially as "cream crackers" – Have another cream cracker Mr Reilly. You'll like a cream cracker with your cheese" – thus glozing over the fact that there was only cheese for supper.'[35] Many an office worker rounded off their day like the respondent to a Mass Observation survey, who spent her evening knitting by the fire listening to the news with a 'cup of "Bourn-Vita" and a biscuit' before getting ready for bed.[36]

In 1939 there were still a sizeable number of unskilled workers who were untouched by these developments, however.[37] For Richard Hoggart, whose widowed mother brought up her three small children on the meagre offerings of public assistance, a 'chrome biscuit barrel' was one of the 'trappings of splendour' that might only be found, along with 'lamps with bobbled fringes…full-length curtains on a rail, hot water systems and inside lavatories', in the remote world of the lower-middle-class houses near his home in Chapeltown, Leeds.[38] Cocoa, cheap blackberry-and-apple jam and the 'cloying, gooey sweetness' of the cheapest, 'grittily sugary' condensed milk were the pleasures of the poorest children. Richard and his siblings could only afford an occasional 'ha'penny of sweets…of peculiar and dubious provenance' between the three of them.[39] In Liverpool on Tuesdays and Thursdays, when the workers at Crawford's biscuit factory were given their bags of broken biscuits, the poor kids used to stand on the corner of Binns Road and beg: 'Biscuits, any biscuits please!'[40] For the children of the deprived, biscuits only featured in their diet as hard ship's biscuits smashed into crumbs and mixed with an Oxo-cube-flavoured broth in a simple version of sailor's scouse, which often was their only warm meal.[41] It took another war to fully democratise biscuit consumption.

In November 1940, Pam Ashford began to feel anxious. She had allowed her hoard of biscuits to run down. Lulled into a false sense of security by the apparently plentiful stocks in the shops, now she was confronted with their sudden disappearance. On the way to work she stopped at Cranston's, which normally had a wide selection, but was disappointed to find that only plain biscuits were left on the shelves. On her way home that evening she was lucky to find chocolate biscuits at Cooper's, but their price had risen from sixpence a pound before the war to a shilling. While she had made substantial savings by stockpiling when war broke out the previous year, it would now be much more expensive to build up a new store. But the expense was the least of her concerns. Pam worked as a secretary in a shipping firm in Glasgow and lived with her 73-year-old mother, who was in charge of the shopping and cooking. Biscuits were central to their diet because her mother was too frail to stand in long food queues. Their household was organised along labour-saving lines, which meant that Pam and her mother had reduced their lunch to only one course, and rather than having a pudding, they finished the meal off with 'coffee and fancy biscuits'. Their supper was biscuits and cheese. On Saturdays, Pam nibbled Healthy Life biscuits in the darkness of the cinema. Even their canary, Charlie, breakfasted on Butterette biscuits, as bird seed was in short supply.[42]

Pam's biscuit-hoarding habits were brought to an end in August 1942, when biscuits were included in the points system. Foods such as tinned meat, fish, dried fruit, tapioca, jelly, suet, rice and dried peas, the supply of which was too unreliable for them to be included as a weekly entitlement in the rationing system, were allocated a certain number of points. According to the vagaries of supply, the Ministry of Food was able to adjust the points value of these items up or down in order to steer demand.[43] Each ration-book holder was allocated sixteen points for four weeks. They could be sensible and spend all of them on a pound of tinned sausage meat, enough to create several main meals with the bonus of a thick layer of nearly half a pound of fat; or they could splurge eight points on half a pound of suet or a packet of biscuits. This allowed people subsisting mainly on unrationed wholemeal bread and potatoes to satisfy their craving for fatty meat or sweetness. Many people around the country would have shared the feelings of one factory manager, who was 'rather annoyed about the biscuits. I eat a lot (any kind) and am very fond of them.'[44] Even though the Ministry of Food tried to curb demand by awarding biscuits an unfavourably high cost in points, they were consistently one of the most preferred goods on the points system.[45]

Sugar rationing meant that cakes and desserts disappeared from the menu. Like Pam Ashford and her mother, many people used biscuits as substitutes for a pudding at the end of a meal or a slice of cake at tea time.[46] And in a development that cemented the new association with tea, biscuits replaced the sugar that people would normally have put in their tea. Before long, however, tea was also rationed, to two ounces per person, about two thirds of the pre-war average. A woman in Stepney told a Mass Observation investigator: 'We've just got used to going without sugar, and then they start rationing tea...I'd sooner they rationed our clothes, and let us have our necessities. I know we're asked to make sacrifices, but it's pretty hard, our tea. I think some of us women live for our cup of tea.'[47]

Sweet tea was the mainstay of the working classes. It gave them energy and boosted their spirits. The government was aware that the mundane things in life gained great power at a time when ordinary life was under siege. The Minister of Food, Lord Woolton, worried that severe tea shortages would damage morale, as people would feel that ordinary life was breaking down. The government therefore went to great lengths to provide tea in every setting: it was served in the canteens run by the various voluntary agencies; factories were encouraged to give their workers tea breaks to increase their productivity; and the Tea Marketing Board funded mobile tea vans to distribute tea to Londoners taking refuge in the air-raid shelters. A hot cuppa entered wartime mythology as a spirit-lifting symbol of the community spirit associated with the idea that all Britons had pulled together to defeat fascism.[48]

Yet many complained that wartime tea was too weak and never as sweet as they would have liked. A sweet biscuit to go with it therefore became a natural compensation, and tea and biscuits became embedded in the national consciousness. The mobile tea vans were stocked with cigarettes, buns and biscuits to accompany the cups of tea. The Ministry of Information identified tea and biscuits as a weapon to deploy against the panic air raids might induce in the civilian population. Leaflets advised people 'to ACCUMULATE A SMALL STORE (say in a biscuit tin) of TEA,

SUGAR, BISCUITS, etc. ready to give light food to neighbours whose homes have been destroyed. Such a store of food must be secured from dust and contamination by being kept in a closed container: i.e. – a biscuit tin.'[49]

By the end of the Second World War, sweet biscuits had completed their transformation from luxury goods eaten only by the privileged few into a mundane food eaten by the masses. On 10 May 1945, just two days after the end of the war in Europe, a teacher described in her diary a visit to some friends, when they chatted about 'clothes, coupons, and people … [and] the arch criminals' and wondered whether Hitler was dead while they drank tea and ate biscuits.[50] A Mass Observation survey of biscuit-eating habits found that by 1945 people from all walks of life ate biscuits at virtually any time of day (see page 8 of the picture section). They might be included with cheese or with a cup of tea to round off either lunch or dinner, or as a snack with coffee or tea between meals. When people put the kettle on to make 'a nice cup of tea', it was now a reflex to also reach for the biscuit tin.[51] And it was with the democratisation of the biscuit and its fixed association with tea that the practice of dunking biscuits in tea came about. Dunking biscuits in wine was an established practice among the middle class, while it was common practice for the labouring classes to their dunk their bread in their drink. In the eighteenth century, William Ellis described how at harvest time on his Hertfordshire farm his wife would time the baking of the sweet buns called wigs so that they came hot out of the oven just as the men came 'home to supper from reaping, when we toss one each of these large Wigs to each Man for his dipping in a Bowl of Ale'.[52] Just as farm labourers dipped their buns in their ale, the working classes dunked their dried bread in their tea. Once biscuits became a widespread accompaniment to tea, it must have been quite natural to dunk them too.

It took eight years for Britain's food supply system to recover from the war. In fact, once the fighting was over, things got worse rather than better. Faced with providing food relief for a starving Europe, where agricultural systems had been devastated, and a recalcitrant United States more interested in feeding its

GENUINE TEA COMPANY

This early nineteenth-century etching of an urban tea stall shows three customers: one is raising the steaming cup to his lips, another has poured the hot tea into his saucer and is cooling it further by blowing on it, the third has just dunked his hunk of bread into his tea.

citizens red meat than sending grain to Europe, Britain now extended rationing to bread and cut the biscuit factories' fat and flour allocations.[53] Plain biscuits remained on points rationing until March 1949, sweet biscuits until May 1950.[54] It was not until 1954 that people were able to buy as much flour, sugar, fat and eggs as they pleased. And they could increasingly afford to buy as much as they liked. Between 1945 and 1970, rising incomes and state welfare provision led to a striking improvement in living standards. People had more disposable income than ever before and, making up for the years of austerity, they spent a good deal of it on confectionery, cakes, pastries and biscuits.[55] Shops sprang up specialising entirely in biscuits. Growing up in Hackney in the 1950s, Norman Jacobs' favourite shop was the Biscuit Box. 'The shop and the pavement outside were piled high with tins of loose biscuits. These were bought by weight, scooped out and placed in a paper bag. The tins of broken biscuits were our favourites, as you got a big variety of different biscuits for a lower price.'[56]

Throughout the war biscuits had functioned as substitute cake, and they continued in this role, especially for children. While the men in a family might be given cake to take to work in their packed lunch, sweet biscuits stood in for cake in the children's lunchboxes.[57] The individually wrapped chocolate biscuits that the manufacturers had begun producing in the 1930s – the Club biscuit, the Kit Kat and the Penguin – now all came into their own. Weston's emerged from the war with a poor reputation. Fifty per cent of the respondents to a Mass Observation survey named it as the 'cheap and nasty' biscuit brand they most disliked.[58] In order to recover, Weston's now looked for a way to appeal to the children's market, and launched their Wagon Wheels, wrapped in a gingham-patterned package featuring cowboys.[59] In 1960, by which time the company had changed its name to Burton's, they launched the Jammie Dodger. With a heart-shaped hole in the centre through which a red jam filling could be glimpsed, it was intended to recall the nursery rhyme when the Knave of Hearts stole the tarts the Queen had baked, 'all on a summer's day'. True to the company's cheapskate reputation, the jam glowed red but was made with cheaper plums rather than raspberries.[60]

Restrictions during the war had meant that manufacturers were forced to drop most of their biscuit lines. In the 1950s, George Miller, sales manager at McVitie & Price's Harlesden factory, was reluctant to return to the company's pre-war practice of selling their most popular biscuits at an artificially high price in order to subsidise the production of less successful lines. Before the war the factory had produced a total of 387 different varieties. Now the company's chairman, Hector Laing, agreed with Miller that it should concentrate on making just four of

McVitie's core sellers: Digestive, Home Wheat, Rich Tea and MacVita. In addition, they overhauled and rationalised the entire production process. These innovations meant that they not only cut costs but also increased output and thereby secured the place of McVitie's Digestive as one of the most popular of all industrial biscuits. The new supermarkets also tended to just take the top five bestsellers of each biscuit company, and as other biscuit lines disappeared from the customer's view, the few that were left rose to dominance.[61]

In post-war Britain there was a complex hierarchy of sweet foodstuffs. Home-made cakes ranked higher than shop-bought; cakes ranked higher than biscuits. In some contexts, to serve shop-bought biscuits suggested laziness and a lack of devotion.[62] In Pennine towns, a child entering a friend's house for 'tea' could tell as soon as they stepped over the threshold whether they were likely to be served biscuits or cake. If the step was smartly donkey-stoned by the proud homeowner, it held out the promise of a 'good tea with plenty of home-made sweet stuff'. A dirty step forewarned that you would probably have to 'make do with a cream cracker or a rich tea biscuit'.[63] Ayub Khan Din played on such perceptions in his film *East is East*: the slovenliness of the mother is suggested when she opens a packet of biscuits, pours them onto a plate and shouts 'Breakfast!' to her children.

Nevertheless, by the 1970s, the anthropologist Mary Douglas observed that 'nowhere else in the world outside the British Isles is there [such] a steady demand for small geometrically-shaped biscuits, with a layer of jam or cream in the middle and coated with icing, at a sufficiently modest price to permit them a regular place in the daily menu'.[64] Despite apparently occupying a lowly position in the hierarchy of sweet foods, shop-bought industrial biscuits played an important role in the food world. Their power rested in the fact that they suggested in desiccated form a whole range of possible sweet dishes and the occasions when such dishes might be eaten.[65]

Tea drunk from a dainty china cup with a Bourbon biscuit for the eleven o'clock tea break marked a moment of rest; it spoke of a leisured life even though it was consumed during a break in a busy morning of housework. A Jaffa cake eaten at the end of a hurried midday meal suggested the trifle that might have taken its place in more leisurely circumstances. A diminutive cake in biscuit form, with its dry sponge base, layer of orange jelly and chocolate coating, the Jaffa cake epitomises the way in which biscuits function as miniature re-enactments of the sweet course. After a tea of ham sandwiches and celery sticks, a mint Viscount with its thick layer of chocolate and fancy foil wrapping could stand in for a slice of ginger or Battenberg cake; its flavour even carried an allusion to an after-dinner mint.[66] A Digestive eaten with a cup of cocoa before bed marked the occasion as a miniature meal, a 'supper' rather than just a hot drink. Just as a coda in a musical movement recalls the whole due to its rhythmic structure or harmony, the biscuit recalled 'all the sequences of puddings through the year, and of wedding cakes and christening cakes through the life-cycle'.[67] When Douglas was writing, the National Food Survey showed a decline in the consumption of bread, cakes, buns, teacakes, scones and pastries. But biscuit sales resisted this trend. Within just two decades after the end of the war, the biscuit had become a 'special kind of necessity' in the British diet, the 'rhyme-end to a line of verse', conjuring up the whole realm of British sweet stuff.[68]

BOURBON BISCUITS

For the dough:

100 g butter
100 g caster sugar
1 egg
150 g plain flour
50 g Bird's Custard Powder
25 g cocoa

For the filling:

100 g icing sugar
25 g butter
2 tbsp cocoa
a few drops milk or water

Preheat oven to 175°C. Line a baking tray with greaseproof paper.

To make the dough: Cream butter and sugar. Stir in the egg. Sift in the flour, custard powder and cocoa, and mix to a dough. Roll out to ½ cm thick and cut into fingers, or cut out

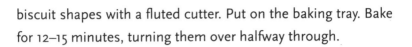

biscuit shapes with a fluted cutter. Put on the baking tray. Bake for 12–15 minutes, turning them over halfway through.

To make the filling: mix all the ingredients together to form a stiff buttercream, adding a drop more liquid if necessary, but don't make too sloppy.

Cool the biscuits thoroughly on a rack and then sandwich together with the filling.

JAMMIE DODGERS

For the jam:

   350 g frozen raspberries, defrosted
   1 tbsp lemon juice
   100–200 g sugar

For the dough:

   100 g unsalted butter, softened
   175 g caster sugar
   1 large egg

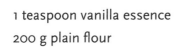

1 teaspoon vanilla essence
200 g plain flour

First make the jam. Heat the raspberries until they form a pulp and pass through a wire sieve to remove the pips. Measure the raspberry pulp and place in a thick-bottomed saucepan. Add the lemon juice and sugar in the ratio 200 g sugar to 300 ml of pulp (or a little less if you don't want the jam to be too sweet).

Heat, stirring, until all the sugar has dissolved. Then bring to a boil and allow to bubble without stirring until it reaches setting point. Test this by putting a small blob on a chilled saucer and pushing gently with your finger. If a wrinkly skin forms on the surface the jam is at setting point.

Now make the dough. Cream the butter and sugar until light and fluffy. Whisk the egg together with the vanilla essence in a separate bowl. Add to the butter/sugar mix and beat until it is incorporated.

Sieve in the flour and fold into the mixture. Shape into a ball and roll out to a thickness of 5 mm. Transfer to a tray and leave in fridge for 10 minutes. Cut out biscuit shapes and

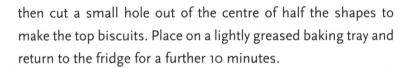

then cut a small hole out of the centre of half the shapes to make the top biscuits. Place on a lightly greased baking tray and return to the fridge for a further 10 minutes.

Bake at 170°C for 10–12 minutes.

Cool on a wire rack and then sandwich together the top and bottom biscuits with the jam.

CONCLUSION

On a hot summer afternoon in 2007, Yashaswini Chandra was canvassing door to door for a relative in a small village in eastern Uttar Pradesh. Considered by many as the badlands of India, this area is one of the poorest in the world. The householders listened politely and, according to the rules of hospitality, offered her glasses of water and sweets; it is considered bad form to only offer water to a guest. As they left the village, her colleague from the election campaign team suggested that they might as well cover a neighbouring hamlet. They followed a path through fields of crops until they reached a tiny hut with a caved-in roof. A stooped old farmer with a weather-beaten face stepped out and listened while Yashaswini sang the praises of the political candidate. 'Please have a glass of water,' he said when she had finished her piece. He gestured through the door of the hut and his grandson, dressed in a torn undershirt and grubby shorts, skipped out. The old man slipped a crumpled five-rupee note into the boy's hand and off he ran. A few minutes later he returned with a tiny packet of Parle-G biscuits, which the farmer offered to Yashaswini to accompany her glass of water.[1]

There is some irony that a campaigner during an election in an independent India should be offered a food stuff that the pageantry of the Raj served as a marker of British distinction. Both India's parliamentary system and industrially manufactured biscuits are legacies of British rule in India. Although Britain's reliance on heavily processed foodstuffs has not enhanced the nation's culinary reputation, its first and most quintessentially industrial food – the biscuit – is its most popular food legacy. Parle-G biscuits, which its Bombay manufacturer claims are 'the world's largest selling biscuit', are descendants of the mass-produced fancy biscuits that were born out of Britain's early industrialisation. The nineteenth-century invention of machine-manufactured sweet biscuits packaged in airtight tins transformed what had been a short-lived bakery product into a commodity that was as durable and transportable as twice-baked ship's biscuits.

By distributing their biscuits to virtually every corner of the globe, Huntley & Palmers created a worldwide taste for industrial biscuits. In their 1938 survey of biscuit consumption, Crawford's biscuit manufacturers claimed that the afternoon pause for a 'tea-time' of a hot drink and something sweet was 'the one meal which the English have created and given to the world'.[2] And not only did they export biscuits: as other countries industrialised, they set up their own biscuit factories modelled on the British template, using British-made machinery and often employing British engineers. Today you can buy packets of industrial biscuits virtually anywhere in the world. Mass-produced biscuits are cheap: an 80 g pack of Parle-G costs about 10 pence. What was once a luxury product for Europe's bourgeoisie is now an affordable food item even for the world's poorest. The British industrial biscuit has indeed become, as that food writer predicted it would in the 1930s, 'among all peoples the most widespread and democratic food'.[3]

Because biscuits are so versatile, they are difficult to define. At one end of the spectrum they merge into bread and at the other into cake. When they are coated in chocolate, the line between biscuit and confectionery becomes blurred. They reflect the culinary conditions of the time and place in which they are made. In classical antiquity biscuits preserved the staple grain; in the early Islamic world they were a vehicle for the consumption of sugar – a magical substance that it was believed helped to keep the body in a state of harmony with the cosmos. Today many industrial biscuits are made with palm oil rather than butter and maize syrup instead of sugar, reflecting the highly processed nature of our food. Their high sugar content means that we identify them as one of the causes of our current epidemic of obesity. But at the same time, low-calorie crackers are now sold as healthy diet foods.

Biscuits are such a malleable foodstuff that they can fit into virtually any food niche. Having begun as a digestive at the end of a meal, they are now eaten at any time of day and can be incorporated into – or indeed replace – virtually any meal. And biscuit eating has its own etiquette. A packet of Rich Tea used as a family breakfast substitute is considered neglectful, but cheese and biscuits at the end of a meal still carries the air of gentility that surrounded the nineteenth-century savoury course. Each host has their own sense of when it would be suitable to serve shortbread or Bourbons. But most of all, biscuits and a cup of tea are a universal comfort food. When he was a small boy in the 1860s, George Sturt would 'hurry home from morning school so as to have a turn at a certain book that was fascinating me; only, being too hungry to wait for dinner I first provided myself with three or four Osborne biscuits … Thus furnished, I made my way into the Front Room … and there I settled down to read.'[4] This is still how many of us prefer to indulge in a biscuit: with a cup of tea and a good book.

ACKNOWLEDGEMENTS

I owe Ivan Day a huge thank you for generously sharing his biscuit and baking knowledge, recipes, and pictures.

A heartfelt cheer of thanks goes out to Sally, Adam and Emily Norris for lending me a computer when mine broke during lockdown.

For their stories and recipes, tasting my baking efforts and trying out often rather odd recipes as well as help with maths and translation I would like to thank Julie Boagey, Yashaswini Chandra, James Clackson, Agnes Donoghue, Jennifer Donkin, Lee Evans, Ruth Goodall, Claire and Lola James, Renate Lauritzen, Frances Magee, Sara Magee, Susan McCrossan, David Mond, Glenda Mooney, Veronique Mottier, Abdul Paliwala, Anne and Jim Secord, Andrea Shimmen, Jessica Sparato, Kathryn Wearing and Alison White.

Jörg Hensgen edited this book with his usual good humour and rigour for which I am extremely grateful. At the Bodley Head I would also like to thank Stuart Williams, Lauren Howard, Jasmine Marsh and Mollie Stewart. I am as always grateful to my agent Clare Alexander for her encouragement and support.

I thank my sister Sarah Burwood for her helpful comments on the first draft, proof reading, and the spirit-lifting presents and conversation. I am as ever grateful to Thomas Seidel, stalwart provider of tea, research and constructive criticism.

NOTES AND REFERENCES

Preface

1 Bligh, *Mutiny on the Bounty*, p.150.
2 Londeix, *Le Biscuit et son Marché*, p.185.
3 Statista.

Chapter 1: In which the slaves in the Modestus bakery over-bake their bread

1 Cited by Knapp, *Invisible Romans*, p.133.
2 Beard, *Pompeii*, pp.120–21, 172.
3 Higman, *How Food Made History*, p.12.
4 Hornsey, *A History of Beer and Brewing*, pp.83–4.
5 Dalby, *Siren Feasts*, pp.164–5.
6 Thévenot, *The Travels of Monsieur de Thévenot*, pp.106–7.
7 Garnsey, *Food and Society in Classical Antiquity*, p.120.
8 Beard, *Pompeii*, p.170.
9 Garnsey, 'Malnutrition in the Ancient World', p.31.
10 Spit bread is the ancestor of the German speciality *Baumkuchen*.
11 Athenaeus, *The Deipnosophistae*.
12 Ibid.
13 Pitassi, *The Roman Navy*, p.78.
14 Jones, *Feast*, p.263.
15 Cited by Athenaeus, *The Deipnosophistae*.
16 Jones, *Feast*, pp.267–8.

17 Walters, 'The world, the flesh and the Devil', pp.194–5.

18 Dembinska, 'Diet', p.439; The Rule of Pachomius.

19 Walters, 'The world, the flesh and the Devil', pp.194–5.

20 Dembinska, 'Diet', p.447.

21 Aglaia, 'Paximadia (Barley Biscuits)', p.208.

22 Dembinska, 'Diet', p.439.

23 Dalby, *Siren Feasts*, p.197.

24 *OED*. The *Promptorium Parvulorum* (*Storehouse for Children*), by a friar from Lynn, Norfolk, was completed in 1440 and published repeatedly in the early 16th century. It is regarded as a major reference work for the vocabulary of late-medieval England.

25 Mason, 'By bread alone?', p.70.

26 Polo and Boni, *The Travels of Marco Polo*, p.59.

27 Fiennes, *Through England on a Side Saddle*, pp.152–3.

28 Brears, 'Traditional food in the Lake Counties', p.88.

29 Fermor, *Words of Mercury*.

30 Louis, 'Paximadia'.

31 Ibid.

Chapter 2: In which Ibrahim bin al-Mahdi writes a poem about sweet biscuits

1 Nasrallah, *Annals of the Caliph's Kitchens*, pp.124–5.

2 Alcock, '"All sugar from the waves"', p.11.

3 Mason, *Sugar-plums and Sherbet*, p.44.

4 Sato, *Sugar in the Social Life of Medieval Islam*, pp.15–22.

5 Ibid., pp.41–6.

6 Laudan, *Cuisine and Empire*, p.138.

7 Schoenfeldt, 'Fables of the belly in early modern England', p.253.

8 Winter, *Spices and Comfits*, p.345; Savage-Smith, 'Medicine in medieval Islam', pp.145, 167; Ragep, 'Islamic culture and the natural sciences', pp.27–40.

9 Sato, *Sugar in the Social Life of Medieval Islam*, pp.142–7.

10 Nasrallah, *Annals of the Caliph's Kitchens*, pp.94, 100–4, 113, 165.

11 His proper name was Abu al-Hasan al-Mukhtar al-Hasan. Ibid., pp.158–62.

12 Nasrallah, *Annals of the Caliph's Kitchens*, pp.562–3.

13 Laudan, *Cuisine and Empire*, p.139.

14 Nasrallah, *Annals of the Caliph's Kitchens*, pp.426–7.

15 Ibid., pp.124–5.

16 Sato, *Sugar in the Social Life of Medieval Islam*, pp.66, 76.

17 Ibid., pp.58, 122–4.
18 Ibid., pp.154, 166–7.
19 Nasrallah, *Annals of the Caliph's Kitchens*, pp.562–3.

Chapter 3: In which Bartolomeo Scappi serves Pope Pius IV *mostaccioli* biscuits

1 Astarita, *The Italian Baroque Table*, p.64.
2 Sato, *Sugar in the Social Life of Medieval Islam*, p.30.
3 Grewe, 'Catalan cuisine', p.163.
4 Ibid.
5 Parry, *The Age of Reconnaissance*, pp.39–44.
6 Burnett, 'Translation and transmission of Greek and Islamic science', p.344; Kedar and Kohlberg, 'The intercultural career of Theodore of Antioch', pp.169–70.
7 Ballerini (ed.), *The Art of Cooking*, p.15; Milham, *Platina*, p.51.
8 Milham, *Platina*, pp.52, 55.
9 Ibid., p.157.
10 Ballerini (ed.), *The Art of Cooking*, p.29.
11 Milham, *Platina*, p.157.
12 Ballerini (ed.), *The Art of Cooking*, p.19.
13 Miller, *A Modern History of the Stomach*, p.7.
14 Milham, *Platina*, p.463.
15 Riley, *The Oxford Companion to Italian Food*, p.334.
16 Stefani, *L'Arte di ben cucinare*, p. 77; Astarita, *The Italian Baroque Table*, p.49.
17 Ibid., pp.49, 85, 210.
18 Stefani, *L'Arte di ben cucinare*, p.77.
19 Astarita, *The Italian Baroque Table*, p.212.
20 Ballerini (ed.), *The Art of Cooking*, p.87.
21 Milham, *Platina*, p.337.
22 Goldstein, *The Oxford Companion to Sugar and Sweets*, p.779.
23 Abbott, *Sugar*, p.22.
24 Astarita, *The Italian Baroque Table*, p.111; McIver, *Cooking and Eating*, p.121.
25 Astarita, *The Italian Baroque Table*, p.221.
26 Ibid., pp.4–5.
27 Evangelisti, 'Monastic poverty and material culture', pp.2–5.
28 Laudan, *Cuisine and Empire*, pp.175–7; Goldstein, *The Oxford Companion to Sugar and Sweets*, pp.181–2.
29 Simeti and Grammatico, *Bitter Almonds*, p.13.
30 Ibid., p.32.

31 Ibid., p.22.
32 Ibid., p.51.
33 Ibid., p.32.
34 Ibid., pp.33–4.
35 Ibid., p.30.
36 Schino, 'The waning of sexually allusive monastic confectionery', pp.69–71.
37 Thanks are due to Ivan Day for telling me about this recipe. A clip of him making these biscuits can be found at 'Pride and Prejudice: having a Ball', https://www.bbc.co.uk/programmes/p018rdvx. See also Ivan Day, 'Biscuits'.

Wafers and Waffles

1   Brears, *Cooking and Dining*, p.355.
2   Moor, 'The wafer and its roots', p.123.
3   Ibid.
4   Ibid., p.125.
5   Ibid., p.120.
6   Day, *Eat, Drink and Be Merry*, p.55.
7   Alcock,"All sugar from the waves"', p.12; Walvin, *How Sugar Corrupted the World*, p.9.
8   Hieatt and Butler, (eds.), *Curye on Inglysch*, p.3.
9   Power, *The Goodman of Paris*, pp.238, 306; Brears, *Cooking and Dining*, p.355.
10 Brears, *Cooking and Dining*, p. 343.
11 Moor, 'The wafer and its roots', p.120.
12 Barnes and Rose, *Matters of Taste*, p.24.

Chapter 4: In which Lady Elinor Fettiplace bakes 'stif bisket bread'

1   Spurling; *Elinor Fettiplace's Receipt Book;* Mason, 'William Alexis Jarrin', p.55; Moody, *The Private Life of an Elizabethan Lady*, p.xxxiv.
2   Colquhoun, *Taste*, p.105.
3   Spurling, *Elinor Fettiplace's Receipt Book*, pp.98, 113, 161–70.
4   Day, *Eat, Drink and Be Merry*, p.59.
5   Alexis of Piemont, *The Secrets of Maister Alexis of Piemont*; Astarita, *The Italian Baroque Table*, p.49.
6   Spurling, *Lady Fettiplace's Receipt Book*, pp.117–22.
7   Alexis of Piemont, *The Secrets of the Reverende Maister Alexis of Piemont*, pp.89–90.
8   Hamlyn, *The Recipes of Hannah Woolley*, p.138.
9   Spurling, *Elinor Fettiplace's Receipt Book*, pp.1–10, 29.

10 Astarita, *The Italian Baroque Table*, p.6.
11 Spurling, *Elinor Fettiplace's Receipt Book*, pp.1–3.
12 Thirsk, *Food in Early Modern England*, pp.9–10.
13 Astarita, *The Italian Baroque Table*, p.10.
14 Spurling, *Elinor Fettiplace's Receipt Book*, pp.244–5.
15 Curtin, *The Rise and Fall of the Plantation Complex*, pp.18–26.
16 Stols, 'The expansion of the sugar market in Western Europe', pp.243–8, 275; Laudan, *Cuisine and Empire*, p.190; Thirsk, *Food in Early Modern England*, p.56.
17 Winter, *Spices and Comfits*, p.132.
18 Brears, *The Gentlewoman's Kitchen*, p.6.
19 Masson, *The Compleat Cook*, p.5 (my italics)
20 Spurling, *Elinor Fettiplace's Receipt Book*, p.165.
21 Ibid., pp.115, 158.
22 Day, *Eat, Drink and Be* Merry, p.47.
23 Zahedieh, *The Capital and the Colonies*, p.221.
24 Masson, *The Compleat Cook*, pp.15–16.
25 The spelling has been modernised. Masson, *The Compleat Cook*, p.275.
26 Ibid., p.11.
27 Ibid, pp.12–13.
28 Ibid., pp.256–8.
29 Ibid., pp.259, 262–4.
30 Spurling, *Elinor Fettiplace's Receipt Book*, pp.118–19.
31 Masson, *The Compleat Cook*, pp.266, 275–6.
32 Ibid., p.259.
33 Ibid., pp.266–7.
34 Ibid., p.259.
35 Mintz, *Sweetness and Power*, p.135.
36 Zahedieh, *The Capital and the Colonies*, p.225.
37 Driver and Berredale-Johnson, *Pepys at Table*, p.112.
38 Prochaska and Prochaska, *Margaretta Acworth's Georgian Cookery Book*, pp.120, 124.

Gingerbread

1 Morley, *Memoirs of Bartholomew Fair*, pp.161–2.
2 Mason and Brown, *Traditional Foods*, p.252.
3 Stellingwerf, *The Gingerbread Book*, p.10.
4 Morley, *Memoirs of Bartholomew Fair*, pp.16–24.
5 Chapman, *Patrons and Patron Saints*, p.56.

6   Hopkins and Ostovich, *Magical Transformations*, p.210.
7   Hess, *Martha Washington's Booke of Cookery*, p.343.
8   Parry, *The Age of Reconnaissance*, pp.39–44; Stellingwerf, *The Gingerbread Book*, p.10.
9   Kelly, *Festive Baking*, p.50.
10 Riley, 'Eat Your Words!', p.56; Stellingwerf, *The Gingerbread Book*, p.9.
11 Mason and Brown, *Traditional Foods*, pp.249, 256.
12 Stead, 'Prodigal Frugality', pp.161–2.
13 Griffin, 'Venetian treacle', pp.117–18.
14 Hess, *Martha Washington's Booke of Cookery*, p.201.
15 Hopkins and Ostovich, *Magical Transformations*, p.203.
16 Stead, 'Prodigal Frugality', pp.182–3.
17 Pollard, 'Lancashire's Heritage', p.136.
18 Willcox, *The Bakers' Company of Coventry*, p.20.
19 Sturt, *A Small Boy in the Sixties*, p.105.
20 Morley, *Memoirs of Bartholomew Fair*, pp.161–2.
21 Brears, *The Gentlewoman's Kitchen*, pp.72–3.

Chapter 5: In which Spanish fishermen make biscuit soup on the Barbary coast

1   St Bernadino of Siena, cited by Fraser, *The Six Wives of Henry VIII*, p.13.
2   Abreu de Galindo, *The History of the Discovery of the Canary Islands*, pp.334–8.
3   Dembinska, 'Diet', p.447.
4   Villamont, *Les Voyages du seigneur de Villamont,* p.329.
5   Stead, 'Navy blues', p.93.
6   Ibid., p.72.
7   Gosnell, *Before the Mast*, pp.40–1.
8   Robertson, 'Mariner's mealtimes', p.15.
9   Lane, *Venice*, pp.43, 58–60.
10 Ibid., p.163.
11 Davis, *Shipbuilders of the Venetian Arsenal*, p.169; Swinburne, 'Dancing with the mermaids', p.309; Rose, *Medieval Naval Warfare*, p.20.
12 Rose, *Medieval Naval Warfare*, p.20.
13 Finkel, *The Administration of Warfare*, p.172.
14 Sezgin, 'The provision of hard biscuits', pp.28–30.
15 Malcolm, *Agents of Empire*, p.37.
16 Parry, *The Age of Reconnaissance*, p.72.
17 Ibid., p.20.
18 Ibid., pp.87–94.

19 Ibid., pp.53–68.
20 Ibid., p.38.
21 Ibid., p.74.
22 Ibid., p.12.
23 Ibid., p.158. The records may have been removed by the Braganza family in an attempt to play down the role of King John II in the discovery of the sea route to India. The Braganzas sought to amplify the achievement of their relation, Manuel I, who was king in 1498 when Vasco da Gama reached India. Coben, 'The Events that led to the Treaty of Tordesillas,' p.157.
24 Parry, *The Age of Reconnaissance*, p.140.
25 Ravenstein, *A Journal of the First Voyage of Vasco Da Gama*, p.166.
26 Parry, *The Age of Reconnaissance*, p.140.
27 Corréa, *The Three Voyages of Vasco da Gama*, pp.71–2.
28 Bergreen, *Over the Edge of the World*, pp.128–202.
29 Keay, *The Spice Route*, pp.179–80.
30 Phillips, *Six Galleons*, pp.97–9.
31 Kistemaker, 'Amsterdam's municipal control of food supplies', p.226.
32 Corréa, *The Three Voyages of Vasco da Gama*, p.143.
33 Macdonald, *From Boiled Beef*, p.5; Phillips, *Six Galleons*, p.169.
34 Collingham, *The Hungry Empire*, pp.115–16.
35 Kaufmann, *Black Tudors*, p.153.
36 Fury, *Tides in the Affairs of Men*, p.139.
37 Robertson, 'Mariner's mealtimes', p.26.
38 Shakespeare, *As You Like It*, Act II, Scene 7.
39 Macdonald, *Feeding Nelson's Navy*, pp.18, 98.
40 Hibbert, *Nelson*, p.11.
41 Macdonald, *Feeding Nelson's Navy*, p.98.
42 Stead, 'Navy blues', p.80.
43 Banks, *Journal of the Right Hon. Sir Joseph Banks*, p.181.
44 Macdonald, *Feeding Nelson's Navy*, pp.9–10.
45 Stead, 'Navy blues', p.86.
46 Knight and Wilcox, *Sustaining the Fleet*, p.22.
47 Baugh, *British Naval Administration*, p.451.
48 Corley, 'Nutrition, technology and the British biscuit industry', p.14.
49 Macdonald, *The British Navy's Victualling Board*, pp.1, 62; Falconer, *A New Universal Dictionary of the Marine*, p.40; Corley, *Quaker Enterprise in Biscuits*, pp.46–8.
50 Shepherd, *Pickled, Potted and Canned*, p.199.
51 Old Sailor, *Greenwich Hospital*, p.27.

52 Smollett, *Roderick Random*.
53 Lloyd, *The British Seaman*, p.208.
54 Knight and Wilcox, *Sustaining the Fleet*, pp.47, 52; Hall, *British Strategy in the Napoleonic* War, pp.37–8.
55 Corley, *Quaker Enterprise in Biscuits*, p.48.
56 Hall, *British Strategy in the Napoleonic War*, p.41.
57 Ibid., p.40.
58 Macdonald, *The British Navy's Victualling Board*, p.79.
59 Knight and Wilcox, *Sustaining the Fleet*, p.86.
60 Ibid., p.93.
61 Collingham, *The Hungry Empire*, pp.174–6.
62 Nowrojee, *Journal of a Residence in Great Britain*, pp.399–401; Corley, *Quaker Enterprise in Biscuits*, pp.51–2.
63 MacDougall, 'William Scamp and his early naval works', p.30.

Chapter 6: In which Joseph Banks enjoys fish and biscuit boiled for about an hour

1   Banks, *Joseph Banks in Newfoundland*, p.137.
2   Collingham, *The Hungry Empire*, pp.3–11.
3   *Henry IV*, Part II, Scene 3.
4   Stavely and Fitzgerald, *America's Founding Food*, pp.95–6.
5   Pope, *Fish into Wine*, p.366.
6   Collingham, *The Hungry Empire*, pp.25–6.
7   Tye, '"A poor man's meal"', pp.338, 340.
8   Lacombe, '"A continuall and dayly table', p.669–87.
9   Clap, *Relating some of God's Remarkable Providence to him in bringing him into New England*, p.14.
10 Vickers, *Farmers and Fishermen*, p.100.
11 Collingham, *The Hungry Empire*, p.38.
12 Stavely and Fitzgerald, *America's Founding Food*, p.89.
13 Melville, *Moby Dick*, p.67.
14 See Hess, *Martha Washington's Booke of Cookery*.
15 Simmons, *American Cookery*; Rutledge, *The Carolina Housewife*; Spaulding and Spaulding (eds.), *Civil War Recipes*.
16 Astarita, *The Italian Baroque Table*, p.221.
17 Shepherd, *Pickled, Potted and Canned*, p.48
18 Schama, *The Embarrassment of Riches*, p.552.

19 Trentmann, *Empire of Things*, pp.54–5.
20 Schama, *The Embarrassment of Riches*, p.165.
21 White, *Good English Food*, p.189.
22 Barnes and Rose, *Matters of Taste*, pp.1–2, 24.
23 Simmons, *American Cookery*; Sellick, *The Imperial African Cookery Book*.
24 Ibid., p.332.
25 Mason and Brown, *Traditional Foods*, p.287.
26 David, *English Bread and Yeast Cookery*, pp.490–2; Mason and Brown, *Traditional Foods of Britain*, pp.241, 263.
27 Simmons, *American Cookery*.
28 Sellick, *The Imperial African Cookery Book*, pp.328–9.
29 Stavely and Fitzgerald, *America's Founding Food*, pp.242–3.
30 Cobbold, 'The rise of alternative bread leavening technologies', p.32.
31 Dale, *The Cross Timbers*, p.40.
32 Ibid., p.45.
33 Barnes and Rose, *Matters of Taste*, p.110.
34 Stellingwerf, *The Gingerbread Book*, p.13.
35 Stavely and Fitzgerald, *America's Founding Food*, pp.246–7.
36 Smith, *Peanuts*, pp.8–15, 62–3.
37 Farmer, *Boston Cooking-School Cook Book* p.408.

Chapter 7: In which Mrs Elizabeth Raffald opens a confectionery shop in Manchester

1 Lehmann, *The British Housewife*, pp.272–3.
2 Ibid, pp. 271–2.
3 Ibid., p.49–50.
4 Mintz, *Sweetness and Power*, p.67.
5 Burnett, *Liquid Pleasures*, p.53.
6 Woodforde, *The Diary of A Country Parson*, p.145.
7 Baretti was later accused of murdering a ruffian who attacked him in the streets of London by stabbing him with the fruit knife he carried to use during the dessert course. Cited by Aulnoy, *The Lady's Travels into Spain*, p.289.
8 Day, 'Biscuits'.
9 Ibid.
10 Astarita, *The Italian Baroque Table*, p.198.
11 Peterson, *Acquired Taste*, p.164.
12 Lehmann, *The British Housewife*, p.52.

13 Astarita, *The Italian Baroque Table*, p.47.
14 Lehmann, *The British Housewife*, p.97.
15 Cited by Prochaska and Prochaska, *Margaretta Acworth's Georgian Cookery Book*, pp.18–19; Lehmann, *The British Housewife*, p.167.
16 Lehmann, *The British Housewife*, p.198.
17 Day, *Eat, Drink and Be Merry*, p.35.
18 Colquhoun, *Taste*, p.108.
19 Spurling, *Elinor Fettiplace's Receipt Book*, p.158.
20 Goldstein, *The Oxford Companion to Sugar and Sweets*, p.741.
21 Colquhoun, *Taste*, p.229.
22 Raffald, *The Experienced English Housekeeper*, p.296.
23 Masson, *The Compleat Cook*, p.261.
24 Mason and Brown, *Traditional Foods of Britain*, pp.285–6.
25 Masson, *The Compleat Cook*, pp.256, 260–1.
26 Day, *Eat, Drink and Be Merry*, p.63; Spurling, *Elinor Fettiplace's Receipt Book*, pp.223–4.
27 Prochaska and Prochaska, *Margaretta Acworth's Georgian Cookery Book*, pp.10–15, 19.
28 *Leeds Intelligencer*, 6 July 1795.
29 Mason, 'William Alexis Jarrin', p.50.
30 Thackeray, *Vanity Fair*.
31 Davidson, *The Oxford Companion to Food*, p.740.
32 Lehmann, *The British Housewife*, pp.303–14.
33 Ibid., p.320.
34 Cited by Ellis et al., *Empire of Tea*, p.145.
35 Lehmann, *The British Housewife*, p.320.
36 Austen, *Emma*.
37 Gaskell, *The Cranford Chronicles*, pp.92–7.
38 Ibid., p.166.
39 Mason and Brown, *Traditional Foods of Britain*, p.254; Alison White in conversation with the author.
40 Jurafsky, 'Macaroons, Macarons and Macaroni'.
41 Grigson, *Good Things*,
42 Scully, *La Varenne's Cookery*, pp.44–7.

Funeral Biscuits

1   Mortan, 'Gastrobamica', p.13.
2   Latham and Matthews (eds.), *The Diary of Samuel Pepys*, 5, p.91.

3 Brears, 'Arvals, wakes and months minds', p.93.
4 Brears, *The Gentlewoman's Kitchen*, p.74.
5 Brears, 'Arvals, wakes and months minds', p.99.

Chapter 8: In which Henry Mayhew marvels at the fabrication of fancy biscuits by a series of cog-wheels and cranks

1 'The Great International Exhibition', *The Lancet*, 15 October 1862, p.432.
2 Mayhew, *The Shops and Companies of London*, p.13.
3 Ibid., pp.13–15.
4 Ibid., pp.15–17.
5 Burnett, 'The baking industry', p.102.
6 Windsor, *The Quaker Enterprise*, p.104; 'The Huntley & Palmers Collection, Reading Biscuit Town'.
7 Windsor, *The Quaker Enterprise*, p.105; Corley, *Quaker Enterprise in Biscuits*, p.20.
8 Corley, *Quaker Enterprise in Biscuits*, p.19.
9 Ibid., p.20; Windsor, *The Quaker Enterprise*, pp.102–3.
10 Forster, *Rich Desserts and Captain's Thins*, p.18.
11 Wilson, *Swindled*, p.82.
12 Burnett, 'The baking industry', p.103.
13 Forster, *Rich Desserts and Captain's Thins*, p.37.
14 Oddy, 'A nutritional analysis', pp.317–18, 321–2.
15 Forster, *Rich Desserts and Captain's Thins*, pp.22–37.
16 Ibid., p.60.
17 Ibid., pp.31, 38, 51–2.
18 Ibid., p.91.
19 Corley, *Quaker Enterprise in Biscuits*, p.36.
20 Ibid., p.38.
21 Londeix, *Le Biscuit et son Marché*, p.42.
22 Corley, *Quaker Enterprise in Biscuits*, pp.59, 72.
23 Ibid., p.77. When Thomas Huntley died in 1857, his son withdrew from the firm, leaving it in the hands of the Palmer family, although the firm continued to use Huntley's name.
24 Forster, *Rich Desserts and Captain's Thins*, p.136.
25 Corley, *Quaker Enterprise in Biscuits*, p.18.
26 Loeb, *Consuming Angels*, pp.8, 43.
27 Mayhew, *The Shops and Companies of London*, p.13.

28 Burnett, 'The baking industry', p.103.
29 Sala, *Lady Chesterfield's Letters*, pp.75–6.
30 Corley, *Quaker Enterprise in Biscuits*, p.6; Fitzgerald, *Rowntree and the Marketing Revolution*, p.25.
31 Fitzgerald, *Rowntree and the Marketing Revolution*, p.11.
32 Broomfield, *Food and Cooking in Victorian England*, p.19.
33 Forster, *Rich Desserts and Captain's Thins*, p.52; Londeix, *Le Biscuit et son Marché*, p.12.
34 Loeb, *Consuming Angels*, p.7.
35 Nowrojee, *Journal of a Residence in Great Britain*, pp.258–9.
36 Broomfield, *Food and Cooking in Victorian England*, p.43.
37 Sala, *Twice Round the Clock*, p.140.
38 Trollope, *The Three Clerks*.
39 Londeix, *Le Biscuit et son Marché*, p.185.
40 Corley, *Quaker Enterprise in Biscuits*, p.75.
41 Dickens, *The Pickwick Papers*.
42 Gaskell, *The Cranford Chronicles*, p.52.
43 Forster, *Rich Desserts and Captain's Thins*, p.93.
44 Bristed, *Five Years in an English University*, pp.21, 50.
45 Thackeray, 'The Book of Snobs'.
46 Dickens, *Letters*, p.624.
47 Fraser, *Roses in December*, p.35.
48 Mason and Brown, *Traditional Foods*, p.250.
49 Hack, *Tunbridge Wells Biscuits*, p.8.
50 Forster, *Rich Desserts and Captain's Thins*, p.170.
51 Mulvihill, *Ingenious Ireland*, p.439.
52 Fitzgerald, *Rowntree and the Marketing Revolution*, pp.28, 48, 52.
53 Corley, *Quaker Enterprise in Biscuits*, p.161.
54 'Photocopy of a printed booklet listing national agents for H7P biscuits', Huntley & Palmers Collection MS 1490.
55 Corley, *Quaker Enterprise in Biscuits*, p.77.
56 Forster, *Rich Desserts and Captain's Thins*, p.38.
57 Corley, *Quaker Enterprise in Biscuits*, p.77.
58 Forster, *Rich Desserts and Captain's Thins*, p.91.
59 Fitzgerald, *Rowntree and the Marketing Revolution*, p.12.
60 Huntley and Palmers Collection MS 1490; Lázaro, 'Tecnología, empresa y mercado en la fabricacíon española de galletas', n.p.

61 Corley, *Quaker Enterprise in Biscuits*, p.135.
62 Hibbert, 'Garibaldi in England', p.597.
63 Sawyer, 'When Britain fell for Garibaldi'.
64 Records of Peek Frean MS 1216; Forster, *Rich Desserts and Captain's Thins*, p.98.
65 Hill, *Biscuits, Banquets and Bollinger*, pp.242–8, 253.
66 Ibid., p.258.
67 Corley, *Quaker Enterprise in Biscuits*, pp.135, 161.
68 Williams, 'Outward facing', p.59.
69 Ibid., p.62.
70 Corley, *Quaker Enterprise in Biscuits*, p.135.
71 Fitzgerald, *Rowntree and the Marketing Revolution*, p.31.
72 Forster, *Rich Desserts and Captain's Thins*, p.149.
73 Williams, 'Outward facing', p.62.
74 Whiteley, General Price List October 1913, Vol. 2, pp.1212–15.
75 Fitzgerald, *Rowntree and the Marketing Revolution*, p.11.
76 Corley, *Quaker Enterprise in Biscuits*, p.97; 'The Huntley & Palmers Collection, Reading Biscuit Town'; Forster, *Rich Desserts and Captain's Thins*, p.55.
77 Fitzgerald, *Rowntree and the Marketing Revolution*, pp.6–7.
78 Forster, *Rich Desserts and Captain's Thins*, pp.64–5.
79 Corley, *Quaker Enterprise in Biscuits*, p.101.
80 Ibid., p.59.
81 Forster, *Rich Desserts and Captain's Thins*, p.211.
82 Orwell, *The Road to Wigan Pier*, p.86.
83 Oddy, 'A nutritional analysis', p.322.
84 Dickens, *Sketches by Boz*.
85 Mayhew, *Selections from London Labour*, pp.13–14.
86 Ibid., pp.94–5.
87 Fitzgerald, *Rowntree and the Marketing Revolution*, p.21.
88 Mayhew, *The Shops and Companies of London*, p.16.
89 Dickens, 'Hard Times'.

Digestive Biscuits

1 Latham and Matthews (eds.), *The Diary of Samuel Pepys*, Vol. 6, p.224.
2 Woolley, *The Queen-like Closet*.
3 Dickens, *Pickwick Papers*.
4 Austen, *Emma*.

5 Rousseau, 'Coleridge's dreaming gut,' pp.106–7.
6 Thornton, *John Abernethy*, pp.72–6; Miller, *A Modern History of the Stomach*, pp.9, 15, 34.
7 Miller, *A Modern History of the Stomach*, p.34.
8 Miller, 'Digesting in the long eighteenth century', p.73.
9 Thornton, *John Abernethy*, p.90.
10 Miller, 'Digesting in the long eighteenth century', p.21.
11 Whiting, *Memoirs of a Stomach*.
12 Thornton, *John Abernethy*, p.114.
13 Ibid., p.127; Mason and Brown, *The Taste of Britain*, p.377.
14 Dacome, 'Useless and pernicious matter', pp.196–7.
15 Whiting, *Memoirs of a Stomach*, p.129.
16 Ibid., p.135.
17 Queen Victoria's Journals, 11 September 1838 and 10 January 1839.
18 Hill, *Biscuits, Banquets and Bollinger*, pp.240–42.
19 Ibid., p.242. In fact, captain's biscuits were also made with leavened or fermented dough.
20 Miller, 'Digesting in the long eighteenth century', pp.67–8.
21 Cobbold, 'The rise of alternative bread leavening technologies', pp.22–5.
22 Ibid., p.29.
23 Ibid., p.33.
24 17 November 1860, cited by ibid., p.36.
25 Forster, *Rich Desserts and Captain's Thins*, p.124.
26 Cobbold, 'The rise of alternative bread leavening technologies', p.26.
27 Pugh, *A Clear and Simple Vision*, pp.1–3.
28 Corley, *Quaker Enterprise in Biscuits*, p.204.
29 'This is why digestives are called digestives'.
30 Smith, *Eating History*, p.33.
31 *The Lancet*, 30 August 1862, p.245.
32 Fitzgerald, *The Knox Brothers*, p.83.
33 Swinburne, 'Nothing but the best', p.198.
34 *Arnott's Biscuits Case Study*, p.2.
35 Corley, *Quaker Enterprise in Biscuits*, p.48.
36 Hill, *Biscuits, Banquets and Bollinger*, p.242.
37 Wiebe, *Benjamin Disraeli*, p.174.
38 Hill, *Biscuits, Banquets and Bollinger*, p.274.
39 Waugh, *Brideshead Revisited*, p.99.

Chapter 9: In which the English drown the French market with cataracts of plain and fancy biscuits

1 Sala, *Paris Herself Again*, p.345.
2 Ibid.
3 Corley, *Quaker Enterprise in Biscuits*, p.85.
4 Bradley, *Enlightened Entrepreneurs*, p.69.
5 Corley, *Quaker Enterprise in Biscuits*, pp.85–9.
6 Sala, *Paris Herself Again*, p.345.
7 Corley, *Quaker Enterprise in Biscuits*, p.84.
8 Sala, *Paris Herself Again*, p.226.
9 Forster, *Rich Desserts and Captain's Thins*, pp.94–5.
10 Sala, *Paris Herself Again*, p.128.
11 Corley, *Quaker Enterprise in Biscuits*, p.91; Forster, *Rich Desserts and Captain's Thins*, p.138.
12 Londeix, *Le Biscuit et son Marché*, p.122.
13 Ibid., pp.43–5.
14 Ibid., pp.22–3; Passemiers, 'A history of De Beukelaer's Fabrieken', p.25.
15 Lázaro, 'Tecnología, empresa y mercado en la fabricacíon española de galletas'.
16 Passemiers, 'A history of De Beukelaer's Fabrieken', p.26.
17 Lázaro, 'Tecnología, empresa y mercado en la fabricacíon española de galletas'.
18 Ibid.; Londeix, *Le Biscuit et son Marché*, pp.27, 33, 43.
19 Passemiers, 'A history of De Beukelaer's Fabrieken', pp.35–9, 42.
20 'The Bahlsen Family'.
21 Londeix, *Le Biscuit et son Marché*, p.132.
22 Ibid., pp.139, 141.
23 Corley, *Quaker Enterprise in Biscuits*, p.89.
24 Londeix, *Le Biscuit et son Marché*, p.98.
25 Ibid., p.99.
26 Corley, *Quaker Enterprise in Biscuits*, pp.159.
27 Brooke, *Relations and Complications*, p.6.
28 Windsor, *The Quaker Enterprise*, p.121; Corley, *Quaker Enterprise in Biscuits*, p.141; 'What happened to Huntley & Palmers Breakfast Biscuits?'.
29 'Zwieback'.
30 'Zwieback, Steine, Schriftchen: Briefbeigaben'.
31 Toettchen, 'Brandt-Zwiebak und westfälischer Zwieback pudding'.
32 'Friedrichsdorf – die Stadt des Zwiebacks'.
33 Brooke, *Relations and Complications*, p.24.

34 Whorton, *Inner Hygiene*, p.167.
35 Corley, *Quaker Enterprise in Biscuits*, p.141.
36 Londeix, *Le Biscuit et son Marché*, p.126.
37 Corley, *Quaker Enterprise in Biscuits*, p.141.
38 Ibid., pp.159, 162.
39 Loeb, *Consuming Angels*, p.32.
40 Londeix, *Le Biscuit et son Marché*, pp.101–2.
41 Loeb, *Consuming Angels*, pp.7–8.
42 Davidoff and Hall, *Family Fortunes*, pp.23–5.
43 Londeix, *Le Biscuit et son Marché*, p.128.
44 Loeb, *Consuming Angels*, p.127.
45 Londeix, *Le Biscuit et son Marché*, p.126.
46 Ibid., p 85.
47 Cited by Aglaia, 'Paximadia (Barley Biscuits)', p.208.
48 Thanks are due to Renate Lauritzen and her dog Cello for this recipe.

Chapter 10: In which King Mwanga puts the lid on one of John Roscoe's last tins of Osborne biscuits and carries them home

1   Sala, *Paris Herself Again*, pp.345–6.
2   Roscoe, *Twenty-five Years in East Africa*, p.117.
3   Ibid.
4   Ibid., p.119.
5   Zahedieh, *The Capital and the Colonies*, p.275.
6   St John, *The Making of the Raj*, pp.72–3.
7   Forster, *Rich Desserts and Captain's Thins*, pp.94–5, 23; Corley, *Quaker Enterprise in Biscuits*, pp.83–4.
8   Corley, *Quaker Enterprise in Biscuits*, p.93.
9   Ibid., p.92.
10 Ibid., pp.90–1.
11 'Travel Diaries of Helen Caddick'.
12 *Cunard Steam Ship Album and Guide* (1875), cited by Corley, *Quaker Enterprise in Biscuits*, p.160.
13 Sala, *Paris Herself Again*, pp.345–6.
14 'About H&P in Scott's last camp and a letter from Scott on 20 October 1911 extolling the virtues of H&P biscuits on Polar Expedition', Huntley and Palmers Collection MS 1490.
15 Lumholtz, *Through Central Borneo*, pp.57–9.

16 Postans, *Hints to Cadets*, pp.14–15.
17 Johnson, *The Stranger in India*, I, p.164.
18 Collingham, *Imperial Bodies*, p.157.
19 Steel and Gardiner, *The Complete Indian Housekeeper and Cook*.
20 Collingham, *Imperial Bodies*, pp.52–3.
21 Morgan, *Sweet and Bitter Island* p.121.
22 Wilk, *Home Cooking in the Global Village*, pp.48–9.
23 *Cunard Steam Ship Album and Guide* (1875), cited by Corley, *Quaker Enterprise in Biscuits*, p.160.
24 Brooks, *Eurafricans in Western Africa*, pp.203–4.
25 Waddell, *Among the Himalayas*, p.48.
26 Ray, *Culinary Culture in Colonial India*, p.23.
27 Collingham, *Imperial Bodies*, p.186.
28 Gandhi, *The Collected Works*, p.22.
29 Collingham, *Curry*, pp.201–4.
30 Tandon, *Punjabi Century*, p.78.
31 Ibid.
32 Collingham, *Curry*, pp.194–7.
33 Jeffrey, *Politics, Women and Well-Being*, p.209.
34 Collingham, *Curry*, p.203.
35 Ray, *Culinary Culture in Colonial India*, pp.56–7.
36 Achaya, *The Food Industries of British India*, pp.194–5.
37 Wickramasinghe, *Dressing the Colonised Body*, p.63.
38 Ray, *Culinary Culture in Colonial India*, pp.89–90.
39 Manji, *Memoirs of a Biscuit Baron*.
40 Abdul Paliwala in conversation with the author.
41 Biney, 'The development of Kwame Nkrumah's political thought in exile', p.86.

Biscuit Tins

1 Franklin, *British Biscuit Tins*, pp.15–19; Franklin, 'Biscuit tins', p.120.
2 Franklin, 'Biscuit tins', p.123.
3 Ibid., p.120.
4 Corley, *Quaker Enterprise in Biscuits*, p.215.
5 Franklin, 'Biscuit tins', p.123.
6 Ibid., p.125.
7 Corley, *Quaker Enterprise in Biscuits*, p.94.
8 Redesdale, *Memories*, II, p.170–1.

9   Diary (No. 7) of the Rev John W Lloyd, Empire online.
10 Corley, *Quaker Enterprise in Biscuits*, p.94.
11 Redesdale, *Memories*, Vol. II, p.740.
12 Sword, Reading Museum.
13 Wenzel, *House Decoration in Nubia*, pp.131–51.
14 Huntley & Palmers biscuit tin reused as the sound box of an African thumb piano, early 20th century, Reading Museum.
15 Muller, Nazma. 'Pan! Our music odyssey: a steelband story', pp.136–9,163.
16 Guise, *Six Years in Bolivia*, pp.117–19.
17 Duff, *The Shy Princess*, p.173.
18 Hands, *Thomas Hardy*, p.31; Tomalin, *Thomas Hardy*, p.372.
19 Greenhalgh, *The Military and Colonial Destruction*, p.285.
20 Ibid., p.74.
21 Queen Victoria's Journals, 12 October 1879, Balmoral Castle.
22 Glover, *The Fateful Battle Line*.
23 Harley, *Bully Beef and Biscuits*.
24 Paxman, *Great Britain's War*.
25 Delaforce, *The Black Bull*, p.69.
26 Crimp, *The Diary of a Desert Rat*, pp.38–9.
27 Carr, 'The archaeology of occupation', p.163–4.
28 MCR-1, Miniature Communications Receiver.
29 Collingham, *The Taste of War*, p.282.
30 Frei, 'Japan remembers the Malaya campaign', p.156.

Chapter 11: In which May Hanaphy gives every penny of the 11s. 6d she earned at Jacob's to her mother

1   For May Hanaphy's interview see Kearns, *Dublin Voices*, pp.143–9.
2   For Harry Brierton's interview see ibid., pp.164–9.
3   Corley, *Quaker Enterprise in Biscuits*, p.97.
4   Mort, *Dangerous Sexualities*, pp.37–8.
5   Corley, *Quaker Enterprise in Biscuits*, p.176.
6   Raymond, 'Responses of female industrial workers', pp.128–9.
7   Londeix, *Le Biscuit et son Marché*, p.63.
8   Forster, *Rich Desserts and Captain's Thins*, pp.137–8.
9   Ibid.; Raymond, 'Responses of female industrial workers', pp.127–30; Santich, *In the Land of the Magic Pudding*, pp.170–2.
10 McCaffrey, 'Jacob's women workers', p.118.

11 Forster, *Rich Desserts and Captain's Thins*, pp.173–4.
12 McCaffrey, 'Jacob's women workers,' p.121.
13 Arrington, 'Revolutionary Genesis?' pp.42–3.
14 Ibid.
15 Foy and Barton, *The Easter Rising*, Ch. 5.
16 'The Huntley & Palmers Collection, Reading Biscuit Town'.
17 'Recollections, Crawford's Biscuits, Elbe Street, Leith'.
18 Pugh, *A Clear and Simple Vision*, p.29.
19 Corley, *Quaker Enterprise in Biscuits*, p.278.
20 Pugh, *A Clear and Simple Vision*, p.40.
21 Botton, *The Pleasures and Sorrows of Work*, p.92.
22 Ibid., p.76.
23 Ibid., pp.76–8.
24 Ibid., pp.80–4.
25 Mulvihill, *Ingenious Ireland*, p.439; Cahn, *Out of the Cracker Barrel*, p.101–103.

Chapter 12: In which Private G. L. Verney has fried corned beef and biscuit for breakfast, cold bully beef and biscuit for lunch and bully beef and biscuit stew for supper

1 Reynolds, *Anzac Biscuits*, p.42.
2 Roth, *The Logistics of the Roman Army*, pp.50, 77–8.
3 Garnsey, *Food and Society in Classical Antiquity*, p.120; Krentz, 'War', pp.151, 165.
4 Pitassi, *The Roman Navy*, p.78.
5 Roth, *The Logistics of the Roman Army*, p.45.
6 Déry, 'Food and the Roman army,' p.84.
7 Roth, *The Logistics of the Roman Army*, pp. 71–2.
8 Ibid., p.69.
9 Ibid., pp.70–4; Pryor, 'Introduction', p.15.
10 Goldsworthy, 'War', pp.103–4.
11 Erdkamp, *Hunger and the Sword*, p.36; Pollard, *Soldiers, Cities and Civilians in Roman Syria*, pp.108, 225; Greatrex, *Rome and Persia at* War, p.111.
12 Warner, *Richard II*, p.10.
13 Harari, 'Strategy and supply', pp.323–4.
14 Russell, *Who Made the Scottish Enlightenment?*
15 Roth, *The Logistics of the Roman Army*, pp.68–9.
16 Perjés. 'Army provisioning', p.26.
17 Ibid., p.25.

18 Grimmelshausen, *Der abenteuerliche Simplicissimus.*
19 Perjés, 'Army provisioning', pp.33–4.
20 Firth, *Cromwell's Army*, p.211.
21 Nusbacher, 'Civil supply in the civil war', p.147.
22 Ibid., p.150.
23 Ibid., pp.155–6.
24 Ibid., p.153.
25 Ibid., p.156.
26 Ibid., p.155.
27 Ibid., p.148; Firth, *Cromwell's Army*, pp.224–5.
28 Firth, *Cromwell's Army*, p.223.
29 Perjés, 'Army provisioning', p.27.
30 Erdkamp, *Hunger and the Sword*, p.36.
31 Blaze, *Life in Napoleon's Army*, p.22.
32 Ibid., p.32.
33 Knight and Wilcox, *Sustaining the Fleet*, p.82.
34 Duffett, *The Stomach for Fighting*, pp.29–31.
35 Ibid., pp.37–8.
36 Ibid., p.109.
37 Ibid., p.27.
38 Corley, *Quaker Enterprise in Biscuits*, p.182.
39 Duffett, *The Stomach for Fighting*, p.38.
40 Smith, 'Narrative and identity at the Front', p.138.
41 Ibid., pp.137–8.
42 Corley, *Quaker Enterprise in Biscuits*, p.182.
43 'Chiltonian Ltd'.
44 Corley, *Quaker Enterprise in Biscuits*, pp.137, 200.
45 Waterhouse, 'Rail-Head'.
46 Duffett, *The Stomach for Fighting*, p.122.
47 Ibid., p.160.
48 Ibid., pp.114–15.
49 Ibid., pp.167–70.
50 Reynolds, *Anzac Biscuits*, pp.42–3.
51 Duffett, *The Stomach for Fighting*, pp.109, 114–16.
52 Private Offe made it home with trench fever in 1917. Reynolds, *Anzac Biscuits*, pp.50–1.
53 Ellis, *World War II*, p.274.
54 G. L. Verney, *The Desert Rats* (1954), cited in ibid., pp.272–3.

55 R. P. Evans Papers, Imperial War Museum, p.25.
56 Page, 'Six Years of my Life', Imperial War Museum, p.30.
57 Collingham, *The Taste of War*, p.403–4.
58 Page, 'Six Years of my Life', Imperial War Museum, p.47.
59 Cross, *Jungle Warfare*, p.34.
60 Stauffer, *The Quartermaster Corps*, p.231.
61 Collingham, *The Taste of War*, p.443.
62 Duffett, *The Stomach for Fighting*, pp.128–9.
63 Wyatt, 'The Great military beans fatigue'.
64 Ibid.

Anzac Biscuits

1   Andrea Shimmen in conversation with the author.
2   Supski, 'Anzac biscuits', p.51.
3   Gofton, 'The Anzac Biscuit myth'.
4   Reynolds, *Anzac Biscuits*, p.65.
5   Ibid., p.62.
6   Ibid., pp.35–7.
7   Gofton, 'The Anzac Biscuit myth'.
8   Reynolds, *Anzac Biscuits*, p.9.
9   Ibid., pp.84–6.
10 Ibid., p.72.

Chapter 13: In which Pam Ashford anxiously stockpiles biscuits

1   Dunbar, *More Than a Puff of Smoke*, p.17.
2   Londeix, *Le Biscuit et son Marché*, p.153.
3   Corley, *Quaker Enterprise in Biscuits*, p.197.
4   Crawford and Broadley, *The People's Food*, p.61.
5   Forster, *Rich Desserts and Captain's Thins*, pp.202–11.
6   Howard, *The Light Years*, p.72.
7   Hack, *Tunbridge Wells Biscuits*; Forster, *Rich Desserts and Captain's Thins*, p.235.
8   Graves and Hodge, *The Long Week-End*, p.14; Corley, *Quaker Enterprise in Biscuits*, p.221.
9   Elizabeth David, *Spices, Salt and Aromatics*, p.230–1.
10 Russell, 'History Cook', p.34.
11 Fitzgerald, *Rowntree and the Marketing Revolution*, p.22.

12 Hyslop, *Made in London*.
13 Hill, *Biscuits, Bollinger and Banquets*, p.274.
14 Fitzgerald, *Rowntree and the Marketing Revolution*, pp.318–34.
15 Crawford and Broadley, *The People's Food*, p.45. Forster, *Rich Desserts and Captain's Thins*, p.261.
16 Corley, *Quaker Enterprise in Biscuits*, p.219.
17 Crawford and Broadley, *The People's Food*, pp.11, 173.
18 Ibid., pp.102–3; Rappaport, *The Thirst for Empire*, p.318.
19 Gill, *The C.W. S. Crumpsall Biscuit Factory*.
20 Spark, *Curriculum Vitae*, pp.29–30.
21 Fraser, *The Coming of the Mass Market*, p.29.
22 Mathias, *Retailing Revolution*, pp.x, 41–5.
23 Ibid., pp.103–9.
24 Dunkerley, *To-Day A Weekly Magazine Journal* (1896).
25 Corley, *Quaker Enterprise in Biscuits*, p.74.
26 Fraser, *The Coming of the Mass Market*, pp.23–4, 41.
27 Corley, *Quaker Enterprise in Biscuits*, pp.216, 221, 228, 233.
28 Shears, *Tapioca For Tea*, p.99.
29 Reynolds, *A Poor Man's House*, p.71.
30 Warren, *The Foods We Eat*, p.7.
31 Fraser, *The Coming of the Mass Market*, p.39.
32 Mathias, *Retailing Revolution*, pp.24–5.
33 Corley, *Quaker Enterprise in Biscuits*, p.256.
34 Reynolds, *A Poor Man's House*, pp.71–2.
35 Orwell, *The Road to Wigan Pier*, p. 14.
36 Day Survey Respondent 083, October 1937–January 1938, Mass Observation Archive.
37 Crawford and Broadley, *The People's Food*, p.173; Fitzgerald, *Rowntree and the Marketing Revolution*, p.22.
38 Hoggart, *A Local Habitation*, p.38.
39 Ibid., p.48.
40 Frances Green talks about Crawfords biscuit factory.
41 Inglis, *The Children's War*, pp.41–2, 164.
42 Garfield, *Private Battles*, p.18.
43 Burnett, *Plenty and Want*, pp.293–4.
44 ARP Worker and Food Packing Manager, Belmont, Surrey, b.1908, Diarist 5004. Mass Observation Online.
45 Corley, *Quaker Enterprise*, p.256.
46 Oddy, *From Plain Fare*, p.157.

47 Cited by Rappaport, *A Thirst for Empire*, p.309.
48 Ibid., p.305.
49 'Topic Collection', Mass Observation Online.
50 Sheridan, *Wartime Women*, p.239.
51 *BISCUITS*, Mass Observation Online.
52 Ellis, *The Country Housewife's Family Companion*, p.75.
53 Collingham, *The Taste of War*, pp.477–81.
54 Corley, *Quaker Enterprise in Biscuits*, pp.245–6.
55 Trentmann, *Empire of Things*, p.10.
56 Jacobs, *Pie 'n' Mash*, p.89.
57 *BISCUITS*, Mass Observation Online.
58 *BISCUITS*, Mass Observation Online.
59 Nicey and Wifey, *Nice Cup of Tea and A Sit Down*, p.95.
60 Ibid., p.88.
61 Pugh, *A Clear and Simple Vision*, pp.17, 25–7.
62 Hardyment, *A Slice of Life*, p.107.
63 Nicholson, *Perfect Wives*.
64 Douglas and Nicod, 'Taking the biscuit', p.746.
65 Ibid., p.747.
66 Nicey and Wifey, *Nice Cup of Tea and A Sit Down*, p.116.
67 Douglas and Nicod, 'Taking the biscuit', p.746.
68 Ibid., p.747.

Conclusion

1 Yashaswini Chandra in conversation with the author.
2 Crawford and Broadley, *The People's Food*, p.64.
3 Londeix, *Le Biscuit et son Marché*, p.185.
4 Sturt, *A Small Boy in the Sixties*, p.199.

BIBLIOGRAPHY

Online Sources

Athenaeus, *The Deipnosophistae* (Loeb Classical Library, 1928), penelope.uchicago.edu/Thayer/E/Roman/Texts/Athenaeus/3D*.html

The Bahlsen Family, https://www.bahlsen.co.uk/our-story

Chiltonian Ltd: record held by Lewisham Local History and Archives Centre, Ref: A80/28, https://discovery.nationalarchives.gov.uk/details/r/4cfee82b-31e4-4901-8e61-3987be6ce2a6

Day, Ivan 'Biscuits' https://foodhistorjottings.blogspot.com/search/label/Biscuits

Downey, Mike, www.mikedowney.co.uk/blog/food_and_drink/ato_z/IOW_cracknel

Friedrichsdorf – die Stadt des Zwiebacks, https://www.friedrichsdorf.de/lebeninfriedrichsdorf/unserestadt/geschichte/stadtundstadtteile/zwiebackstadt.php

Frances Green talks about Crawfords biscuit factory (5 August 2009), http://www.edgehillstation.co.uk/resources/francis-green-03/

Gofton, Allyson, 'The Anzac Biscuit myth', https://web.archive.org/web/20060612232250/http://ecook.co.nz/index.php/ps_pagename/featurearticles/pi_articleid/57

'The Huntley & Palmers Collection, Reading Biscuit Town', http://www.huntleyandpalmers.org.uk/

Jurafsy, Dan, 'Macaroons, Macarons and Macaroni' https://languageoffood.blogspot.com/2011/04/macaroons-macarons-and-macaroni.html

Louis, Dianna Farr, 'Paximadia Cretan twice-baked bread', *The Art of Eating*, https://www.prosphatos.com/gastronomy

Mass Observation Online: http://www.massobservation.amdigital.co.uk.ezp.lib.cam.ac.uk/Documents/Details/Diarist-5004.

Mass Observation Online: *BISCUITS*. [File Report], University of Sussex Special Collections, Mass Observation Online, http://www.massobservation.amdigital.co.uk.ezp.lib.cam.ac.uk/Documents/Details/FileReport-2240 and http://www.massobservation.amdigital.co.uk.ezp.lib.cam.ac.uk

Mass Observation Online: Day Survey, Mass Observation Archive, University of Sussex Special Collections, Mass Observation Online, http://www.massobservation.amdigital.co.uk.ezp.lib.cam.ac.uk/Documents/Details/DaySurvey

Mass Obserbvation Online: 'Topic Collection', http://www.massobservation.amdigital.co.uk.ezp.lib.cam.ac.uk/Documents/Details/TopicCollection-23

MCR-1, Miniature Communications Receiver, https://www.cryptomuseum.com/spy/mcr1/

Passemiers, Lazlo, 'A history of De Beukelaer's Fabrieken, with specific reference to its corporate social responsibility (1885–1929)', thesis presented in fulfilment of the requirements for the degree Masters of Arts (History) in the Faculty of Arts at the University of Stellenbosch, December 2011, https://core.ac.uk/download/pdf/37345310.pdf

'Pride and Prejudice: having a Ball', https://www.bbc.co.uk/programmes/p018rdvx

Queen Victoria's Journals, www.queenvictoriasjournals.org/search/displayItem.do?FormatType=fulltextimgsrc&QueryType=articles&ResultsID=3124959377747&filterSequence=0&PageNumber=1&ItemNumber=1&ItemID=qvj01163&volumeType=ORIG

'Recollections, Crawford's Biscuits, Elbe Street, Leith', www.edinphoto.org.uk/1_edin/1_edinburgh_history_-_recollections_employment_crawfords_biscuits_leith.htm

The Rule of Pachomius, Part 1, trans. Esmeralda Ramirez de Jennings and ed. Rev. Daniel R. Jennings, http://www.seanmultimedia.com/Pie_Pachomius_Rule_1.html

Sawyer, Patrick, 'When Britain fell for Garibaldi', *The New European*, 18 March 2019, https://www.theneweuropean.co.uk/top-stories/when-britain-fell-for-garibaldi-1-5938195 accessed 11 October 2019

Sezgin, Ibrahim, 'XVII–XVIII. Yüzyillarda Karadendz Sehdrlerdnden Donanma Dçdn Peksdmet Tedardkd ('The provision of hard biscuits for the Ottoman Fleet from the Black Sea Cities in the 17th and 18th centuries'), *International Journal of Black Sea Studies*, http://www.seranderyayinevi.com//wp-content/uploads/2011/09/335D-7.-SAYI-BASILAN-DOSYA1.pdf

Simmons, Amelia, *American Cookery: The Art of Dressing Viands, Fish, Poultry, and Vegetables* (4 July 2004 EBook), http://www.gutenberg.org/cache/epub/12815/pg12815-images.html

Statista, https://www.statista.com/

'This is why digestives are called digestives', https://metro.co.uk/2016/12/25/this-is-why-digestives-are-called-digestives-6343329/?ito=cbshare

'"Tiddy Doll" – famous London gingerbread street vendor', https://researchingfoodhistory.blogspot.com/2018/02/tiddy-doll-famous-london-gingerbread.html

Toettchen, 'Brandt-Zwiebak und westfälischer Zwieback pudding', http://toettchen.eu/brandt-zwieback-und-eine-kleine-geschichte-des-zwiebacks/

Villamont, Jacques de, *Les Voyages du seigneur de Villamont* 3 vols. (1607), https://books.google.co.uk/books?id=KDT64kYbRywC&pg=PA228&dq=De+Villamont,+L+S&hl=en&sa=X&ved=0ahUKEwiIpPWz9NTkAhWEcAKHcSuA_IQ6AEIOTAC#v=onepage&q=biscuit&f=false

Waterhouse, Gilbert, 'Rail-Head' (1916), https://warpoets.org.uk/worldwar1/blog/poem/rail-head

What happened to Huntley & Palmers Breakfast Biscuits? https://forums.doyouremember.co.uk/threads/11088-What-happened-to-Huntley-amp-Palmers-Breakfast-biscuits

Whiteley, William, General Price List, October 1913, Vol. 2, https://books.google.co.uk/books?id=IyJFAQAAMAAJ&pg=PA1171&dq=William+Whiteley,+General+Price+List+October+1913,+Vol.+2&hl=en&sa=X&ved=0ahUKEwiKpeG_5fjoAhU4RxUIHcaXC5MQ6AEIKDAA#v=onepage&q=William%20Whiteley%2C%20General%20Price%20List%20October%201913%2C%20Vol.%202&f=false

Woolley, Hannah, *The Queen-like Closet or Rich Cabinet*, http://www.gutenberg.org/ebooks/14377

Wyatt, Caroline, 'The Great Military Beans Fatigue', http://news.bbc.co.uk/1/hi/magazine/7472887.stm

'Zwieback', https://www.patrimoineculinaire.ch/Produkt/Zwieback/163

'Zwieback, Steine, Schriftchen: Briefbeigaben', https://www.goethehaus-frankfurt.de/ausstellungen_veranstaltungen/ausstellungen/wechselausstellung/leseheft-briefbeigaben.pdf

Empire Online Database

Caddick, Helen, Travel Diaries of Helen Caddick, Vol. 5, 1898, manuscript diary, Birmingham Central Library, MS 908, Vol. 5

Lloyd, Rev. John W., Diary (No. 7), University of Birmingham Library, G3 A 9 0, 1908

Imperial War Museum, London

G. R. Page Papers, Department of Documents

R. P. Evans Papers, Department of Documents

Reading Museum

Huntley & Palmers biscuit tin reused as the sound box of an African thumb piano, early 20th century, REDMG: 1997.162.17

Sword, REDMG: 1997.84.2

Reading University Special Collections

Photocopy of a printed booklet listing national agents for H7P biscuits *c.*1850, HP 130 Huntley and Palmers Collection MS 1490

Records of Peek Frean MS 1216

Books and Articles

Abbott, Elizabeth, *Sugar. A Bittersweet History* (Duckworth Overlook, London, 2010)

Abreu de Galindo, Juan de, *The History of the Discovery of the Canary Islands:* translated from a Spanish manuscript lately found in the island of Palma (trans. George Glass, London, 1764)

Achaya, K. T., *The Food Industries of British India* (Oxford University Press, New Delhi, 1994)

Aglaia, Kremezi, 'Paximadia (Barley Biscuits): Food for sailors, travellers and poor islanders', in Harlan Walker (ed.), *Food on the Move. Proceedings of the Oxford Symposium on Food History 1996* (Prospect Books, Totnes, Devon, 1997), 208–11

Alcock, Joan P., '"All sugar from the waves": the changing concept of sugar', in Harlan Walker (ed.), *Look and Feel: Studies in Texture, Appearance and Incidental Characteristics of Food. Proceedings of the Oxford Symposium on Food 1993* (Prospect Books, Totnes, Devon, 1994), 11–25

Alexis of Piemont, *The Secrets of Maister Alexis of Piemont, by hym collected out of divers excellent authors, and translated into English, by William Warde and Richard Anglosse* (Atenar Publishing, Oxford, 2000)

Allen, Brigid, *Food. An Oxford Anthology* (Oxford University Press, Oxford, 1994)

Arnott's Biscuits Case Study: 140 Years of Change and Innovation to Maintain Market Leadership (Datamonitor, 1 September 2008)

Arrington, Laura, 'Revolutionary Genesis? Jacob's Biscuit Factory and the transformation of Ireland', *History Ireland* 21 4 (2013), 42–3

Astarita, Tommaso, *The Italian Baroque Table: Cooking and Entertaining from the Golden Age of Naples* (Arizona Center for Medieval and Renaissance Studies, Temple, Arizona, 2014)

Aulnoy, Madame d', *The Lady's Travels into Spain* (London, 1774)

Austen, Jane, *Emma* (Richard Bentley, London, 1882)

Ballerini, Luigi (ed.), *The Art of Cooking: The First Modern Cookery Book. Composed by the eminent Maestro Martino of Como, a most prudent expert in this art, once cook to the most reverend Cardinal Trevisan, patriarch of Aquileia* (University of California Press, Berkeley, 2005)

Banks, Joseph, *Joseph Banks in Newfoundland and Labrador, 1766: His Diary, Manuscripts and Collections* (University of California Press, Berkeley, 1971)

Banks, Joseph, *Journal of the Right Hon. Sir Joseph Banks Bart., K.B., P.R.S.: During Captain Cook's First Voyage in HMS Endeavour in 1768–71 to Terra Del Fuego, Otahite, New Zealand, Australia, the Dutch East Indies etc.* (Cambridge University Press, Cambridge, 2011)

Banks, Joseph, *The Letters of Sir Joseph Banks: A Selection, 1768–1820* (ed. Neil Chambers, Imperial College Press, London, 2000)

Barnes, Donna R. and Peter G. Rose, *Matters of Taste. Food and Drink in Seventeenth-Century Dutch Art and Life* (Albany Institute of History of Art, Albany, 2002)

Barr, Rebecca Anne, Sylvie Keiman-Lafon and Sophie Vasset (eds.), *Bellies, Bowels and Entrails in the Eighteenth Century* (Manchester University Press, Manchester, 2020)

Baugh, Daniel A., 'Naval power: what gave the British navy superiority?', in Leandro Prados de la Escosura, *Exceptionalism and Industrialisation. Britain and its European rivals, 1688–1815* (Cambridge University Press, Cambridge, 2004), 235–60

Baugh, Daniel A., *British Naval Administration in the Age of Walpole* (Princeton University Press, Princeton, NJ, 2015)

Beard, Mary, *Pompeii. The Life of a Roman Town* (Profile Books, London, 2009)

Bergreen, Laurence, *Over the Edge of the World: Magellan's Terrifying Circumnavigation of the Globe* (William Morrow, London, 2003)

Biney, Ama, 'The development of Kwame Nkrumah's political thought in exile, 1966–72', *The Journal of African History* 50/1 (2009), 81–100

Blaze, Elzéar, *Life in Napoleon's Army* (Frontline Books, London, 2015)

Bligh, William, *Mutiny on the Bounty* (Courier Corporation, 2012)

Borella, Mr, *The Court and Country Confectioner* (G. Riley at his Circulating Library, London, 1772)

Botton, Alain de, *The Pleasures and Sorrows of Work* (Hamish Hamilton, London, 2009)

Bradley, Ian Campbell, *Enlightened Entrepreneurs* (Weidenfeld & Nicolson, London, 1987)

Brears, P. C. D., *The Gentlewoman's Kitchen: Great Food in Yorkshire 1650–1750* (Wakefield Historical Publications, Wakefield, 1984)

Brears, Peter, 'Arvals, wakes and month minds: food for funerals', in Laura Mason (ed.), *Food and the Rites of Passage* (Prospect Books, Totnes, Devon, 2002), 87–114

Brears, Peter, *Cooking and Dining in Medieval England* (Prospect Books, Totnes, Devon, 2008)

Brears, Peter, 'Traditional food in the Lake Counties', in C. Anne Wilson, *'Traditional Food East and West of the Pennines'. Papers by Peter Brears, Lynette Hunter, Helen Pollard, Jennifer Stead and C. Anne Wilson* (Edinburgh University Press, Edinburgh, 1991), 66–116

Bristed, Charles Astor, *Five Years in an English University* (first published 1852; Applewood Books, 2010)

Brooke, G. M., *Relations and Complications: Being the Recollections of H. H. the Dayang Muda of Sarawak* (John Lane the Bodley Head, London, 1929)

Brooks, George E., *Eurafricans in Western Africa: Commerce, Social Status, Gender and Religious Observance from the Sixteenth to the Eighteenth Century* (James Currey, Oxford, 2003)

Broomfield, Andrea, *Food and Cooking in Victorian England* (Praeger, London, 2007)

Burnett, Charles, 'Translation and transmission of Greek and Islamic science to Latin Christendom', in David C. Lindberg and Michael H. Shank (eds.), *The Cambridge History of Science*, Vol. 2. (Cambridge University Press, Cambridge, 2013)

Burnett, John, 'The baking industry in the nineteenth century', *Business History* 5 (1963), 98–108

Burnett, John, *Liquid Pleasures: A Social History of Drinks in Modern Britain* (Routledge, London, 1999)

Burnett, John, *Plenty and Want: A Social History of Food in England from 1815 to the Present Day* (Routledge, London, 1989)

Cahn, William, *Out of the Cracker Barrel: the Nabisco Story from Animal Crackers to Zuzus* (Simon and Schuster, New York, 1969).

Carr, Gillian, 'The archaeology of occupation, 1940–2009: a case study from the Channel Islands', *Antiquity* 84/ 323 (2010), 163–4

Chapman, Alison, *Patrons and Patron Saints in Early Modern English Literature* (Routledge, London, 2013)

Clap, Roger, Memoirs of Capt. Roger Clap: *Relating Some of God's Remarkable Providence to him in Bringing him into New England* (T. Prince, Boston, 1731)

Cobbold, Carolyn Ann, 'The rise of alternative bread leavening technologies in the nineteenth century', *Annals of Science* 75/1 (2018), 21–39

Coben, Lawrence A., 'The Events that led to the Treaty of Tordesillas', *Terrae Incognitae* 47/2 (2015), 142–62

Collingham, Lizzie, *Curry: A Biography* (Chatto & Windus, London, 2005)

Collingham, Lizzie, *The Hungry Empire. How Britain's Quest for Food Shaped the Modern World* (The Bodley Head, London, 2017)

Collingham, Lizzie, *Imperial Bodies: the Physical Experience of the Raj, c.1800–1947* (Polity Press, Cambridge, 2001)

Collingham, Lizzie, *The Taste of War: World War II and the Battle for Food* (Penguin, London, 2011)

Colquhoun, Kate, *Taste: The Story of Britain Through its Cooking* (Bloomsbury, London, 2007)

Corley, T. A. B., *Quaker Enterprise in Biscuits: Huntley and Palmers of Reading 1822–1972* (Hutchinson, London, 1972)

Corley, T. A. B., 'Nutrition, technology and the growth of the British biscuit industry 1820–1900', in Derek Oddy and Derek Miller (eds)., *The Making of the Modern British Diet* (Croom Helm, London, 1976), 13–25.

Corréa, Gaspar, *The Three Voyages of Vasco da Gama, and his Viceroyalty* (B. Franklin, London, 1869)

Crawford, William and H. Broadley, *The People's Food* (William Heineman, London, 1938)

Crimp, R. L., *The Diary of a Desert Rat* (Leo Cooper, London, 1971)

Cross, J. P., *Jungle Warfare: Experiences and Encounters* (Arms and Armour Press, London, 1989)

Curtin, Philip D., *The Rise and Fall of the Plantation Complex* (Cambridge University Press, Cambridge, 1990)

Dacome, Lucia, 'Useless and pernicious matter: Corpulence in eighteenth-century England', in Christopher E. Forth and Ana Carden-Coyne (eds.), *Cultures of the Abdomen: Diet, Digestion and Fat in the Modern World* (Palgrave Macmillan, London, 2005), 185–204

Dalby, Andrew, *Siren Feasts. A History of Food and Gastronomy in Greece* (Routledge, London, 1996)

Dale, Edward Everett, *The Cross Timbers: Memories of a North Texas Boyhood* (University of Texas Press, London, 1966)

David, Elizabeth, *English Bread and Yeast Cookery* (Penguin, London, 1979)

David, Elizabeth, *Spices, Salt and Aromatics in the English Kitchen* (Penguin, London, 1970)

Davidoff, Leonore and Catharine Hall, *Family Fortunes: Men and Women of the English Middle Class, 1780–1850* (Hutchinson, London, 1988)

Davidson, Alan (ed.), *National and Regional Styles of Cookery. Proceedings of the Oxford Symposium on Food 1981* (Prospect Books, Totnes, Devon, 1981)

Davidson, Alan, *The Oxford Companion to Food* (ed. Tom Jaine), 3rd edition, (Oxford University Press, Oxford, 2014)

Davis, Robert C., *Shipbuilders of the Venetian Arsenal* (Johns Hopkins University Press, London, 1991)

Day, Ivan (ed.), *Eat, Drink and Be Merry. The British at Table 1600–2000* (Philip Wilson Publishers, London, 2000)

Delaforce, Patrick, *The Black Bull* (Pen and Sword, Barnsley, 2010)

Dembinska, Maria, 'Diet: a comparison of food consumption between some eastern and western monasteries in the 4th–12th centuries', *Byzantion* 55 (1985), 431–462

Déry, Carol A., 'Food and the Roman army: travel, transport, and transmission (with particular reference to the province of Britannia)', in Harlan Walker (ed.), *Food on the Move. Proceedings of the Oxford Symposium on Food History 1996* (Prospect Books, Totnes, Devon, 1997), 84–96

Dickens, Charles, 'Hard Times', in *Household Words* 26 (1854)

Dickens, Charles, *Letters of Charles Dickens*. 1833-1870 (Cambridge University Press, Cambridge, 2011)

Dickens, Charles, *The Pickwick Papers* (Hurd and Houghton, London, 1876)

Dickens, Charles, *Sketches by Boz* (Peterson, London, 1837)

Douglas, Mary and Michael Nicod, 'Taking the biscuit: the structure of British meals', *New Society* 30/637 (December 1974), 744–7

Driver, Christopher and Michelle Berredale-Johnson, *Pepys at Table: Seventeenth-century Recipes for the Modern Cook* (Bell & Hyman, London, 1984)

Duff, David, *The Shy Princess. The Life of Her Royal Highness Princess Beatrice, the youngest daughter and constant companion of Queen Victoria* (Evans Brothers, London, 1958).

Duffett, Rachel, *The Stomach for Fighting: Food and the Soldiers of the Great War* (Manchester University Press, Manchester, 2012)

Dunbar, Ian, *More Than a Puff of Smoke: A Life in General Medical Practice* (Raleigh NC, 2009)

Dunkerley, W. A., *To-Day A Weekly Magazine Journal* (1896)

Ellis, John, *World War II: The Sharp End of War* (Windrow and Green, London, 1990)

Ellis, Markman, Richard Coulton and Matthew Mauger, *Empire of Tea: The Asian Leaf that Conquered the World* (Reaktion Books, London, 2015)

Ellis, William, *The Country Housewife's Family Companion* (J. Hodges, London, 1750)

Erdkamp, Paul, *Hunger and the Sword: Warfare and Food Supply in Roman Republican Wars (264–30 BC)* (J. C. Gieben, Amsterdam, 1998)

Escosura, Leandro Prados de la, *Exceptionalism and Industrialisation. Britain and its European rivals, 1688–1815* (Cambridge University Press, Cambridge, 2004)

Evangelisti, Silvia, 'Monastic poverty and material culture in early modern Italian convents', *The Historical Journal* 47/1 (March 2004), 1–20

Falconer, William, *A New Universal Dictionary of the Marine* (Now modernised and much enlarged by William Burney), (T. Cadell, London, 1815)

Farmer, Fannie Merritt, *Original 1896 Boston Cooking-School Cook Book* (Courier Corporation, 1997)

Fermor, Patrick Leigh, *Words of Mercury* (Hachette, London, 2010)

Fiennes, Celia, *Through England on a Side Saddle* (Penguin, London, 2009)

Finkel, Caroline, *The Administration of Warfare: The Ottoman Military Campaigns in Hungary 1593–1606* (VWGÖ, Vienna, 1988)

Firth, C. H., *Cromwell's Army: A History of the English Soldier during the Civil Wars, the Commonwealth and the Protectorate* (Greenhill Books, London, 1992)

Fitzgerald, Penelope, *The Knox Brothers: Edmund 1881–1971, Dillwyn 1884–1943, Wilfred 1886–1950, Ronald 1888–1957* (Coward, McCann and Geoghegan, New York, 1977)

Fitzgerald, Robert, *Rowntree and the Marketing Revolution, 1862–1969* (Cambridge University Press, Cambridge, 1995)

Forster, Margaret, *Rich Desserts and Captain's Thins. A Family and their Times* (Chatto & Windus, London, 1997)

Forth, Christopher E. and Ana Carden-Coyne (eds.), *Cultures of the Abdomen: Diet, Digestion and Fat in the Modern World* (Palgrave Macmillan, London, 2005)

Foy, Michael T. and Brian Barton, *The Easter Rising* (The History Press, Stroud, 2011)

Franklin, M. J., *British Biscuit Tins 1868–1939* (New Cavendish Books, London, 1979)

Franklin, M. J., 'Biscuit tins – a lost Christmas tradition', *The V&A Album 5* (V&A, London, 1986)

Fraser, Amy Stewart, *Roses in December: Edwardian Recollections* (Routledge & Kegan Paul, London, 1981)

Fraser, Antonia, *The Six Wives of Henry VIII* (Weidenfeld & Nicolson, London, 1992)

Fraser, W. Hamish, *The Coming of the Mass Market, 1850–1914* (EER, Brighton, 2017)

Frei, Henry P., 'Japan remembers the Malaya campaign', in Paul H. Kratoska, *Malay and Singapore during the Japanese Occupation* (Singapore University Press, Singapore, 1995), 148–68.

Fury, Cheryl A., *Tides in the Affairs of Men: the Social History of Elizabethan Seamen, 1580–1603* (Greenwood Press, London, 2002)

Gandhi, M. K., *The Collected Works of Mahatma Gandhi*, Vol. I, 1884–June 1896 (Ministry of Information and Broadcasting, Government of India, 1969)

Garfield, Simon, *Private Battles. How the War Almost Defeated Us* (Ebury Press, London, 2006)

Peter Garnsey (ed.), *Food, Health and Culture in Classical Antiquity* (Cambridge Department of Classics Working Papers, Cambridge, 1989)

Garnsey, Peter, *Food and Society in Classical Antiquity* (Cambridge University Press, Cambridge, 1999)

Garnsey, Peter, 'Malnutrition in the Ancient World or Was Classical Antiquity a Third World?', in Peter Garnsey (ed.), *Food, Health and Culture in Classical Antiquity* (Cambridge Department of Classics Working Papers, Cambridge, 1989), 36–49

Gaskell, Elizabeth, *The Cranford Chronicles* (Vintage Books, London, 2007)

Gill, Andrew, *The C. W. S. Crumpsall Biscuit Factory through the Magic Lantern* (ebook)

Glover, Michael (ed.), *The Fateful Battle Line: The Great War Journals and Sketches of Captain Henry Ogle* (Cooper, London, 1993)

Goldstein, Darra (ed.), *The Oxford Companion to Sugar and Sweets* (Oxford University Press, Oxford, 2015)

Goldsworthy, Adrian, 'War', in Philip Sabin, Hans van Wees and Michael Whitby (eds.), *The Cambridge History of Greek and Roman Warfare, Vol. II, Rome from the Late Republic to the late Empire* (Cambridge University Press, Cambridge, 2007), 76–121

Gosnell, Harpur Allen (ed.), *Before the Mast in the Clippers: The Diaries of Charles A. Abbey 1856 to 1860* (Dover Publications, New York, 1989)

Graves, Robert and Alan Hodge, *The Long Week-End: A Social History of Great Britain 1918–1939* (Cardinal, London, 1985)

Greatrex, Geoffrey, *Rome and Persia at War, 502–532* (Francis Cairns, Leeds, 1998)

Greenhalgh, Michael, *The Military and Colonial Destruction of the Roman Landscape of North Africa, 1830–1900* (Brill, Leiden, 2014)

Grewe, Rudolf, 'Catalan cuisine, in an historical perspective', in Alan Davidson (ed.), *National and Regional Styles of Cookery. Proceedings of the Oxford Symposium on Food 1981* (Prospect Books, Totnes, Devon, 1981), 157–65

Griffin, J. P., 'Venetian treacle and the foundation of medicines regulation', *British Journal of Clinical Pharmacology* 58/3 (2004), 317–25

Grigson, Jane, *Good Things* (Michael Joseph, London, 1971).

Grimmelshausen, Hans Jakob Christoph von, *Der abenteuerliche Simplicissimus* (Winkler, München, 1967)

Guise, Anselm Verener Lee, *Six Years in Bolivia: The Adventures of a Mining Engineer* (T. F. Unwin, London, 1922)

Hack, Ann Grimble, *Tunbridge Wells Biscuits: The Story of Romary's* (Tunbridge Wells Museum and Art Gallery, Tunbridge Wells, 2000)

Hall, Christopher D., *British Strategy in the Napoleonic War 1803–15* (Manchester University Press, Manchester, 1992)

Hamlyn, Matthew (ed.), *The Recipes of Hannah Woolley: English Cookery of the Seventeenth Century* (Heinemann, Kingswood, London, 1988)

Hands, Timothy, *Thomas Hardy* (Macmillan, London, 1995)

Harari, Yuval Noah, 'Strategy and supply in fourteenth-century western European invasions', *The Journal of Military History* 64/2 (2000), 297–333

Hardyment, Christina, *Slice of Life. The British Way of Eating Since 1945* (Penguin Books/ BBC Books, London, 1995)

Harley, John, *Bully Beef and Biscuits: Food in the Great War* (Pen and Sword, London, 2015)

Hess, Karen, *Martha Washington's Booke of Cookery* (Columbia University Press, New York, 1981)

Hibbert, Christopher, 'Garibaldi in England', *History Today* 15/9 (1965), 595–604

Hibbert, Christopher, *Nelson. A Personal History* (Viking, London, 1994)

Hieatt, Constance B. and Sharon Butler (eds.), *Curye on Inglysch. English Culinary Manuscripts of the Fourteenth Century* (The Early English Text Society, Oxford University Press, Oxford, 1985)

Higman, B. W., *How Food Made History* (Wiley-Blackwell, London, 2012)

Hill, Andrew, *Biscuits, Banquets and Bollinger. The History of Cater, Stoffell and Fortt Ltd* (ELSP, Bradford on Avon, 2015)

Hillman, David and Carla Mazzio (eds.), *The Body in Parts: Fantasies of Corporeality in Early Modern Europe* (Routledge, London, 1997)

Hoggart, Richard, *A Local Habitation: Life and Times, Volume I: 1918–40* (Chatto & Windus, London, 1988)

Hopkins, Lisa and Helen Ostovich, *Magical Transformations on the Early Modern Stage* (Ashgate Publishing, London, 2014)

Hornsey, Ian Spencer, *A History of Beer and Brewing* (Royal Society of Chemistry, London, 2003)

Howard, Elizabeth Jane, *The Light Years* (Pan Macmillan, London, 1992)

Hyslop, Leah, *Made in London* (Bloomsbury, London, 2018)

Inglis, Ruth, *The Children's War: Evacuation 1939–1945* (Collins, London, 1989)

Jacobs, Norman, *Pie 'n' Mash & Prefabs: My 1950s Childhood* (John Blake, London, 2015)

Jeffrey, Robin, *Politics, Women and Well-Being: How Kerala Became 'a Model'* (Palgrave Macmillan, London, 1992)

Johnson, G. W., *The Stranger in India, or three years in Calcutta* (2 vols, London, 1843)

Jones, Martin, *Feast: Why Humans Share Food* (Oxford University Press, Oxford, 2008)

Kaufmann, Miranda, *Black Tudors: the Untold Story* (Oneworld, London, 2017)

Kearns, Kevin, *Dublin Voices: An Oral Folk History* (Gill & Macmillan, Dublin, 1998)

Keay, John, *The Spice Route: A History* (John Murray, London, 2005)

Kedar, Benjamin Z. and Etan Kohlberg, 'The intercultural career of Theodore of Antioch', *Mediterranean Historical Review* 10/1–2 (1995), 164–76

Kelly, Sarah, *Festive Baking in Austria, Germany and Switzerland* (Penguin, London, 1985)

Kessel, Peter van and Elisja Schulte (eds.), *Rome – Amsterdam. Two Growing Cities in Seventeenth-Century Europe* (Amsterdam University Press, Amsterdam, 1997)

Kistemaker, Renée, 'Amsterdam's municipal control of food supplies', in Peter van Kessel and Elisja Schulte (eds.), *Rome – Amsterdam. Two Growing Cities in Seventeenth-Century Europe* (Amsterdam University Press, Amsterdam, 1997), 221–34

Knapp, Robert, *Invisible Romans: Prostitutes, Outlaws, Slaves, Gladiators, Ordinary Men and Women… the Romans that History Forgot* (Profile Books, London, 2013)

Knight, Roger and Martin Wilcox, *Sustaining the Fleet, 1793–1815: War, the British Navy and the Contractor State* (The Boydell Press, Woodbridge, 2010)

Kratoska, Paul H., *Malay and Singapore during the Japanese Occupation* (Singapore University Press, Singapore, 1995)

Krentz, Peter, 'War', in Philip Sabin, Hans van Wees and Michael Whitby (eds.), *The Cambridge History of Greek and Roman Warfare, Vol. I: Greece, the Hellenistic World and the Rise of Rome* (Cambridge University Press, Cambridge, 2007), 147–85

Lacombe, Michael, "'A continuall and dayly table for Gentlemen of Fashion": humanism, food and authority at Jamestown 1607–09', *American Historical Review* 115/3 (June 2010), 669–87

Lane, Frederic C., *Venice: A Maritime Republic* (Johns Hopkins University Press, London, 1973)

Latham, Robert and William Matthews (eds.), *The Diary of Samuel Pepys*, 10 vols. (G. Bell and Sons, London, 1971)

Laudan, Rachel, *Cuisine and Empire: Cooking in World History* (University of California Press, Berkeley, 2013)

Lázaro, Javier Moreno, 'Tecnología, empresa y mercado en la fabricacíon española de galletas,1790–1936', *Revista de Historia Industrial* 17/2 (2008), 15–55

Lehmann, Gilly, *The British Housewife: Cookery Books, Cooking and Society in Eighteenth-Century Britain* (Prospect Books, Totnes, Devon, 2003)

Lindberg, David C. and Michael H. Shank (eds.), *The Cambridge History of Science*, Vol. 2 (Cambridge University Press, Cambridge, 2013)

Lloyd, Christopher, *The British Seaman 1200–1860* (Collins, London, 1968)

Loeb, Lori Anne, *Consuming Angels: Advertising and Victorian Women* (Oxford University Press, Oxford, 1994)

Londeix, Olivier, *Le Biscuit et son Marché. Olibet, LU et les autres marques depuis 1850* (Presse universitaire de Rennes/Presses universitaries François-Rabelais de Tours, Rennes/Tours, 2012)

Lumholtz, Carl, *Through Central Borneo: An Account of Two Years' Travel in the Land of the Head-Hunters between the Years 1913 and 1917* (first published 1921; Cambridge University Press, 2012)

McCaffrey, Patricia, 'Jacob's women workers during the 1913 lockout', *Saothar* 16 (1991), 118–29

Macdonald, Janet, *The British Navy's Victualling Board, 1793–1815. Management, Competence and Incompetence* (Boydell Press, Woodbridge, 2010)

Macdonald, Janet, *Feeding Nelson's Navy: The True Story of Food at Sea in the Georgian Era* (Chatham Publishing, London, 2006)

Macdonald, Janet, *From Boiled Beef to Chicken Tikka. 500 Years of Feeding the British Army* (Frontline Books, London, 2014)

MacDougall, Philip, 'William Scamp and his early naval works in the Mediterranean', *Mariner's Mirror* 93/1 (2007), 28–42

McIver, Katherine A., *Cooking and Eating in Renaissance Italy: From Kitchen to Table* (Rowman & Littlefield, London, 2014)

Malcolm, Noel, *Agents of Empire: Knights, Corsairs, Jesuits and Spies in the Sixteenth-Century Mediterranean World* (Penguin, London, 2015)

Manji, Madatally, *Memoirs of a Biscuit Baron* (Kenway Publications, Nairobi, 1995)

Mason, Laura, 'By Bread Alone?', in Ivan Day (ed.), *Eat, Drink and Be Merry. The British at Table 1600–2000* (Philip Wilson Publishers, London, 2000), 70–3

Mason, Laura (ed.), *Food and the Rites of Passage* (Prospect Books, Totnes, Devon, 2002)

Mason, Laura, *Sugar-Plums and Sherbet: The Prehistory of Sweets* (Prospect Books, Totnes, Devon, 2004)

Mason, Laura, 'William Alexis Jarrin: an Italian confectioner in London', *Gastronomica* 1/2 (Spring 2001), 50–64

Mason, Laura with Catherine Brown, *Traditional Foods of Britain. An Inventory* (Prospect Books, Totnes, Devon, 1999)

Masson, Madeline (ed.), *The Compleat Cook or the Secrets of a Seventeenth-Century Housewife by Rebecca Price* (Routledge & Kegan Paul, London, 1974)

Mathias, Peter, *Retailing Revolution. A History of Multiple Retailing in the Food Trades based upon the Allied Suppliers Group of Companies* (Longmans, London, 1967)

Mayhew, Henry, *Selections from London Labour and the London Poor* (Oxford University Press, Oxford, 1965)

Mayhew, Henry (ed.), *The Shops and Companies of London and the Trades and Manufactories of Great Britain*, Part 1 (March 1865)

Melville, Herman, *Moby Dick* (St Botolph Society, 1892)

Milham, Mary Ella, *Platina. On the Right Pleasure and Good Health: A Critical Edition and Translation of* De Honesta Voluptate et Valetudine Bartolomeo (Medieval & Renaissance Texts & Studies, Tempe, Arizona, 1998)

Miller, Ian, 'Digesting in the long eighteenth century', in Rebecca Anne Barr, Sylvie Keiman-Lafon and Sophie Vasset (eds.), *Bellies, Bowels and Entrails in the Eighteenth Century* (Manchester University Press, Manchester, 2020)

Miller, Ian, *A Modern History of the Stomach: Gastric Illness, Medicine and British Society, 1800–1950* (Pickering & Chatto, London, 2011)

Mintz, Sydney, *Sweetness and Power: The Place of Sugar in Modern History* (Penguin, New York, 1985)

Moody, Joanna (ed.), *The Private Life of an Elizabethan Lady: The Diary of Lady Margaret Hoby 1599–1605* (Sutton Publishing, Stroud, 2001)

Moor, Jenny de, 'The wafer and its roots', in Harlan Walker (ed.), *Look and Feel. Studies in Texture, Appearance and Incidental Characteristics of Food. Proceedings of the Oxford Symposium on Food 1993* (Prospect Books, Totnes, Devon, 1994), 119–27

Morgan, Tabitha, *Sweet and Bitter Island: A History of the British in Cyprus* (I. B. Tauris, London, 2010)

Morley, Henry, *Memoirs of Bartholomew Fair* (Chapman and Hall, London, 1859)

Mort, Frank, *Dangerous Sexualities: Medico-Moral Politics in England Since 1830* (Routledge, London, 1987)

Mortan, Mark, 'Gastrobamica', *Gastronomica* 10/1 (2010), 12–13

Muller, Nazma, 'Pan! Our music odyssey: a steelband story', *Caribbean Quarterly*, Mona 61/4 (December 2015)

Mulvihill, Mary, *Ingenious Ireland: A County-by-County Exploration of the Mysteries and Marvels of the Ingenious Irish* (Simon and Schuster, London, 2003)

Nasrallah, Nawal, *Annals of the Caliph's Kitchens. Ibn Sayyar al-Warraq's Tenth-Century Baghdadi Cookbook* (Brill, Leiden, 2007)

Nicey and Wifey, *Nice Cup of Tea and a Sit Down* (Time Warner, London, 2005)

Nicholson, Virginia, *Perfect Wives in Ideal Homes. The Story of Women in the 1950s* (Viking, London, 2015)

Nowrojee, Jehangeer and Hirjeebhoy Merwanjee, *Journal of a Residence of Two Years and a Half in Great Britain* (W. H. Allen, London, 1841)

Nusbacher, Aryeh J. S., 'Civil supply in the civil war: supply of victuals to the New Model Army on the Naseby campaign, 1–14 June 1645', *The English Historical Review* 115 (2000), 145–60

Oddy, D. J., 'A nutritional analysis of historical evidence: the working-class diet, 1880–1914', in Derek Oddy and Derek Miller (eds.), *The Making of the Modern British Diet* (Croom Helm, London, 1976), 214–31

Oddy, Derek J., *From Plain Fare to Fusion Food: British Diet from the 1890s to the 1990s* (The Boydell Press, Woodbridge, 2003)

Oddy, Derek and Derek Miller (eds.), *The Making of the Modern British Diet* (Croom Helm, London, 1976)

Old Sailor, *Greenwich Hospital: A Series of Naval Sketches, Descriptive of the Life of a Man-of-War's Man* (J. Robins and Company, London, 1826)

Orwell, George, *The Road to Wigan Pier* (Penguin, Harmondsworth, 1981)

Parry, J. H., *The Age of Reconnaissance: Discovery, Exploration and Settlement 1450–1650* (Phoenix Press, London, 2000)

Paxman, Jeremy, *Great Britain's War* (Penguin, London, 2013)

Perjés, C., 'Army provisioning, logistics and strategy in the second half of the 17th century', *Acta Historica Academiae Scientiarum Hungaricae* 16 (1970), 1–51

Peterson, T. Sarah, *Acquired Taste: The French Origins of Modern Cooking* (Cornell University Press, Ithaca, 1994)

Phillips, Carla Rahn, *Six Galleons for the King of Spain: Imperial Defence in the Early Seventeenth Century* (Johns Hopkins Press, Baltimore, 1986)

Pitassi, Michael, *The Roman Navy: Ships, Men and Warfare 350 BC–AD 475* (Seaforth Publishing, Barnsley, 2012)

Pollard, Helen, 'Lancashire's Heritage', in C. Anne Wilson, *'Traditional Food East and West of the Pennines'. Papers by Peter Brears, Lynette Hunter, Helen Pollard, Jennifer Stead and C. Anne Wilson* (Edinburgh University Press, Edinburgh, 1991), 117–42

Pollard, Nigel, *Soldiers, Cities and Civilians in Roman Syria* (University of Michigan Press, Ann Arbour, Michigan, 2000)

Polo, Marco and Giovanni Battista Baldelli Boni, *The Travels of Marco Polo* (Harper & Bros, London, 1852)

Pope, Peter E., *Fish into Wine: The Newfoundland Plantation in the Seventeenth Century* (University of North Carolina Press, Chapel Hill, 2004)

Postans, Thomas, *Hints to Cadets, with a Few Observations on the Military Service of the Honourable East India Company* (London, 1842)

Power, Eileen, *The Goodman of Paris (Le Ménagier de Paris): A Treatise on Moral and Domestic Economy by A Citizen of Paris (c.1393)* (George Routledge & Sons, London, 1928)

Prochaska, Alice and Frank, *Margaretta Acworth's Georgian Cookery Book* (Pavilion, Michael Joseph, London, 1987)

Pryor, John H., 'Introduction: modelling Bohemod's march to Thessalonike', in John H. Pryor (ed.), *Logistics of Warfare in the Age of the Crusades* (Ashgate, Aldershot, 2006), 1–24

Pryor, John H. (ed.), *Logistics of Warfare in the Age of the Crusades* (Ashgate, Aldershot, 2006)

Pugh, Peter, *A Clear and Simple Vision* (Cambridge Business Publishing, Cambridge, 1991)

Raffald, Elizabeth, *The Experienced English Housekeeper* (R. Baldwin, London, 1786)

Ragep, F. Jamil, 'Islamic culture and the natural sciences', in David C. Lindberg and Michael H. Shank (eds.), *The Cambridge History of Science*, Vol. 2 (Cambridge University Press, Cambridge, 2013)

Rappaport, Erika, *A Thirst for Empire: How Tea Shaped the Modern World* (Princeton University Press, Princeton, 2017)

Ravenstein, E. G., *A Journal of the First Voyage of Vasco Da Gama, 1497–1499* (Cambridge University Press, Cambridge, 2010)

Ray, Utsa, *Culinary Culture in Colonial India* (Cambridge University Press, Cambridge, 2015)

Raymond, Melanie, 'Responses of female industrial workers: a case study of the Guest Biscuit Factory, 1888–1899', *Labour History* 61 (November 1991), 123–32

Redesdale, Algernon Bertram Freeman-Mitford, Baron, *Memories 1837–1916* (2 Vols.) (London, 1915)

Reynolds, Allison, *Anzac Biscuits: The Power and Spirit of an Everyday National Icon* (Wakefield Press, South Australia, 2018)

Reynolds, Stephen, *A Poor Man's House* (Oxford University Press, Oxford, 1982)

Riley, Gillian, 'Eat Your Words! Seventeenth-century edible letterforms', *Gastronomica* 1/1 (2001), 45–59

Riley, Gillian, *The Oxford Companion to Italian Food* (Oxford University Press, Oxford, 2007)

Robertson, Una A., *Mariners' Mealtimes and Other Daily Details of Life on Board a Sailing Warship* (The Unicorn Preservation Society, Edinburgh, 1979)

Roscoe, John, *Twenty-Five Years in East Africa* (Cambridge University Press, Cambridge, 1921)

Rose, Susan, *Medieval Naval Warfare, 1000–1500* (Psychology Press, London, 2002)

Roth, Jonathan P., *The Logistics of the Roman Army at War: 264 BC–AD 235* (Brill, Leiden, 1999)

Rousseau, George, 'Coleridge's dreaming gut. Digestion, genius, hypochondria', in Christopher E. Forth and Ana Carden-Coyne (eds.), *Cultures of the Abdomen. Diet, Digestion and Fat in the Modern World* (Palgrave Macmillan, London, 2005), 105–26

Russell, Colin, *Who Made the Scottish Enlightenment?* (Xlibris Corporation, London, 2014)

Russell, Polly, 'History Cook: the smart cookies behind the chocolate biscuit', *Financial Times* (22 September 2018)

Rutledge, Sarah, *The Carolina Housewife* (facsimile of the 1847 edition: University of South Carolina Press, Columbia, 1979)

Sabin, Philip, Hans van Wees and Michael Whitby (eds.), *The Cambridge History of Greek and Roman Warfare, Vol. II: Rome from the Late Republic to the Late Empire* (Cambridge University Press, Cambridge, 2007)

St John, Ian, *The Making of the Raj: India under the East India Company* (Praeger, Oxford, 2012)

Sala, George Augustus, *Lady Chesterfield's Letters to Her Daughter* (Houlston and Wright, London, 1860)

Sala, George Augustus, *Paris Herself Again 1878–9* (Vizetelly & Co., London, 1882)

Sala, George Augustus, *Twice Round the Clock; or The Hours of Day and Night in London* (Houlston and Wright, London, n.d.)

Santich, Barbara, *In the Land of the Magic Pudding. A Gastronomic Miscellany* (Wakefield Press, London, 2000)

Sato, Tsugitaka, *Sugar in the Social Life of Medieval Islam* (Brill, Leiden, 2014)

Savage-Smith, Emilie, 'Medicine in medieval Islam', in David C. Lindberg and Michael H. Shank (eds.), *The Cambridge History of Science*, Vol. 2 (Cambridge University Press, Cambridge, 2013), 143–67

Schama, Simon, *The Embarrassment of Riches: an Interpretation of Dutch Culture in the Golden Age* (Fontana Press, London, 1991)

Schino, June di, 'The waning of sexually allusive monastic confectionery in Southern Italy', in Harlan Walker (ed.), *Disappearing Foods. Studies in Food and Dishes at Risk. Proceedings of the Oxford Symposium on Food 1994* (Prospect Books, Totnes, Devon, 1995), 67–72

Schoenfeldt, Michael, 'Fables of the belly in early modern England', in David Hillman and Carla Mazzio (eds.) *The Body in Parts: Fantasies of Corporeality in Early Modern Europe* (Routledge, London, 1997), 243–61

Scully, Terence, *La Varenne's Cookery: The French Cook, The French Pastry Chef, The French Confectioner. A Modern Translation and Commentary* (Prospect Books, Totnes, Devon, 2006)

Sellick, Will, *The Imperial African Cookery Book: Recipes from English-Speaking Africa* (Jeppsestown Press, London, 2010)

Shears, Sarah, *Tapioca for Tea. Memories of a Kentish Childhood* (Elek, London, 1971)

Shepherd, Sue, *Pickled, Potted and Canned: The Story of Food Preserving* (Headline, London, 2000)

Sheridan, Dorothy, *Wartime Women: an Anthology of Women's Wartime Writing for Mass-Observation, 1937–45* (Heinemann, London, 1990)

Sijs, Nicoline van der, *Cookies, Coleslaw, and Stoops: the Influence of Dutch on the North American Languages* (Amsterdam University Press, Amsterdam, 2009)

Simeti, Mary Taylor and Maria Grammatico, *Bitter Almonds. Recollections and Recipes from a Sicilian Girlhood* (Bantam Books, London, 1994)

Smith, Andrew F., *Peanuts. The Illustrious History of the Goober Pea* (Illinois University Press, Urbana, 2002)

Smith, Andrew F., *Eating History: 30 Turning Points in the Making of American Cuisine* (Columbia University Press, New York, 2009)

Smith, Leonard V., 'Narrative and identity at the Front. "Theory and the poor bloody infantry"', in Jay Winter, Geoffrey Parker and Mary R. Habeck (eds.), *The Great War and the Twentieth Century* (Yale University Press, London, 2000), 132–65

Smollett, Tobias, *The Adventures of Roderick Random* (Oxford University Press, Oxford, 1930)

Spark, Muriel, *Curriculum Vitae. A Volume of Autobiography* (Penguin, London, 1992)

Spaulding, Lily May and John Spaulding (eds.), *Civil War Recipes: Receipts from the Pages of Godey's Lady's Book* (The University Press of Kentucky, Lexington, 1999)

Spurling, Hilary (ed.), *Elinor Fettiplace's Receipt Book: Elizabethan Country House Cooking* (Viking Salamander, London, 1986)

Stauffer, Alvin, *The Quartermaster Corps: Operations in the War Against Japan. United States Army in World War II. The Technical Services* (Office of the Chief of Military History, Department of the Army, Washington DC, 1956)

Stavely, Keith and Kathleen Fitzgerald, *America's Founding Food: The Story of New England Cooking* (The University of North Carolina Press, London, 2004)

Stead, Jennifer, 'Navy blues: the sailor's diet, 1530–1830', in C. Anne Wilson (ed.), *Food for the Community. Special Diets for Special Groups* (Edinburgh University Press, Edinburgh, 1991), 69–96

Stead, Jennifer, 'Prodigal Frugality: Yorkshire Pudding and Parkin, Two Traditional Yorkshire Foods', in C. Anne Wilson, *'Traditional Food East and West of the Pennines'. Papers by Peter Brears, Lynette Hunter, Helen Pollard, Jennifer Stead and C. Anne Wilson* (Edinburgh University Press, Edinburgh, 1991), 143–86

Steel, Flora Annie and G. Gardiner, *The Complete Indian Housekeeper and Cook* (3rd edition, 1898)

Stefani, Bartolomeo, *L'Arte di ben cucinare, et instruire i men periti in questa lodeuole professione* (Mantua 1662)

Stellingwerf, Steven, *The Gingerbread Book* (Letts, London, 1991)

Stols, Eddy, 'The Expansion of the Sugar Market in Western Europe', in Stuart B. Schwartz, *Tropical Babylons: Sugar and the Making of the Atlantic World, 1450–1680* (University Of North Carolina Press, Chapel Hill, 2004), 237–88

George Sturt, *A Small Boy in the Sixties* (Cambridge University Press, Cambridge, 1927)

Supski, Sian, 'Anzac biscuits – a culinary memorial', *Australian Studies* 30/87 (2006), 51–9

Swinburne, Layinka, 'Dancing with the mermaids: ship's biscuit and portable soup', in Harlan Walker (ed.), *Food on the Move. Proceedings of the Oxford Symposium on Food 1996* (Prospect Books, Totnes, Devon, 1997), 309–21

Swinburne, Layinka M., 'Nothing but the best: arrowroot – today and yesterday', in Harlan Walker (ed.), *Disappearing Foods. Studies in Food and Dishes at Risk. Proceedings of the Oxford Symposium on Food 1994* (Prospect Books, Totnes, Devon, 1995), 198–203

Tandon, Prakash, *Punjabi Century 1857–1947* (Chatto & Windus, London, 1971)

Thackeray, William Makepeace, 'The Book of Snobs', in *The Works of William Makepeace Thackeray* (Smith, Elder & Co., London, 1869)

Thackeray, William Makepeace, *Vanity Fair: A Novel Without a Hero* (Methuen, London, 1853)

Thevénot, Jean de, *The Travels of Monsier de Thevénot into the Levant*, Vol. I (Faithorne, London, 1687)

Thirsk, Joan, *Food in Early Modern England: Phases, Fads, Fashions, 1500–1760* (Hambledon Continuum, London, 2007)

Thornton, John L., *John Abernethy: A biography* (Simpkin Marshall, London, 1953)

Tomalin, Claire, *Thomas Hardy: the Time-Torn Man* (Penguin, London, 2007)

Trentmann, Frank, *Empire of Things: How We Became a World of Consumers, from the 15th Century to the 21st* (Penguin, London, 2017)

Trollope, Anthony, *The Three Clerks: A Novel* (R. Bentley, London, 1867)

Tye, Diane, '"A poor man's meal": molasses in Atlantic Canada', *Food, Culture and Society* 11/3 (September 2008), 335–53

Vertecchi, Giulia, 'Innovation technique et conservation du biscuit: le cas de Venise au XVIIIe siècle', in Caroline Le Mao and Philippe Meyzie (eds.), *Approvisionnement des Villes Portuaires en Europe du XVI siècle à nos jours* (Paris, 2015), 215–27

Vickers, Daniel, *Farmers and Fishermen: Two Centuries of Work in Essex County, Massachusetts, 1630–1850* (University of North Carolina Press, Chapel Hill, 1994)

Waddell, L. Austine, *Among the Himalayas* (Cambridge University Press, Cambridge, 2015)

Walker, Harlan (ed.), *Look and Feel: Studies in Texture, Appearance and Incidental Characteristics of Food. Proceedings of the Oxford Symposium on Food 1993* (Prospect Books, Totnes, Devon, 1994)

Walker, Harlan (ed.), *Disappearing Foods. Studies in Food and Dishes at Risk. Proceedings of the Oxford Symposium on Food 1994* (Prospect Books, Totnes, Devon, 1995)

Walker, Harlan (ed.), *Food on the Move. Proceedings of the Oxford Symposium on Food History 1996* (Prospect Books, Totnes, Devon, 1997)

Walters, Jonathan, 'The world, the flesh and the Devil: some aspects of early Christian asceticism', in Peter Garnsey (ed.), *Food, Health and Culture in Classical Antiquity* (Cambridge Department of Classics Working Papers, Cambridge, 1989), 193–204

Walvin, James, *How Sugar Corrupted the World: From Slavery to Obesity* (Robinson, London, 2017)

Warner, Kathryn, *Richard II: A True King's Fall* (Amberley Publishing Limited, London, 2017)

Warren, Geoffrey C., *The Foods We Eat* (Cassell, London, 1958)

Waugh, Evelyn, *Brideshead Revisited, The Sacred and Profane Memories of Captain Charles Ryder* (first published 1945; Penguin, London, 1981)

Wenzel, Marion, *House Decoration in Nubia* (Duckworth, London, 1972)

White, Florence, *Good English Food. Local and Regional. Famous Food and Drink of Yesterday and Today. Recorded with Recipes* (Jonathan Cape, London, 1952)

Whiting, Sydney, Minister of the Interior, *Memoirs of a Stomach* (first published 1853, Applewood Books, 2008)

Whorton, James C., *Inner Hygiene. Constipation and the Pursuit of Health in Modern Society* (Oxford University Press, Oxford, 2000)

Wickramasinghe, Nira, *Dressing the Colonised Body: Politics, Clothing and Identity in Sri Lanka* (Orient Blackswan, London, 2003)

Wiebe, Melvin George, *Benjamin Disraeli, Letters: 1860–1864* (University of Toronto Press, Toronto, 2009)

Wilk, Richard, *Home Cooking in the Global Village: Caribbean Food from Buccaneers to Ecotourists* (Berg, Oxford, 2006)

Willcox, Phillip, *The Bakers' Company of Coventry* (Coventry Branch of the Historical Association, Coventry, n.d.)

Williams, Wendy, 'Outward facing: W. & R. Jacob & Co. Biscuit Labels, 1900–1939', *Journal of Historical Research in Marketing* 6/1 (2014), 56–97

Wilson, Bee, *Swindled: From Poison Sweets to Counterfeit Coffee – the Dark History of the Food Cheats* (John Murray, London, 2008)

Wilson, C. Anne, *'Traditional Food East and West of the Pennines'. Papers by Peter Brears, Lynette Hunter, Helen Pollard, Jennifer Stead and C. Anne Wilson* (Edinburgh University Press, Edinburgh, 1991)

Windsor, David Burns, *The Quaker Enterprise. Friends in Business* (Frederick Muller Ltd, London, 1980)

Winter, Jay, Geoffrey Parker and Mary R. Habeck (eds.), *The Great War and the Twentieth Century* (Yale University Press, London, 2000)

Winter, Johann Maria van, *Spices and Comfits: Collected Papers on Medieval Food* (Prospect Books, Totnes, Devon, 2007)

Woodforde, James, *The Diary of a Country Parson 1758–1802* (The Canterbury Press, Norwich, 1999)

Zahedieh, Nuala, *The Capital and the Colonies: London and the Atlantic Economy, 1660–1700* (Cambridge University Press, Cambridge, 2010)

INDEX

penguin.co.uk/vintage